The Well-Ordered Police State

THE WELL-ORDERED POLICE STATE

Social and Institutional Change through
Law in the Germanies and Russia,
1600–1800

Marc Raeff

*Es ist der Geist der
sich den Korper baut*
—Goethe

Yale University Press

New Haven and London

Published with assistance from the foundation established in the memory of Philip Hamilton McMillan of the Class of 1894, Yale College.

Designed by Nancy Ovedovitz and set in VIP Baskerville type by Coghill Composition Co. Printed in the United States of America by Halliday Lithograph, West Hanover, Mass.

Library of Congress Cataloging in Publication Data

Raeff, Marc.
    The well-ordered police state.

    Bibliography: p.
    Includes index.
    1. Law—Germany—History and criticism. 2. Law—Soviet Union—History and criticism. 3. Sociological jurisprudence. I. Title.
    LAW   349.43′09   82-19980
    ISBN 0-300-02869-5   344.3009

2   4   6   8   10   9   7   5   3   1

To the memory of my first mentors
A. S. Hackel (Mother Alexia)
K. V. Mochulskii
H. Wildangel
and to Lillian, Anne, and Catherine, my latest teachers,
for their love and encouragement

Contents

Acknowledgments

A fellowship from the National Endowment for the Humanities (1975–76), complementing a sabbatical leave, enabled me to formulate the basic ideas of this study. Research was carried on under the auspices and with material support of All Souls College (Trinity term 1976), the Max Planck Institut für Geschichte in Göttingen (1972 and 1974), and the Herzog August Bibliothek in Wolfenbüttel (1978, 1980). I am most grateful to the officers and staff of these institutions for their interest, encouragement, and generous assistance. The final typing was completed thanks to Miriam Levy's efficient competence and the generosity of the Dunning and Dean's Funds of Columbia University.

I thank my friends Professors Orest Ranum and Rudolf Vierhaus for their critical reading of the original typescript, and I am also much obliged to my anonymous referees for several useful suggestions. They are not responsible for my failure to accept all their advice; the remaining mistakes and errors in judgment are strictly my own.

My editor Charles Grench and copy editor Christie Lerch are to be thanked for having greatly contributed to producing a well-organized book in readable prose.

Introduction

The central issue that the present essay endeavors to explore is that of the making of the modern world and of the implications that the ways of its making had for the society that emerged in the process in the West. Simply, the fundamental problem is to define the nature of the political attitudes and administrative practices of the seventeenth and eighteenth centuries and their role in shaping the kind of Europe that imposed its pattern on the rest of the world.

Even the casual observer will notice that the history of Europe and of the Western world in the last two or three centuries has shown a striking departure from all other known patterns of social and economic development. The originality of the pattern lies in the extraordinary speed of the social transformation that resulted from the dynamic, conscious, and purposeful action of the creative, enterprising, and acquisitive elements of society— elements that were more numerous and more influential than in other societies. It would not be far wrong to say that it is the breakneck speed and dynamics of the rate of material growth and economic expansion during the period that characterizes the modernity of the Western world. Dynamic creativity marked the behavior of those conscious and purposeful individuals and groups, while opposing their efforts was the static, enduring force of traditions, and customs. The efforts of the innovators therefore needed the support and protection of political institutions in order to have a social and cultural effect. It is no accident that the foundation and rise of the so-called modern state and the very process of its formation gave the political establishment a role of leadership in the development of society and the evolution of culture. The fact now finds recognition and acceptance even among those historians who started out by almost entirely denying this role to the modern state.[1] Neither can long-range economic developments be understood if one ignores or denies the conspicuous part played by the attitudes and actions of elite individuals and their ability to introduce innovative patterns of social and economic behavior, thanks to the protection and support provided by the political authorities.[2]

There are many ways of defining modernity, of course. The most simple-minded is to equate modernity with the present, in contrast to the past, the old, but such a definition lacks analytical and heuristic value. As some have suggested, it may be a sign of arrogance and sociocentrism to claim for the culture of the Western world—that is, the culture that emerged in central and Western Europe in the course of the seventeenth and eighteenth centuries and then spread to North America and to most of the world—the distinction of being peculiarly modern. Yet there is no denying that from about the dawn of the sixteenth century (with origins going farther back, of course), Europe embarked on an extraordinary departure from the traditional cultural patterns that one observes in its own past and in most of the world prior to its contact with the West. The most outstanding and characteristic feature of the pattern that makes Western Europe exceptional and that eventually subjected to its sway most societies the world over is an extraordinary dynamism, an entrepreneurial spirit,

---

1. Pierre Chaunu and Richard Gascon, eds., *De 1450 à 1660*. Pt. 1 of *Histoire économique et sociale de la France*, edited by Fernand Braudel and Ernest Labrousse. See especially vol. 1, *L'État et la ville*, particularly "L'État," by Chaunu (Paris: Presses Universitaires de France, 1977). See also Geoffrey Parker and Lesley M. Smith, eds., *The General Crisis of the Seventeenth Century* (London: Routledge & Kegan Paul, 1978) and the peculiar Marxist approaches in Perry Anderson, *Lineages of the Absolutist State* (London: NLB; reprint ed., Atlantic Highlands, N.J.: Humanities Press, 1974) or Theda Skocpol, *States and Social Revolutions: A Comparative Analysis of France, Russia, and China* (Cambridge, England: Cambridge University Press, 1979).

2. For example, Douglass C. North and Rovert Paul Thomas, *The Rise of the Western World: A New Economic History* (Cambridge, England: Cambridge University Press, 1973). This is also one of the points in Alexander Gerschenkron's many essays on the development of modern economies.

and the willingness to take risks for results in the distant future. This creative energy and dynamism (some would call it arrogance and aggressiveness) were predicated on an essential assumption: that the resources at man's disposal are greater than perceived, that they may be unlimited, and that it is the task of man's rational and purposeful action to discover, develop, and make use of these resources that lie more or less fallow in the natural state.[3]

From today's perspective it is particularly interesting to observe the means used by European man to effectuate this transformation in his outlook and behavior. The present essay will examine one of the most significant means that was extensively resorted to. As we are aware today—and as contemporaries were not, or only exceptionally so—the pattern of Europe's transformation and the institutional means employed to that end developed in unforeseen ways. The means became ends, practical goals turned into ultimate purposes, and the original subordination to transcendental spiritual values was lost or stifled. It is precisely such contradictions and ambiguities that help explain the dynamic form and ultimate results of the process of modernization, as well as the emergence of some problems faced by our own generation. This essay* will therefore have as an ancillary purpose, or paradoxical result, to show how an institutional instrument devised to enforce the will of the sovereign or of an elite itself became a formative factor in the subsequent dynamics of transformation. A further background theme, or *basso continuo*, of this essay will be the hypothesis that the authorities' conscious

---

*The book has been conceived as an essay rather than as a monograph in the traditional sense. Since most of the observations and interpretations especially in parts 1 and 3, represent my own synthesis of many scholars' ideas, it is impossible to give all specific references. The secondary literature cited in the notes to parts 1 and 3 points to those works, preferably recent, that I believe have the most relevant information and offer the most stimulating analyses and interpretations. The reader should view these references merely as suggestions for further reading and not as an attempt to give comprehensive bibliographical coverage.

3. A hint of such attitudes is to be detected in classical Greece and to a lesser degree in the Hellenistic and Roman worlds. This is perhaps one of the reasons why the rediscovery and revival of the classical heritage in the fifteenth and sixteenth centuries may be an essential factor in explaining Europe's dynamic reorientation.

desire to transform society and its modes of behavior resulted in
the development of administrative and legal tools that, in turn,
displayed their own inherent dynamic. As a consequence, society
had to submit to an ever-expanding interference with patterns of
everyday life and to the professionalization of its cultural and
economic activities. On their part, these trends ultimately had a
stifling effect on the dynamic forces of society; the efforts to raise
society's productive potential meant the absorption of part of
society's manpower and productivity to support the institutional
tools that had themselves been created to foster productivity,
giving rise to one of the ironies of contemporary history, an irony
I wish to illustrate in the following pages in the particular context
of *Polizei-* and *Landes-ordnungen.*

Such paradoxes and ambiguities become more glaringly apparent, and prove quite instructive, when the methods and goals
originally developed in one society or historical context are later
transferred to another less complex or different one. An object
lesson of this phenomenon is offered by the history of Russia
after Peter the Great (reign, 1689–1725) had compelled it to
follow in the footsteps of Western and central Europe. Peter's
innovations, at first imposed ruthlessly and accepted reluctantly
and superficially, came to acquire a dynamic force of their own.
Their effects differed from the effects of the same innovations in
the West, because the social and historical context had changed
the thrust and valence of the borrowings. The successors of
Peter I, more particularly Catherine II, endeavored to grapple
with the problems created by the imported innovations and in so
doing came to realize the necessity of a much more thoroughgoing transformation of Russian society. A study of the policies of
Peter I and Catherine II, therefore, forms an interesting point of
departure for a comparative analysis of the immanent dynamics
of development released by the police ordinances *(Polizeiordnungen)* in the German territories.

In keeping with these various focuses of interest, the present
study consists of three essays, interrelated but separate in form,
and of unequal length and detail. In the first part, on the basis of
a broad rather than deep reading of secondary sources and of
well-known primary literature, I shall try to sketch the intellectual

background that provided the framework and defined the purposes of the practical legislation contained in the *Polizei-* and *Landes-ordnungen*. These were ordinances that contained regulations pertaining to the police and the government of the land (in the sense of *pays*, territorial unit). *Police* had the connotation of administration in the broadest sense, that is, institutional means and procedures necessary to secure peaceful and orderly existence for the population of the land (that is, territory). Police in this sense, obviously a sense derived directly from *polis*, was apparently first used in Burgundy (hence the original German spelling *policie* and *policey)* in the late fifteenth century, from where it passed to the Hapsburg chanceries. Normally, *Polizeiordnungen* were regulations concerning specific areas of administration and public life; *Landesordnungen*, on the other hand, were more comprehensive in scope, frequently summarizing all the administrative rules in force. It is only in the course of the eighteenth century, especially toward its end, that *police (Polizei)* came to acquire the more restricted and specialized meaning of today: crime control and maintenance of law and order.

The second, and longest, part of the book examines the methods used by elite members of society and political authorities to transform society and inculcate the values of a dynamic, productive, and enterprising culture. If successful, their policies were expected to result in the creation of new material and spiritual goods and to permit an almost unlimited and infinite increase in the subjects' welfare and happiness, while at the same time securing the power, wealth, and glory of the country and of its rulers.

Finally, in the third and last part (largely based on my research in Russian institutional history) I will examine critically the transfer of these goals and policies to eighteenth-century Russia and their impact there. This exercise in comparative historical analysis should throw light on the nature of the well-ordered police state and its effect on the course of modern European history.

The question of the role of political action in transforming society and culture is not a new one in European historiography, of course. The relative neglect of this question in recent historical writing is in part to be explained by its having been overstressed, in too simplistic a manner, by positivist and nationalist historians at the turn of the century. These historians ascribed the determining role of the political factor to an abstraction, the state, without adequately taking into consideration the fact that this abstraction was the institutional outcome of the actions of many individuals (and not only rulers) in the pursuit of specific values and goals. Nor does it do much good to say that the individuals acted merely in the interest of a social stratum or class, for these are as much of an abstraction as the state. Earlier historians were primarily interested in what they believed to be the "natural," permanent interests of the state, interests conceived in terms of an alleged national purpose that was consciously pursued by those holding supreme power—for example, the "better" monarchs and their ministers. But this conception only reified such vague entities as "national interest," the securing of "natural" borders, and the idea of the "destiny" or "purpose" of an entire people.[4]

Despite their well-known and frequently denounced biases and prejudices, these historians made available much important documentary material and contributed to a better knowledge of institutional aspects of Europe's history in the last three centuries. Their main failing, as we see it today, was that they did not come to grips with the effects that political, administrative, economic, and cultural policies had in transforming society. Concerned exclusively with legislation emanating from the center, the earlier historians viewed specific institutions or policies in isolation, oblivious of their relationship to the nature and development of society as a whole.

The older monographs (and there are but few recent ones) dealing with specific issues of economic or social policy in the German territories have a narrow focus: they are either strictly legalistic or written from the slanted perspective of some alleged national destiny.[5] They do not relate specific policy questions to

4. Marxist historians followed the same logic, ascribing interests and ultimate goals to social classes in the same manner as their conservative nationalist competitors assigned motives and ends to states and nations.

5. The work of Gustav Schmoller can stand as paradigmatic of that of many others. A model of this orientation in the publication of legislative sources is *Acta Borussica. Denkmäler der preussischen Staatsverwaltung im 18. Jahrhundert.* (Berlin:

the broader issues of a transformation of society to make it more dynamic and productive of material and spiritual goods. They ignore the striving for dynamic and productive behavior in all realms of public and social life that constitutes the modernity of post-Renaissance Europe. Clearly, for such an impulse to be husbanded and directed in an efficient manner, it had to have a goal. To set specific goals became the task of the political institutions and administrators of European sovereignties. Understandably, such efforts are most readily identified and described on the scale of the smaller, more homogeneous political units, and it is there, too, that the influence of individuals, elites, and purposeful thought are most easily discerned and traced. The effect of such efforts may be better documented for a small and particularistic society than for multiethnic empires or large national states where many domestic and external factors complicate the picture and interfere with analytical clarity.

Originally my intention had been to undertake several case studies. But this proved impractical, for in every instance it would have meant painstaking, narrow investigation of local conditions and problems, an investigation that would overemphasize the specific, often exceptional, features and obscure the more general trends. Although quite desirable in themselves (and I hope that German historians will undertake such studies), my general analytical and interpretative purpose would be poorly served by several specialized local histories, a task which, moreover, would be beyond my resources. But my preliminary research efforts pinpointed sources that proved most fruitful for my study, the set of administrative regulations and ordinances—Polizei- und Landes-ordnungen—issued by various territorial units and institutions in Germany in the seventeenth and eighteenth centuries and the legislative efforts of eighteenth-century Russia. These ordinances and laws make it possible to come to grips directly with the nature and effect of the role played by political authorities and elites in the transformation of European societies from premodern to modern cultures.

Preussische Akademie der Wissenschaften, 1892–1970). Series A, *Die Behördenorganisation und die allgemeine Staatsverwaltung Preussens im 18. Jahrhundert,* 16 vols. (vol. 16, first pt. only published). Berlin: 1894–1970.

The body of Polizei- und Landes-ordnungen is unmanageably large. As the diligent Mylius admitted in collecting the ordinances and decrees for the Mark Brandenburg, it is almost impossible to find all the documents, so that as he went on publishing his collection he had to issue supplements for additional ordinances and acts that he had not found originally but later discovered or that were sent to him later by volunteer correspondents.[6] There can be no question of an exhaustive analysis of this material, even for a few political units and for a limited period (which again would narrow the focus and hide the broader implications with which I am concerned). It should also be mentioned that the degree of availability of this material—by publication, collection, or preservation—varies a great deal, so that there rarely exists a complete record for a given territory or period; in any case, because of the wealth of material, it would be impossible for one searcher to work through most of it to make a "characteristic" or "typical" selection for closer scrutiny. But for a team equipped with computer tools and techniques, the huge body of ordinances for the German territories (and others as well) may offer interesting research perspectives and tasks. For example, ordinances could be analyzed for their language, verbal frequencies, patterns of symbolization, and the effectiveness of their messages. My own aim has been much more modest and limited, though perhaps by the same token also more questionable methodologically. Through a critical reading of ordinances ranging over many territories and spanning a period of almost two centuries (as the resources of the libraries accessible to me permitted), I have tried to identify and analyze those broad trends that appear to have been common to practically all the ordinances and expressive of their basic policy thrust.

6. Christian Otto Mylius, *Repertorium Corporis Constitutionum Marchicarum* (1755). In his preface (vol. 1, no pagination), he writes: "Es wird mir hoffentlich auch nicht als eine Negligentia imputiret werden, wenn der Leser einige wenige constitutiones allegiret findet, welche in dem Werke selbst nicht anzutreffen sind. Denn ob wohl es scheinen möchte, dass solcher Defect aus dem Archiv oder Registratur leichtlich hätte suppliret werden können. So ist es doch allezeit nicht zu erlangen gewesen . . . so ist auch kein Zweifel, dass von denen Rescriptis Decisivis noch viele fehlen, welche aus der Menge derer in causis privatorum ergangenen Special Acten herfür zu suchen, wo ich keine Spur gehabt, meine Zeit nicht gelitten hat."

As the notes will show, the ordinances cited are mainly illustrative; similar examples could be multiplied almost ad infinitum for every point made.* The examples cited are not presented as proofs, in the strict sense, but merely as instances of trends and attitudes. Clearly not every theme found in them was necessarily present in every case, in every territory, or at all times. Only a computer would provide a full description of the importance and significance of any one theme at a given time in each territory. I have also tried to bring out the evolutionary trends and patterns that the ordinances reflect. When such evolutionary trends are not discussed specifically in the text, references in the notes are given in chronological order to show the pattern or development over a period of time.

A final technical point should be touched upon: the legal nature of the documents. Following in the footsteps of the great compilers and editors of ordinances for specific territories— Mylius for Brandenburg and Magdeburg, Kleinschmidt for Hesse, Freyberg for Bavaria, and Bergius for the whole Empire— I have not distinguished between edicts, acts, decrees, ordinances, or statutes. During the period under consideration, the distinction was quite arbitrary; the terms employed in the titles of the documents reveal neither the source nor the authority of the documents, nor do they provide a specific, stable, and standard concept of the mode and institution of enforcement of the regulations. The legal force of these ordinances was the same, and their geographic jurisdiction, made clear in each instance, did not depend on the formal nature of the documents.

A review of the existing monographic literature on our main subject of study and related topics will show that much of the critical analysis offered there is based on theoretical writings of the time and contemporary plans and projects, rather than on concrete legislative measures.[7] I have made an effort to rely

*References to ordinances and treatises are given in abridged form in the footnotes; the abbreviated titles are to be found in full in the bibliography. Ordinances are dated: day, Arabic numerals; month, Roman numerals; year, Arabic numerals.

7. A recent exception is the work of Reiner Schulze that unintentionally, but obviously compelled by his analysis of similar evidence, corroborates the main argument of the present essay, though it puts it in the narrower framework of the

almost exclusively on ordinances and laws that were actually implemented, or at any rate that we assume were enforced. I have, of course, read and made use of theoretical treatises, projects, and pamphlets when they contributed to rounding out the picture, especially with respect to the intentions and remote aims of the legislators. My main concern, however, lies with practical efforts rather than with theoretical arguments and projects, though the latter are valuable for an understanding of the legislators' intellectual horizons.

---

traditional issue of the role of estates and their relationship to centralizing monarchical absolutism. Reiner Schulze, *Die Polizeigesetzgebung zu Wirtschafts- und Arbeits-ordnung der Mark Brandenburg in der früheren Neuzeit*, Untersuchungen zur deutschen Staats- und Rechts-geschichte, n.s., vol. 22. (Aalen: Scientia Verlag, 1978).

PART ONE
Intellectual Background to Change

All periodizations are inherently misleading; the web of history is seamless. Yet there occur in specific periods and places events that in retrospect appear to have been genuine watersheds, whether as active factors or because new developments were beginning to make themselves felt, preparing the ground for a novel type of society, culture, or policy. For central and Western Europe (and, *mutatis mutandis,* for Eastern Europe as well) such a watershed was reached in the last quarter of the fifteenth century. Let us try to enumerate the major elements that characterized this period as a distinct break with the past, the order of listing implying neither logical connection among the elements named nor a status of priority among them in shaping the emerging new forms of European polity. It is easier, as well as traditional, to start out with the broader and less precisely describable phenomena of economic and social life, to pass on to the spiritual and moral aspects of institutional developments, and to end by examining specific activities leading to new political and cultural creations.

It is now fairly well established that Western and especially central Europe witnessed a great upswing in economic activity and prosperity at the end of the fifteenth century. The economic renewal ended, for most classes of the population, the long period of decline, stagnation, and poverty ushered in by the Black Death and its manifold consequences. This upswing made possible the dynamic expansion of European creative efforts in practically all domains—the arts, exploration, politics—which, since Michelet and Burckhardt, we label the Renaissance. Ulrich von Hutten's ringing declaration "Es ist eine Lust zum Leben" best captured the optimistic and energetic mood that gripped most of Europe at

11

the turn of the fifteenth century. This optimism, buoyancy, *Tätigkeitslust,* found expression not only in the intellectual, artistic, and political domains but served also as the precondition both of Europe's expansion beyond the sea and its "Reformation" from inside—a double revolution that, in turn, ushered in a new period of disarray and conflict that led to a new watershed in the course of the seventeenth century, as I will try to show below.

Economic growth and revival were particularly noticeable in the towns. In central Europe, the Germanies in particular, the period saw the bloom and fruition of seeds sown in the Middle Ages. It was the height of the wealth, political influence, and social prestige of the patriciate of the Imperial Free Cities, especially in the south and west (but even the Hansa towns were to recoup their fortunes, in part thanks to the intensification of the Baltic trade). The economic activity of the towns—their greater output of handcrafted and manufactured products, coupled with the increased needs of princes and public institutions—all made for a great spurt in quantity and level of consumption. Since labor was relatively scarce, wages were high, which in turn made for higher prices on basic items of consumption, especially foodstuffs and clothing. This trend served the interests of agriculture as well, raising rural production even though it did not necessarily lead to the prosperity of individual peasants. The consequences were somewhat complex, since the classical medieval domainal system had already been weakened beyond repair or was in the process of disappearing altogether in the western parts of the continent. We observe a change in economic structure that is not easily summarized, for various parts of Europe—even of central Europe—responded differently. In broad terms, however, we may speak of an expansion and improvement of the rural economy, with rising productivity that was great enough to satisfy the increased demand yet not sufficient to depress prices. In the northeastern regions of the continent, rising rural production was accompanied by a shift to the exclusive production of grain for the active export market to meet the demands of cities further west and along the Atlantic seaboard. The result was to solidly anchor *Gutsherrschaft* on the estates of noble landowners.

On the other hand, in areas less exclusively devoted to the

cultivation of grain, a decline set in eventually. Many peasants moved to towns, where good wages and other opportunities beckoned because the urban population had declined in the aftermath of invasions, wars, and epidemics. The unrest that led to and was produced by the Reformation in Germany and that resulted in part from opposition to the imposition of new "rational" and legal relationships (for example, the reception of Roman law, which displaced customary norms regulating the peasants) only intensified the depopulation and flight from rural areas. As a consequence, we observe the spread of *Wüstungen,* or deserted communities, throughout Germany. The population loss led to a decline in agricultural production, a rise in prices (stimulated also by the inflationary pressures of the urban economy), and a general decline of prosperity and production in the rural economy that became noticeably significant from the middle of the sixteenth century on. To this trend, once it was perceived, the political and administrative establishments reacted with a series of measures and policies aimed at reinvigorating the rural economy.[1]

A striking characteristic of the intensification of economic life in Europe at the turn of the fifteenth to the sixteenth centuries, and as a matter of fact throughout most of the sixteenth century,

1. I base my comments mainly on the work of Friedrich Lütge: "Das 14/15 Jahrhundert in der Sozial- und Wirtschafts-geschichte," in his *Studien zur Sozial- und Wirtschafts-geschichte (Gesammelte Abhandlungen)* (Stuttgart: G. Fischer, 1963), pp. 281–335; "Strukturwandlungen im ostdeutschen und osteuropäischen Fernhandel des 14. bis 16. Jahrhundert," in his *Beiträge zur Sozial- und Wirtschafts-geschichte (Gesammelte Abhandlungen),* edited by E. Schremmer (Stuttgart: G. Fischer, 1970), 2d ed.? pp. 95–133; "Strukturelle und konjunkturelle Wandlungen in der deutschen Wirtschaft vor Ausbruch des 30. jährigen Krieges," *Sitzungs-berichte,* Bayerische Akademie, Philosoph. Histor. Klasse, vol. 5 (Munich: Bayerische Akademie, 1958). And for summary see his *Deutsche Sozial- und Wirtschafts-geschichte (Ein Überblick),* 3d ed. (Berlin and Heidelberg, New York: Springer Verlag, 1966; reprint ed., 1979) originally published as vol. 5 of W. Kunkel, H. Peters, and E. Preiser, eds., *Enzyklopädie der Rechts- und Staats-wissenschaft* (Abt. Staatswissenschaft) based largely on his monograph *Die mitteldeutsche Grund-herrschaft und ihre Auflösung,* 2d ed. (Stuttgart: G. Fischer, 1957). For a summary of recent work in the economic history of Europe, see vol. 2 of Carlo M. Cipolla, ed., *The Fontana Economic History of Europe* (London: Collins/Fontana Books, 1974).

was the great expansion of consumption. It was a period of rising population, the spread (albeit very limited by modern standards) of Europe's colonial expansion into overseas territories, and of feverish cultural creativity and politico-military activity. These new demands could be more or less easily and regularly satisfied by making full use of available resources and patterns of economic organization. Although new resources were discovered and exploited (especially in mining, in central Europe and beyond the seas) and the existing forms of organization were improved and made more efficient, there was as yet no basic transformation of the essential characteristics of economic life and organization that Europe had inherited from the heydays of medieval expansion. Only gradually, and increasingly from the end of the sixteenth century onward, did Europeans note the depletion of some resources and develop the feeling that at existing levels of consumption the ultimate limit of local possiblities might soon be reached. But it was also beginning to be recognized that the experiences and lessons of colonial expansion could be applied to the situation at home. With the colonial world providing new material resources but also requiring more products from Europe, the realization grew that consumption had to be balanced by efforts to produce. A gradual shift to an emphasis on production began to emerge and to take the upper hand after the devastations of the Thirty Years War and the "crisis" of the mid-seventeenth century. We may thus divide the period from about 1500 to about 1740 into two major epochs: in the first, emphasis was placed on the organization and regulation of consumption (since this belongs mainly to the sixteenth century, we shall not be directly concerned with it here); in the second epoch (mainly the second half of the seventeenth century), stress was put on the promotion and stimulation of production in order to make possible the resumption of a high level of consumption without threatening existing limited resources.

We have just referred to the expansion of Europe beyond the seas. The event was of major significance in several ways. In the first place, it brought to Europe a new supply of various raw materials, first of all minerals and spices, soon to be followed in the seventeenth century by timber, sugar, tobacco, and indigo, as well as furs. These things were welcome to European consumers, especially to those wealthy enough to also afford raw materials and the limited amount of manufactured luxury goods from the Far East. In return, and as time went on increasingly so, the traders and settlers overseas became the purchasers and consumers of manufactured articles and supplies from Europe, especially those in the colonies of the United Provinces of the Netherlands. The economic dimensions of the expansion and its effects on the development of trade, industry, and finances, have been much studied, though there remain areas of controversy into which a nonspecialist would be foolhardy to stray.

From the perspective of the present essay, however, Europe's expansion overseas offers some other interesting questions for analysis and reflection. In the first place, overseas colonies and settlements provided scope for experimenting with new organizational practices, especially in administration and commerce. To be sure, most conquerors and settlers endeavored to transplant to the colonies the basic traditions and institutional structures they were familiar with. But such an effort could not stop at mere transplanting. New circumstances and needs required innovative approaches. We need not go into the varieties of responses, each conditioned by the cultural predispositions and political predilections of the colonials. Suffice it to mention that the colonial experience, though transmitted sometimes at second hand and after a lapse of time, provided comparative material and the elements of cultural relativism in Europe. They helped to make European political and administrative thinking more flexible, more varied and sophisticated.

Last, but perhaps not least, the new colonialism offered an opportunity for attempting practical experimentation with theoretical conceptions of government, administration, and social organization. We shall return to this aspect later. In any event, Europe was expanding; its possibilities were increasing, potential new resources were becoming available. The continent as a whole was becoming more aware of itself in contrast to other worlds heretofore unknown. The sense of European identity, in turn, created a new awareness of the varied potentials of human nature. The sense of European identity seemed to justify the effort and energy that had led to the discoveries of new lands and to European expansion; it vindicated Western man's drive and spirit of adventure. These distinctive features of Western man could also be turned inward, so to speak, to enhance more thorough study and promotion of the material potential available at home and to support the quest for a better understanding of the workings of the universe.

The economic events of the early and middle sixteenth century have to be seen against the background of an even more significant crisis and transformation in the role of government within the general culture. Naturally the major reason for this change was the crisis in the Catholic Church that culminated in the Lutheran Reformation, the wars of religion, and the emergence of other Protestant denominations, sects, and institutions. The institutional crisis of the Roman Church served to weaken much of the framework that had supported the major elements of the social and cultural structure of Europe. The Church had not only been entrusted with the education of the population, with the task of forming the people's ethical values and cosmological outlook; it had also served to keep social discipline (for example, by virtue of its role in family relations), to preserve orthodoxy, and to provide a sense of cultural identity. The weakening and in some cases the utter disappearance of the Church's institutional authority after the Reformation forced the temporal powers to take over and to involve themselves actively in areas that heretofore had not been of immediate concern to them. Not only did this promote secularization; it also saddled the temporal powers with specific tasks of a legal and political, as well as cultural and moral nature for which new approaches had to be devised and new institutions set up. Since the temporal powers' technical, financial, and human resources were limited, there arose the danger of a moral and cultural disarray or vacuum.

Of critical significance was the Church's withdrawal, voluntary or forced, from such vital realms of social and cultural life as education and the care of the poor. The pedagogic role of the Church, however constricted and biased, had been quite significant; it had helped to impart basic literacy to a number of people, those who later would be able to accept and follow Luther's teachings. The welfare function of the Church had been equally important, for it had provided asylum and succor to many by setting up a system for keeping indigents under supervision and for mitigating the effects of economic and family disasters. Now all of these functions had to devolve on temporal authorities that were not always prepared for them, though they managed to finance these new tasks by confiscating or appropriating Church property. The secular power's taking on of such tasks was welcome and in the long run quite beneficial; however, it also made for extreme rigidity and control, smothering initiative and creativity. And, even more significant in our context, compared to the Church, temporal authorities displayed much less tolerance and understanding for human and cultural frailties; they bore down much more harshly on traditions and folkways that perhaps had no theological or dogmatic validity but that had been accepted and hallowed by tradition as the people's normal behavior.

The moral vacuum and cultural disarray created by the decline or withdrawal of the Church was filled in large measure, at least for the upper classes and a goodly portion of the urban population, by the creative explosion in the arts and in letters. Only a few aspects of this development need be mentioned here. In the first place, focus on the aesthetic led to an emphasis on public and outward display of the artistic potentialities of individuals, groups, and societies. At the same time artistic creation became secularized, in that it became a major function of art to beautify individual and group secular activities rather than the religious life of society. Art served to glorify individual creative drive and success, emphasizing the personal moral and spiritual factors, while classical antiquity, popularized by Humanism, provided the models. These new features of public culture did not disappear with the coming of Protestantism; although it spiritualized public activities to a degree, the Reformation continued to stress individual accomplishment and commitment and advocated secular forms of patronage and display, while at the same time disapproving the pomp of Catholic ritual.

The impact of Humanism was to enhance society's perception of the value of the individual's inner life. By recapturing the world of classical antiquity, Humanism rediscovered the value of personal glory and creative accomplishment, as well as the moral worth and dignity of the individual's handling of the existential predicament. At the same time, the Humanists stressed the intellect's rationality and its ability to assess and develop the ideas found in both classical and scriptural sources. Finally, and it is perhaps its most significant aspect, the orientation inspired by Humanism had an inherent dynamic force that furthered continued development and progress of individual rationality and creativity. To be sure, this was not an entirely novel phenomenon. The tensions between the classical heritage and Christian and Germanic folkways had stimulated the extraordinary dynamism of medieval culture in Germany, more particularly its innovative contributions to philosophic and legal discourse. With the weakening and virtual disappearance of the theological scaffolding of the Roman Church, however, it became possible to strike out in new directions by subjecting to scrutiny all the areas of thought into which man's intellect and curiosity might lead him. Building on the literary scholarship of the Humanists, continuing the innovations introduced by the jurists, and bringing to its logical fulfillment the critical stance of theologians and philosophers, the men of the sixteenth century went on to discover new domains of human interest, to analyze and explain an increasing range of phenomena, and to put man into the center of the universe. In short, the new culture of the sixteenth century provided the mental tools for expanding man's intellectual, philosophic, and, ultimately, scientific horizons and enabled the aggressive efforts of some individuals to obtain new control over the natural environment.

We are accustomed to think that since the Renaissance modern politics in Europe has consisted merely in a struggle for power: temporal rulers, whether princes or oligarchs, were bent on centralizing and expanding their power by restricting that of local authorities and the Church in order to impose their will on ever-larger numbers of people and ever-expanding territory. This is certainly not a completely false view, for such a development did play a significant part in the shaping of Europe in early modern times. However, it is only a partial view, and it fails to put the realm of politics into its broader cultural context. The observations that follow are not meant to deny either the medieval antecedents or the role that the quest for individual glory and search for fame played in animating men in Europe. Did not the mythology of chivalry, the ideals sung by the troubadours and celebrated in epic poetry all stress the moral value of the individual's pursuit of renown, recognition, and power, however one defined the ingredients of fame and power? Nor did the institutional framework of the Middle Ages lack the sense of political organization and power necessary to create a stable system of interpersonal and intergroup relationships. Adventure, conquest, expansion, thirst for glory and power—they were all known to the Middle Ages, even though in the minds of contemporaries they were subordinated to higher spiritual and religious values. In practice their effect was still to display force and power and to satisfy utterly mundane interests.[2]

Yet in the sixteenth century, and continuing through the seventeenth, new elements did appear in politics. One may question in this regard the importance of the decline of church sanctions and restraints, the more so since the papal government itself became heavily involved in diplomacy and warfare in the first half of the sixteenth century. Of greater significance was the widening area of competence that the secular power arrogated to itself, an arrogation that not only bespoke increased power and strength in the material sense but also the innate self-perpetuating tendency of social, political, or economic public functions to create further demands and grounds for political intervention and control. We have noted that the elimination of the Church as an active provider of education and of aid to the poor transferred these functions to the temporal sovereignties. The necessities of warfare, of maintaining a large and luxurious court, of colonial expansion, and the like, led governments to seek greater tax returns and also to involve themselves directly in developing new sources of revenue and economic activities from which they hoped to profit. This meant an expansion of the ruler's role as

2. On the medieval background of Renaissance political thought, see now Quentin Skinner, *The Foundations of Modern Political Thought*, vol. 1 (Cambridge, England: Cambridge University Press, 1978).

legislator, since these activities, on such a scale, were neither traditional nor the result of the forceful seizure of territory and jurisdiction, or of confiscation. The spread of religious conflict, accompanied if not actually caused by social clashes, also further involved the secular authorities, putting still greater strain on their resources and requiring their active participation in the organization and accomplishment of many enterprises.

The policies of centralization of authority pursued by the larger territorial rulers, policies in which they were imitated by their smaller brethren, also increased the tendency of individual governments to extend their control over the lives of their subjects. Centralization had the paradoxical result of fostering greater separation and division within Europe. It is anachronistic to label this result as the "emergence of the nation state," since the new units were not necessarily based on the nation (by whatever criteria the latter may be defined). Its effect was to break up Europe not so much into small feudal or medieval suzerainties and dominions as into larger entities striving for economic, cultural, and political autarky and eager to assert their distinctiveness. With the intensification of political rivalries and conflicts, exacerbated by religious strife and its accompanying social turmoil, the new political units aimed at being self-sufficient and at avoiding dependency on others. They were consequently bent on extending their own power and influence as much as possible, and in order to increase their strength and resources their governments were compelled to be more actively involved in their subjects' economic as well as social and cultural behavior. Efforts at regulating major social, religious, and economic activities forced governments into planning for the future and structuring social and institutional relationships.

Such trends, natually, led to an increase in the number of people involved in government and administration. It meant that personnel had to be recruited outside the traditional groups of *ministeriales* of all stripes. The notion (by now a cliché) that new administrative and political personnel were recruited among the bourgeoisie is largely true, but it is the less significant aspect of the phenomenon. The important issue was not merely social origin and numbers; still more important were the qualitative changes in the behavior and intellectual outlook of new administrators. Their transformation in this respect had begun long before the sixteenth century, at the height of medieval civilization, and in many ways was the direct product and reflection of that culture. One of the characteristic traits of the new political and administrative style was an effort to bring about coherence, regularity, and continuity over a long period of time. This could be much supported by logically coherent and self-contained systems of law; hence the revival and reception of Roman canon law as a result of the experience and reflection of medieval philosophers, jurists, canonists, and chancery practitioners—especially in Italy. It is of particular note that this so-called reception of Roman law was primarily the outcome of procedural requirements and developments. Roman law proved highly effective because its strict procedural norms made for consistency and stability, which in turn permitted the formulation of coherent juridical principles and theories. The turning of political and administrative issues into questions of law that could be resolved procedurally produced a stress on formalism and rationalization. As a result, a generalized sense of political stability and social permanence developed; it provided the prime condition for reasonably consistent ongoing policies aimed at increasing resources and revenues and at controlling the population for productive purposes. Not surprisingly, the lawyers, successors to the French *légistes*,[3] came to play a greater and greater role in the administrative life of such territories. These lawyers were of varied social background; as time went on, more and more nobles joined their ranks, but in the earlier stages lawyers tended to be from the clergy, the academic world, and the urban bourgeoisie in the loosest sense of the term. In any case, since similar education, practical training, and experience were necessary, the administrators developed a degree of coherence, consistency, and stability in their outlook and behavior. Professionalization of government

---

3. Carl Schmitt, "Die Formung des französischen Geistes durch den Legisten," in Deutschland—Frankreich, vol. 1, no. 2 (Paris: Institut allemand, 1942), pp. 1–30, and William Bouwsma, "Lawyers in Early Modern Culture," *American Historical Review* 78 (1973): 303–27.

administration and the establishment of technical qualifications for administrators had now arrived.[4]

It did not take long before the administrators began to develop into an interest group of their own. In order to prosper, they needed to expand their functions and role in the polity. This, in turn, helped to accelerate the dynamics of the administrative system and to expand the areas of administrative concern and government competence. Thus it was not the state's growing requirements for diplomacy, war, and public display alone but also the selfish interests of the administrators (who constituted the apparatus of government) that made for an increase in government functions and their steady penetration into new areas of public life and social concern. For the administrators, training in the law became a prime requirement, and in the long run this requirement pushed out the nonprofessionals—more specifically, the landowning warrior–noblemen—and this, in turn, contributed to the transformation of the government into a self-sufficient institution. At the same time it also provided a new avenue of social promotion for those who by virtue of their education and experience in the techniques of administration and law could participate in government.

A last point with respect to the new intellectual orientation of the administrators may be in order. Administrators were not merely technicians for whom procedure was of prime importance and who pursued the interests (as they understood them) of an institution, for the latter was intimately bound up with their own socioeconomic standing and role in society. Administrators came to conceive of their public task as that of guiding and shaping the

4. For the development of legal thought and its implications, see John P. Dawson, *The Oracles of the Law,* (Westport, Conn.: Greenwood Press, 1978); Paul Koschaker, *Europa und das römische Recht,* 4th ed. (Munich and Berlin: C. H. Beck, 1966); Michel Villey, *La Formation de la pensée juridique moderne,* Cours d'histoire de la philosophie du droit 1961–1966. (Paris: editions Montchrestien, 1968); Franz Wieacker, *Privatrechtsgechichte der Neuzeit,* 2d. ed. (Göttingen: Vandenhoeck & Ruprecht, 1967). The literature on the reception of Roman law in Germany is immense, best garnered in standard histories of German law and in the encyclopedic Stintzing-Landesberg: Roderich von Stintzing, *Geschichte der deutschen Rechtswissenschaft,* pt. 3, by Ernst Landsberg (Munich and Leipzig: R. Oldenbourg, 1898; reprint ed., Aalen: Scientia Antiquariat, 1957).

polity, or at any rate its public life. Frequently they had to turn
their energies to completely new areas of public concern, to
organize and structure social reality so as to obtain from the
population and institutions the resources deemed necessary by
the state. In its purest form, such a role could best be performed
in totally new (virgin) territory, either to impose a ruler's domin-
ion over newly settled lands (especially colonial lands) where
existing institutional structures and social traditions need not be
respected or, as in the case of conquests and annexations, to
supplant traditional native legal and social systems by integrating
them into those of the conqueror.

In this respect the colonial experience was of particular interest
and relevance, since it gave the administrator from the homeland
virtually free rein to shape the life of the natives for the purposes
the colonial government demanded and expected. The most
striking instance, though it was not the work of professional
administrators, was the rule of the Jesuits in South America. What
lessons colonial rule could have for the administration of the
homeland, how the feedback mechanism worked, and what its
effects outside the economic and ideological realms were are
topics that deserve more attention than they have received. We
know well the indirect consequences of colonialism in the late
eighteenth century, but most likely the feedback started earlier.
Even those countries that were not directly involved in colonial
enterprises seem to have behaved in the light of the knowledge
and experience provided by imperial administrations overseas.
Quite clearly the notions of levels of culture, of anthropological
and moral relativism, and the very ideas of the "noble savage" and
socioeconomic and cultural backwardness (all of them arising in
the seventeenth century) are all inconceivable without the colonial
experience.

An enormous shift in man's conception of the universe and of
man's position in relation to nature also was a factor that
ultimately expanded the role of government in society. In spite of
the spurt of economic and creative energy in the second half of
the sixteenth century, mainly the result of the moral and spiritual
turmoil accompanying the Reformation but also as we have seen,
a product of expanding aesthetic, scholarly, and geographic

horizons, this period was, for intellectuals, one of profound malaise and philosophic disarray. Cultural creativity alone, directed as it increasingly was to the minority of wealthy people who could afford its works, could not compensate for the loss of a stable, vital center brought about by the collapse of the hallowed framework of the Roman Church, a collapse that had put in question so many beliefs about the physical universe and man's cultural and social character. A turning inward into excessive individualization and scepticism, so well exemplified by Montaigne in his *Essais,* and a frantic search for tranquility of mind and security of body dislodged the exuberantly creative optimism of the earlier decades of the century. The clamor for some sort of discipline was heard everywhere more and more insistently.

For many minds in Europe it was especially hard to face the loss of belief in the stability and orderliness of the physical universe. To be sure, earlier generations may not have had adequate notions of regularity and law to explain and predict the phenomena of the physical environment either. But their ignorance of what we now call scientific laws was compensated for by a faith in God's higher purpose and a belief that He runs the world according to harmonious principles and that His miraculous interventions occur only for the ultimate sake of salvation. The optimistic faith and comforting feeling that the goal of nature was the welfare and salvation of man were now put in question or even destroyed by the realization that the world was much vaster than formerly believed and that it was populated with animals and men who seemingly did not reflect a divine purpose.

The unexpected, the tragic, the catastrophic came to be experienced as single, inexplicable events reinforcing the sense of disarray or instability and heightening men's fear of nature and of their own potential for evil, neither redeemed by a higher divine purpose. At the end of the sixteenth century we observe widespread belief in astrology, necromancy, magic, sorcery. The intellectual and cultural stage of the late Renaissance came to be dominated by a naturalistic cosmology that gave pride of place to irrational as well as arbitrary (or at any rate unpredictable) interventions of supernatural forces, frequently personified. Belief in unknown or impersonal forces shattered the sense of harmony and stability and undermined the security and feeling of identity of Western man. The role believed to be played by stars, planets, and other celestial or terrestrial bodies in men's fates removed their individual responsibility for their own actions and their faith in the possibility of shaping their own lives and of being the captains of their own fates. Moreover, such human irresponsibility appeared in flagrant contradiction to Western man's creative potential, in the aesthetic and intellectual as well as material realms, a potential whose scope had just revealed itself in the first half of the sixteenth century. Lastly, the Christian Weltanschauung was grounded in the belief that regularity and harmonious stability were manifestations of God's omnipotence and underlay the principles that also gave meaning to human relationships. Naturalism came too close for comfort to sceptical paganism and in so doing threatened the equally strong and deeply felt conviction that the individual possessed a moral identity and a purposeful role in the divinely ordained economy of the universe.[5]

At the end of the sixteenth century, the task of Western man was to reconcile the felt sense of permanent religious and ethical principles with the empirical experience of a chaotic, meaningless physical environment. To fail in this task was to perpetuate political, economic, social, and religious conflicts and to prevent constructive channeling of man's energy and resourcefulness. The challenge stimulated Western intellectuals to use their speculative and imaginative talents to make an active effort to understand the workings of the natural universe and to define the individual's role so as to enhance his or her creative potential in all domains. This search held the attention of thinkers, writers, and statesmen in the first half of the seventeenth century.[6]

The search for stability and discipline following the disruptions created by the wars of religion in Western and central Europe may first be recognized in the intellectual domain. R. Lenoble has

5. For a convenient summary and full bibliography, see R. J. W. Evans, *Rudolf II and his World* (Oxford: Clarendon Press, 1973).

6. The implications for the second half of the seventeenth century have been well brought out by Theodore K. Rabb, *The Struggle for Stability in Early Modern Europe*, (New York: Oxford University Press, 1975).

shown convincingly that the efforts of M. Mersenne's circle, in which Descartes played an active role, were directed precisely at overcoming the superstitious naturalism of the late sixteenth century and its belief in the influences of stars and in arbitrary divine interventionism.[7] A similar intention albeit not as consciously religious and theological, informed the labors of Bruno, Kepler, Galileo, and many other scientific and philosophic minds. The significance of this cultural environment and of the socioinstitutional setting for scientific accomplishments of the early seventeenth century has now been clearly demonstrated by historians and philosophers of science.[8]

The outcome of these efforts, by the middle of the seventeenth century, was a new image of the universe that provided both a sense of stability and a basis for understanding its dynamic aspects. The discovery of the laws of motion, both terrestrial and celestial, as well as the speculations about the fundamentally mathematical nature (or description) of matter and of its behavior not only gave a stable and coherent conception of the working of the universe but also, by asserting its predictability, enabled men to plan for purposeful action. The rationalism and the experimental validation of mathematically expressed descriptions of the behavior patterns of matter provided a tool that could be effectively used for further discoveries and applications. The mathematical and logical tools devised and improved by seventeenth-century scientists were felt to provide not only the means for the discovery of further laws of nature but also the framework for purposeful and predictable human action. Their apparent general validity and applicability naturally give rise to the temptation of applying them to the social, moral, and political spheres as well.

7. Robert Lenoble, *Mersenne et la naissance du mécanisme* (Paris: J. Vrin, 1943) and also his *Histoire de l'idée de nature* (Paris: Albin Michel, 1969). In her recent books, Dame Frances Yates makes similar points from a different and stimulating perspective.

8. One thinks of the classical works of A. Koyré on Galileo, E. Cassirer on the philosophical implications, Thomas Kuhn on methodology, and more recently Gerald Holton, *Thematic Origins of Scientific Thought—Kepler to Einstein* (Cambridge, Mass.: Harvard University Press, 1973). Also the somewhat idiosyncratic panorama by P. Kondylis, *Die Aufklärung im Rahmen des neuzeitlichen Rationalismus* (Stuttgart: Klett-Cotta, 1981).

The desire to ensure the stability and predictability of human action was as great as the need to know and understand the laws governing the physical environment. The irrational forces within man—human passions and emotions—were regarded as the main enemies of controlled and disciplined human activity. On the other hand, reason, and more particularly will, were felt to be forces that could supply the necessary controlling and stabilizing elements. To this end, in the first half of the seventeenth century (though the beginnings may be traced back to the last quarter of the sixteenth), Europe's intellectual leaders directed their energies and efforts toward subduing and husbanding passions and emotions so that rational will might prevail. But in order for individual wills to act in harmony, social relationships had to provide a well-balanced social environment within which individual reason and will could be displayed; to this end a hierarchical and stable social order was regarded as a necessary prerequisite. A polity based on order and discipline was taken for granted, and one of its primary functions was to maintain checks on and present barriers to the manifestation of disruptive passions and emotions. The political theories formulated in justification assumed that the social contract was devised primarily for subduing brutal, aggressive instincts (Hobbes, Spinoza) or for taming the passions and emotions to bring about a balance of interests (Locke).[9]

Controlling man's passions and instincts through reason and will implied subjection to sempiternal laws of the universe, which in turn required a knowledge and acceptance of such predictable and stable natural laws. This was the ground for the great popularity and impact of neo-Stoicism as a system of ethics and practical conduct. Neo-Stoicism proclaimed man's submission to the laws of the universe; its very definition of Natural Law was based on the laws of nature, so that those who accepted the precepts of neo-Stoicism were believed to have placed themselves knowingly and willingly under the rational guidance of these

9. There are suggestive ideas and arguments in Albert O. Hirschman, *The Passions and the Interests: Political Arguments for Capitalism before its Triumph* (Princeton, N.J.: Princeton University Press, 1977). See also Jacob Viner, *The Role of Providence in the Social Order* (Princeton, N.J.: Princeton University Press, 1972).

laws. This implied deliberate choice and the pursuit of rational action by dominating the passions and emotions. There was a further dimension to neo-Stoic ethics: it stressed the fact that all men belong to society and, derived from that fact, the necessity of each person's acting for the common good. This trait of neo-Stoic social philosophy made it particularly attractive at the end of the sixteenth century, for it justified a new order of stability and discipline. It proved especially appealing to energetic and action-oriented individuals or groups concerned to preserve their independence and freedom of purposeful action for the common good. It was no accident that neo-Stoicism provided the philosophic underpinning for the military revolution wrought by William and John of Orange in the Dutch fight for independence. The example of effective institutional reform and organization given by the princes of Orange and their military policies spread to other domains of public life and found many imitators, in particular in France and Prussia, the future leading military powers in Europe.[10]

The disciplining ethics of neo-Stoicism also inspired the institutional reforms of the absolute monarchies; one thinks, for example, of Richelieu's curbing the anarchy that had prevailed since the Wars of Religion and of the aesthetic expression of his policies in Corneille's theater and in contemporary novels.[11] Such ethics naturally appealed to the new military, in particular to its modernizing noble officers, because of its stress on leadership and discipline and the premium put on initiative, enterprise, and action. It corresponded also to the ethics of Calvinist Protestantism, an ethics of the active and creative life as propounded by members of the middle classes engaged in economic, aesthetic, and intellectual pursuits.[12] Even more significant was the fact that neo-Stoicism gave philosophic as well as psychological justification for the growing role played by the political establishment and its

10. Günter Abel, *Stoizismus und frühe Neuzeit: Zur Entstehungsgeschichte modernen Denkens im Felde von Ethik und Politik* (Berlin and New York: Walter de Gruyter, 1978), and Gerhard Oestreich, *Geist und Gestalt des frühmodernen Staates: Ausgewählte Aufsätze* (Berlin: Duncker & Humblot, 1969).

11. Paul Bénichou, *Morales du grand siècle* (Paris: Gallimard, 1948).

12. Ch. G. B[essel], *Schmiede des politischen Glücks* (1669).

increasingly professionalized officialdom in the productive life of a society oriented to the future. Surely neo-Stoic ethics found itself at almost the polar opposite to the traditional behavior that had predominated throughout the Middle Ages, a behavior that seemed to lack a sense of purposeful, future-oriented action for betterment in this world.

Closely related to these new attitudes and values was the popularity of the idea of·utopia—another manifestation of the changing outlook of European man. As is well known, *utopia* means "nowhere," but it does not mean outside human (historical) time, in sharp distinction from medieval (or religious) chiliasm, which sees the realization of its ideal beyond humanly known or knowable historical time. Moreover, following the prototype of Thomas More's conception of it, utopian polities are characterized by a conscious, voluntaristic constructivism based on rational principles or a rational interpretation of the dogmas of faith. Utopias were *à la mode* in the seventeenth century, especially in its first half; they proposed polities organized along rational and efficient lines that would give practical expression to moral and religious principles (which varied, of course, depending on the author's preferences and which need not detain us).[13] Again, these utopias were situated in the known world, though not in the present one. Unlike the chiliastic vision of Joachino da Fiore, for example, of a world that was to come into being at the end of time, the utopias of seventeenth-century writers were put into the future of our own historical time. Utopias, in short, provided both a foretaste of what should be achieved and a blueprint or recommendation as to how it might be accomplished. The utopia is a prognosis, a forecasting of desirable and positive things to come, provided men are willing to prepare for them by taking appropriate steps.[14] The literature of utopias bore witness to a

13. Johann Valentin Andreae, *Christianopolis* (1619), ed. Dülmer. A well-known German example of utopia, *Der Wohleingerichtete Staat Des bishero von vielen gesuchten aber nicht gefundenen Königreichs Ophir . . .* (1699). For a general survey of all kinds of utopias, see now Frank E. Manuel, *Utopias* (Cambridge, Mass.: Harvard University Press, 1979).

14. Thomas Nipperdey, "Die Funktion der Utopie im politischen Denken der Neuzeit," in his *Gesellschaft, Kultur, Theorie: Gesammelte Aufsätze* (Göttingen: Van-

new awareness, namely that it was possible to give specific institutional shape to the society man desired for the purpose of maximal prosperity, happiness, and benefit for all.[15]

A specific and concrete undertaking to implement this new attitude to "social engineering" may be found in South America in the rule exercised by Jesuit missionaries. The Jesuits went to Paraguay not only to convert the native Indians but also to "raise" them to the level of Western Christian civilization by establishing a polity that would prove most efficient in the pursuit of that end. Our purpose here cannot be to give a description of the so-called Jesuit states in what are now Paraguay and southern Brazil. They were not states in the strict sense of the term, of course, but communities (under the sovereignty of the king of Spain and his viceroy in Buenos Aires) organized by the Jesuit fathers to (in their view) structure the lives of the christianized Indian tribes, protect them from foreign enemies, secure them against the exactions and exploitation of Spanish colonial authorities and settlers, organize communal and family life so as to eradicate all manifestations of earlier religious beliefs and practices, introduce and enforce Christian patterns of behavior and to devise a rational and efficient economic system that would raise the Indians' cultural level and prepare them for joining the world of civilized Christendom. The Jesuits, naturally, were to provide guidance, teaching, and supervision, exercising full control with the help of willing native leaders (chieftains and heads of families). Value judgments apart, it was a serious and relatively successful effort at setting up a utopian community (at least until the decline of the Jesuit order at the beginning of the eighteenth century). It was not utopian in the sense of expressing an ideal normative system of values, nor was it a communistic (or socialistic) experiment, as some writers would have it. The Jesuit "re-

---

denhoeck & Ruprecht, 1976), pp. 74–88; Reinhart Kosellek, "Vergangene Zukunft der frühen Neuzeit," in his *Vergangene Zukunft: Zur Semantik geschichtlicher Zeiten* (Frankfurt am Main: Suhrkamp Verlag, 1979), pp. 17–37.

15. Utopias become largely negative and pessimistic in the late eighteenth and in the nineteenth centuries, probably to escape the predictable consequences of historical time and of man's acting in pursuit of seventeenth-century utopian goals.

ductions" were utopian in the specific sense mentioned above of providing a blueprint for a possible and indeed desirable form of social, economic, and political organization that, within the limitations of physical circumstances, would make for the greatest common good and the broadest spread of happiness to its individual members. With the benefit of hindsight it is amazing to note to what extent the Jesuits in Paraguay prefigured the outlook, aims, and policies of enlightened absolutism in Austria and Russia (especially with respect to peoples deemed to be on a lower level of culture) and those of the well-organized police state—naturally with quite a different role assigned to religion and its ministers.[16]

Was the Jesuit experiment known and absorbed, and consciously imitated, by European administrators in the late seventeenth and early eighteenth centuries? I have not been able to find any direct evidence for such influence. It is certain that many of the features of the experiment became known in Europe in the second half of the seventeenth century. Reports by Jesuits and other missionaries, as well as descriptions by travelers, were published and did circulate; there are occasional references to jesuitic organization and policies in the learned geographic and anthropological literature of the time.[17] However, I could find no documentary evidence of direct impact or deliberate borrowing and imitation. It is hard, though, to escape the impression of a basic similarity of attitude toward administrative leadership on the part of Jesuit fathers and contemporary secular officials in Europe. Both were eager to bring about a higher and uniform level of culture and economy by means of education, prescription, regulation, and control.

16. Of the abundant literature, the best monograph and introduction is Magnus Mörner, *The Political and Economic Activities of the Jesuits in the LaPlata Region: The Hapsburg Era* (Stockholm: Ibero Amerikanska Bibliotek och Institut, 1953). Also useful are Gerhard Aigner, *Der Jesuitenstaat in Paraguay und seine Wirtschaft* (Ph.D. diss., Hochschule für Welthandel, Vienna, 1959, privately printed) and Maria Fassbinder, *Der "Jesuitenstaat" in Paraguay* (Halle: M. Niemayer, 1926).

17. Most widely known is Anton Sepp and Anton Böhm, *RR.PP. Antonii Sepp und Antonii Böhm Der Societät Jesu Priestern . . . Reiss-Beschreibung/wie dieselben aus Hispanien in Paraquarien kommen . . .* (1696); later editions with slightly varied title (Passau, 1698; Ingolstadt, 1710, for example).

The anticlerical and antijesuitic propaganda of the philosophes
has resulted in an uncritical and emotional condemnation of the
Paraguay settlements as a poorly disguised device to exploit and
maltreat the Indians. In the light of incomplete evidence, this
seems to be misdirected criticism, for, paradoxical as it may
sound, philosophes and Jesuits had too much in common to get
along, both being products of the intellectual attitudes and
political practices that had arisen in the course of the seventeenth
century. In their South American experiment, the Jesuit fathers
had illustrated one way by which the intellectual transformation
of the seventeenth century could be translated into practical social
policy. The missionary fathers were the professional experts who
had made it their task to raise the cultural level, as well as religious
consciousness, of a native population. It is a striking feature of the
seventeenth century that its active elites, in all realms, were
endeavoring to devise institutional structures to implement their
"professional" conceptions and values.

As might be expected in the first stages of this endeavor, the
boundaries between most disciplines and activities were still
rather blurred. As yet we have none of the highly specialized,
strictly compartmentalized social organizations and professional
associations that begin to appear in the eighteenth century and
reach their full development in the nineteenth and twentieth.
Members of one elite might easily be called upon to participate
actively in or even to take control of enterprises in a completely
different domain. The Jesuits were but a special instance: priests
and missionaries, they took on social and economic leadership as
teachers, administrators, entrepreneurs, and rulers.

By mid–seventeenth century, the intellectual elites, especially
those in science and philosophy, were finding a new institutional
and organizational framework: academies, literary or learned
societies (among which the French Academy and the Royal
Society in England were the best known and most prestigious), as
well as private circles associated with outstanding personalities
(for example, M. Mersenne) or religious and educational institutions (Port Royal). The phenomenon spread beyond Western
Europe and found many imitators in central Europe and ultimately in the Slavic East as well. Standards and solidarity were

maintained by self-policing, unless the state took the institution under its wing, which also entailed control. The educational institutions that fell under the influence of the new intellectual elites set the required levels of preparation and performance. In France this was accomplished by the schools set up by progressive religious orders or associations (Jesuits, the Congregation of the Oratory, Port Royal, and so forth). In the Germanies this role was usually played by the universities, since many were founded to suit the particular religious preferences and interests of princes and territorial sovereignties. Later on, with the rise of new religious preoccupations and philosophical concerns, more schools and learned societies were established under the aegis of innovators: one thinks in particular of the role of Pietism in establishing universities, schools, publishing houses, and welfare institutions or of the founding of academies, colleges, and societies for the promotion of learning by prominent philosophers and scholars such as Leibniz. Finally, the new media of communication, in particular journals, newspapers, and publishing enterprises, served as rallying centers for the new intellectual elites. Administrators and statesmen were frequently drawn from among the ranks of these elites; even more frequently, prominent military and political leaders sought membership in these distinguished societies and intellectual circles, either as patrons or as active participants in their work and discussions. All this resulted in lively interaction between intellectual and cultural concerns and economic and social policies.

The situation with respect to the administrative leadership of the government was much the same. Many administrators came from the legal profession, or at any rate had had legal training, so that they carried on the intellectual concerns that had initiated the revival of Roman canon law. As just mentioned, many administrators had the same background as the scientists, philosophers, and writers who came together in the circles, academies, or literary societies, and some administrators were instrumental in founding such institutions as well. Not only do we observe an overlapping membership; what is more important, we notice that the same intellectual attitudes and cultural values were shared by members of the intellectual elite in the several areas of public life.

Mutatis mutandis, the same may be said of entrepreneurial, economic, and technological elites, although only in the Netherlands
and in England did the average businessman have direct contact
with the intellectual elites. Of still greater significance were the
contact and mutual involvement between intellectual elites and
prominent dignitaries of princely courts, of whom the most
outstanding example was Prince Eugene of Savoy in Vienna, but
he was certainly not the only aristocrat to play this role. Little
wonder that administrators readily shared in the new intellectual
trends and endeavored to give a practical and political expression
to the prevailing philosophy and social theory.

The basic intellectual attitudes directly relevant to administrative policy of the seventeenth century had been in the making
since the late fifteenth century. To be sure, instead of an uninter-
rupted linear progression there had been much hesitation and
many twists and turns, nor did every state or society have the
means to implement the new concerns or develop them fully.
What is strikingly particular to the seventeenth century, however,
and in this respect the century proved genuinely seminal, were
the efforts at *routinizing* (to use Max Weber's term) the new
attitudes by devising practical institutional means for preserving
and developing the intellectual and cultural stirps. To the extent
that such efforts were successful, they created the institutional
framework for policies that served to promote the movement
toward modernization that we are tracing.

In a society that believed God to be the source and center of all
things and that accepted unquestioningly the basic dogmas of the
Christian faith (whatever their denominational form or interpretation), the routinization of piety came first. Church and religion
as organizing and disciplining institutions dated from the conver-
sion to Christianity, of course. Heretofore, however, this function
had taken the form of providing a stable framework and calendar
for man's secular activities and traditions. But from the late
sixteenth century on, religious life itself was to become an
instrument for the organization, structuring, and setting of goals
of the earthly existence of the faithful. To this end piety had to
prescribe conduct and behavior that would serve to discipline
society, to promote its productive activities, and to keep the
faithful obedient. The Jesuits pioneered in formalizing piety in

such a manner that it became a set of "do it yourself" rules for attaining the form and level of religious experience deemed desirable for society's purposes. The Counter-Reformation codified this approach and reinforced it by institutionalizing the routine of rituals of piety (through organizations such as the Society for the Perpetual Adoration of the Holy Sacrament, the Congregation of the Oratory, and others). Similar patterns developed in most Protestant denominations: the codification and prescription of pious exercises (such as the taking of communion or attending sermons), strictly supervised by the pastors, were deemed to be essential to a well-organized, disciplined, and productive community. Frequently this emphasis on ritualized piety, which in Protestant culture also took the form of Bible reading and Bible classes, resulted in the establishment of pietistic conventicles and similar associations. The supervised performance of ritual piety became a regular feature of daily life. This did not preclude individual mystical experiences and spiritual pursuits, but these could involve only the elect few and the authorities, both Catholic and Protestant, always viewed this type of religiosity with suspicion and misgiving, for it gave pride of place to individualistic factors not readily controlled or husbanded and potentially conducive to a relaxation of social discipline.

Closely related to the ritualization of piety—and, not unexpectedly, originating in Spain—was the revival of scholasticism in modernized shape to provide useful intellectual instruments for religious and social discipline. Neoscholasticism revitalized the study of Aristotle in the universities (Protestant as much as Catholic, especially in Germany), not so much because of his philosophy's cosmological (scientific) or metaphysical relevance as for its logic and psychology to underpin rhetoric and dialectic as tools of the mind. The rationalism of modern science and mathematics required coherent, step-by-step reasoning, while an elegant presentation and effective persuasion were essential to the dissemination of the new intellectual attitudes, as well as to further discoveries and advances.[18] For this reason, too, the

18. For example, Christian Weise, *Politischer Academicus* . . . (1685); *Der Adeliche Hofmeister* (1693); Spaeth, *Der Teutsche Advocat* (1678); and also the brilliant account and analysis in M. Fumaroli, *L'Âge de l'éloquence: Rhétorique et "res literaria" de la Renaissance au seuil de l'époque classique* (Geneva: Librarie Droz, 1980).

pedagogy of the major educational establishments aimed at
imparting the skills of clear and cogent reasoning—logic (after
the Ramist treatises had introduced dialectic, the most widely
used textbook of logic was the *Logique de Port Royal* of Arnaud and
Nicole[19]) and rhetoric—that is, accurate and simple exposition of
ideas in words, written or oral. Reliance on observation and
experimentation were not yet the central concerns of intellectual
training, but the need to check on results and to formulate laws
brought additional disciplining of the life of the mind. The
organization of sense data and experience in meaningful, permanent, and repeatable ways was the accomplishment of the late
seventeenth and early eighteenth centuries. It added a sense for
perceptual and experienced reality to the theoretical and deduc-
tive systematization of seventeenth-century natural philosophy.

The increase in the number of people involved in the productive tasks of society, the desire to instill the new intellectual
attitudes, and the expectation that in so doing the chaos and
anarchy of the sixteenth and early seventeenth centuries could be
surmounted combined to give high priority to education. Clearly
the growth in numbers of educable men explains the founding of
many new schools and the widespread discussion of pedagogical
issues. The schools of the seventeenth century, of whatever
denomination and under whatever auspices, set themselves the
task of teaching those techniques that would help routinize and
implement the intellectual attitudes we have been describing. The
Protestant reformations, with their stress on reading the Bible
and their reliance on the individual's understanding of the
Scriptures, were not alone in furthering a spread and expansion
of education, at least on the elementary levels. The Catholic
Counter-Reformation followed suit to maintain or recapture the
Church's position. In addition, the elites themselves wanted to
perpetuate acquired knowledge and intellectual mastery in their
own children and train an expanding membership.

Recognizing the special aspects of children's learning patterns

19. Antoine Arnauld and Pierre Nicole, *La logique ou l'art de penser* (1st ed.
1660; 5th ed. 1683). Most recently edited by Louis Marin (Paris: Flammarion,
1970).

and the desirability of complementing the theoretical with the practical, the pedagogy of the times made sure to effectively develop the necessary intellectual skills.[20] The large number of students of different levels of aptitudes and interests forced the pedagogues to devise methods for reaching them effectively and made school itself a conditioning and disciplining as well as learning experience for the future leaders of society. Disciplining meant not only teaching passive acceptance of authority and controls but also, in the neo-Stoic military sense, the formation of individuals capable of initiative, of relying on their own minds and wills, and capable of cooperating with others for a common goal. Instead of physical coercion and punishment, shame—moral suasion enforced by the group—and emphasis on visual and sense perception in learning (rather than rote memory) were the methodological innovations of the pedagogic efforts that laid the foundation for the routinization of the new intellectual trends. The new pedagogy stressed the study of logic, rhetoric, mathematics, physics, and the vernacular, as well as continuing the traditional emphasis on Latin. In the case of the social elites, learning the academic disciplines was complemented by training in socially useful arts and graces (music, art, riding, modern foreign languages). The well-educated, well-rounded gentleman, *l'honnête homme*, was not only the ideal set by salons and polite court society; he was also the essential ingredient and active leader in a disciplined society that endeavored to combine stability and order with dynamic progress. Besides formal schooling, for members of the elite travel also became a major instrument for the acquisition of the mental and social leadership skills.[21]

20. E. Weigel, *Aretologistica* (1687); A. F. Glaffley, *Anleitung* (1747), and of course the great influence of the pedagogic writings of A. Comenius. The literature on education is limitless; one of the most interesting monographs to my knowledge, dealing particularly well with principles and methods, is Georges Snyders, *La Pédagogie en France aux XVII et XVIIIe siècles* (Paris: Presses Universitaires de France, 1965). A most influential treatise incorporating the new views was J. P. de Crousaz, *Traité de l'éducation des enfans* (LaHaye: 1722), German translation by Menantes, *Neuer und besonderer Unterricht von Auferziehung der Jugend nach heutiger Manier* (Halle: 1720).

21. For example, Wolff Bernhard von Tschirnhaus, *Getreuer Hofmeister auf Academien und Reisen . . .* (1727); [author unknown], *Die rechte Reisekunst* (1674).

One of the principal notions the *honnête homme* had to absorb in order to fulfill his elite function was that he and other members of society constituted an organic whole and that the welfare of the polity took precedence over the selfish interests of its individual members. The notion of the common good and a keen awareness of the obligations, duties, as well as rights, of every member of the polity was to be uppermost in the education and thinking of members of the elites. These notions, too, provided the norms and overall goals for the administrative leadership's direction of and attempts to refashion society. The ideas of general welfare and of the individual's duty and obligations to the community were not only ethical concepts to be found in neo-Stoicism; they also derived from the traditional concept of natural law.[22] German philosophers and jurists, in particular, developed the proposition that the rights of the community take precedence over the rights of its individual members, with consequences and implications that have been splendidly drawn by G. Gurvitch in his *L'Idée du droit social* and which we therefore need not repeat.[23] The welfare of the whole could easily be interpreted as meaning the happiness of all, of each and every one; this step was taken in the eighteenth century when the belief in the world as a creation with a divinely ordained purpose receded. The welfare of the commonweal, the subordination of individual interests and passions to the needs of the community, were rationally justified as a necessary framework for every person's existence. These were the singularly important elements of seventeenth-century thinking that intellectual and institutional means were to fix in the consciousness and behavior of contemporaries by routinizing them.

A final word: we have spoken of routinization, that is the giving of a readily acceptable and implementable form to intellectual orientation and moral values, as the task of the seventeenth century. Codification was one such significant method of routiniz-

22. Christian Thomasius, *Summarischer Entwurf derer Grundlehren, die einem studioso Juris zu wissen und auff Universitäten zu lernen nöthig* (1699).
23. Georges Gurvitch, *L'Idée du droit social: Notion et système du droit social— Histoire doctrinale depuis le 17e siècle jusqu'à du 19e siècle* (Paris: Librarie Recueil Sirey, 1932; reprint ed., Aalen: Scientia Verlag, 1972).

ing that made principles and norms readily available for application. Codification, the collection and systematization of the ruling norms of society, as exemplified by the *Grandes ordonnances* of Colbert, not only made the body of laws readily accessible to all those who needed it but also endowed this body of rules with the potential for further development, releasing an immanent dynamics whose ultimate consequences could not be foreseen.[24] The seventeenth century was also the age of great cosmological and metaphysical systematizations, putting every proposition and law about the universe into a coherent whole to permit their convenient use. This was accomplished by the formulation of laws of nature, of international law, or by restating the basic principles of Natural Law.[25] A similar trend may be observed in theology, in systems and interpretations of dogma, and in aesthetics (as seen in the rules of the three unities, and so forth). The imposition of coherent patterns, even at the risk of oversimplification and of doing violence to specifics, was a characteristic feature of the mentality of the seventeenth century. To contemporaries this necessarily justified controls, strict supervision, and overall guidance exercised by powerful institutions or the sovereign ruler; these alone, it was felt, could preserve both harmonious stability and dynamic progress in the body politic.

The trends we have reviewed all too briefly and superficially not only added up to a new conception of man and the universe (whose features have been well and thoroughly described in the literature); they also implied a novel approach to social relationships and political organization and tasks. Indeed, it is not only a question of secularization, whatever that might mean in a specific context, nor is it a question of the "Machiavellian moment." Secularism and Machiavellianism were certainly both present. What was more significant, and implicit in the autonomy of the political, was a realization that the social and political structuring

24. This is not to say that there were no earlier efforts. But the "coutumiers" were collections of laws without the systematizing aspects of the codification, while such acts as the Imperial Police Ordinances partook of new statutory law.

25. In the context of international law, see the as usual very stimulating book by Carl Schmitt, *Der Nomos der Erde im Völkerrecht des Jus Publicum Europaeum* (Berlin: Duncker & Humblot, 1950).

of human activities was to take place *hic et nunc,* within the
broader framework of a conception of the universe which asserted that nature could be understood and acted upon through
discovery of laws or patterns that could be expected to apply not
only in the present but also in the future. The function of politics
(in the widest sense) was more than negative actions to preserve
peace, law, and order so as to enable everyone to live according to
his best lights and ability to merit salvation in the hereafter.
Within the broad context of Natural Law and the laws of nature,
social organization and action provided a purpose for man's
existence on this earth; administrative and political action prepared the future shape of society. Such a view implied voluntary,
rational taking of decisions with a "high time horizon," that is,
with the expectation of the results becoming manifest at some
remote future moment.[26]

This new attitude marked a major departure in European
political thinking and practice. The present may be a given, but
the future is not; people no longer could automatically assume
that the future could be extrapolated from the present and
contain no new elements. The perception of the past as distinct
and different from the present (a notion that was launched by the
Humanists in the fifteenth century and which most people took a
long time to accept) also suggests that the future will be quite
different from the present and that, consequently, if one knows
how the physical universe works, the future can be prepared for
or even shaped. Such a perception demanded drastic transformation of people's attitudes and behavior. In particular, it meant
prying people loose from the constricting, semiautomatic patterns of behavior and thought based purely on tradition—that
is, on the instinctively, unreflectingly accepted notion of the
present as entirely constituted from the past. The most significant
blow (though not the only one, and certainly not the first) to
the traditional attitude was dealt by the Reformation. It put
in question the old conception that the ways of this world are

26. On the notion of "high time horizon," see Alexander Gerschenkron,
"Time Horizon in Russian Literature," *Slavic Review* 34 (1975): 692–715, and
"Time Horizon in Balzac and Others," *Proceedings of the American Philosophical
Society* 122 (1978): 75–91.

subordinated to expectations in the hereafter. In so doing the Reformation shattered the feeling of security and permanence that underlay the unquestioning acceptance of tradition and custom. Something had to be substituted to fill the void.

In the seventeenth century replacements for this shattered image and new goals and purposes for man's activity on this earth were being defined. A direction that suggested itself almost automatically in view of the expanded needs of society and institutions was to increase the potential resources of society, to make the fallow productive and the hidden accessible.

Such an orientation suggested itself because of improved knowledge of the physical world, a better understanding of the varied potentials of human nature, and greater joy and pleasure in rational thought, discovery, and human creativity. Men were finding the natural environment potentially richer than they had thought, less threatening because more understandable, and they were discovering that they were in a position to manipulate and control it better for their own benefit and interests—to be, in Descartes' words, "maîtres et possesseurs de la nature." It was this new attitude that had to be instilled in the common people through the routinization of basic cultural, intellectual, and institutional activities. To this end, the customs, ideas, and activities of the ordinary people had to be transformed, and in order to accomplish this, new forms of administrative action had to be devised.

Police ordinances of a new type were drafted and promulgated to fulfill this purpose. No longer did they consist of moral injunctions supported by the sanctions of religious belief and the potential threat of punishment in the hereafter. They were, rather, pragmatic statements, orders, or counsels designed to have an immediate and direct effect in reshaping patterns of public behavior and social action. As in the case of the routinization of intellectual tools and approaches through codification of law, this rational, purposeful, and voluntaristic administrative policy possessed an inherent dynamic force. Once the police ordinances had been issued, through the institutions they structured and controlled they generated a movement that released new social forces. These, in turn, by creating unforeseen problems, set new tasks that, again, had to be resolved by administrative measures. The legislator's leadership role became increasingly important, beginning a process that eventually transformed the political as well as social and cultural life of Europe.

PART TWO
Transforming German Society

1. The Ordinances *(Landes-* and *Polizei-ordnungen)*

From the late sixteenth century onward, throughout the seventeenth and well into the eighteenth centuries, the chanceries of the host of German territorial sovereignties both great and small churned out a steady stream of *Landesordnungen* and *Polizeiordnungen.* Partaking of the character of both general laws and specific regulations or instructions, these ordinances expressed the government's philosophy, goals, and methods with respect to matters of international policy. Whether the laws dealt with broad issues, such as the organization of the judicial system and state finance, or, as they did more frequently, with specific problems of limited scope (for example, the need for building permits in a town, or market or shipping regulations), the ordinances also set forth what institutional measures had to be taken for their practical implementation. By so doing the ordinances shed light on the technical and human instruments available to the governments at the time. Since many of the problems met by the ordinances were coming within the competence of the government for the first time or in new form, the authors of the regulations could not take traditional modes of operation or established institutional practices for granted. They had to spell out the concrete manner of action and to set forth the principles and rules by which the given aspect of public life was to be handled and resolved in the future. Thus the ordinances also served as the framework within which new bureaucratic practices and a professionalized and functionally specialized administrative personnel developed.

43

While it is quite true that many ordinances were not actually implemented and many regulations more often breached than obeyed, they do, nonetheless, provide evidence of the efforts made by rulers and administrators to move their societies in specific ways and directions, to shape their population, economies, and cultural life according to set standards and norms. In the long run, in spite of resistance and failures, there did emerge an active, productive, efficient, and rationalistic style of economic and cultural behavior,* and in this development the constant prodding and structuring by administrative action played a significant, or rather an essential and seminal role. If with nothing else, the ordinances provide us with a record and testimony of the conscious efforts made, on a national as well as local scale, by the leaders of society to bring about those results and transformations they deemed desirable.

Because of seventeenth- and eighteenth-century Germany's variegated patchwork of states and sovereignties, the authorities that issued police ordinances were numerous and equally varied. Most ordinances, of course, were drafted in the sovereign's council and issued in his or her name. They were enforced (with what success may be questioned at times) within the ruler's entire territory or any particular part of it, as the ordinances might specify. On occasion, however, subordinate authorities also issued ordinances; these were enforced only within the particular jurisdiction of the issuing institution. Such was the case with ordinances pertaining to specialized aspects of public life, such as medicine, education, or, most frequently, religion. In towns and

*Lest *rationalistic* and terms derived from *ratio* give rise to confusion or misunderstanding, I hasten to clarify my use of them. *Rationalistic* is used to refer to measures that have rational grounding, or are based on the systematic application of reason (rather than tradition, custom, emotion, or religious sentiment). Perhaps it might be better to say *rationalized*, except that in contemporary American usage there is the danger of a pejorative implication, i.e., *ex post facto*, spurious, rational justification, which is not intended here. In any event, *rational* as used here is to be distinguished from the anthropological meaning of functionally rational *(zweckrational)*, where everything becomes rational within the terms of its own closed system. In this latter sense even the most emotional and sometimes unpredictable outburst may be "rational" in that it has a social function in a structured context (e.g., the "world turned upside down" in carnivals).

cities possessing a fair degree of self-government, whatever their size or juridical character, it was the mayor or city council that issued ordinances binding on their fellow townsmen. Finally, there are a few instances when individual estate holders or landowners issued similar regulations for their subjects and peasants.[1]

The degree of implementation and effectiveness of ordinances naturally depended very much on the authorities' ability to enforce their will. This varied greatly, not only with respect to the particular sphere of life affected by the ordinances but also with respect to the size of the territory and the comprehensiveness of the administrative network. Large entities, the Empire being the largest, depended for enforcement of ordinances on the help and cooperation of many social and legal bodies, such as estates, municipalities, guilds, universities, and communal jurisdictions. By and large, the greater the territory and the more complex its social and legal structure, the less rewarding the central authorities' efforts.[2] The ordinances of the medium- and small-sized sovereignties in the Germanies were most effective in achieving their purpose, while measures taken by the most tiny ones had such limited impact in Germany as a whole as to be disregarded here.

In point of fact, it was not so much a sovereign's or political entity's ability to centralize and monopolize power that mattered for the successful implementation of its ordinances. It was rather a government's ability to reach out to local communities and subordinate institutions, through effective channels of communi-

---

1. Local urban ordinances, for example *Minden Policey Ordnung* (Lemgo: 1613), *Northausen Policey Ordnung* (Northausen: 1668), *Hildesheimb Policey Ordnung* (Hildesheim: 1665), or the Kleiderordnung of the city of Braunschweig (Braunschweig: 26 Nov. 1650). Technical and institutional ordinances are reprinted, for example, in Bergius, *Sammlung*, and may also be found in manuscript form for pedagogic use (e.g., in the collection in the Göttingen Staats-und Universitäts-bibliothek). Examples of private ordinances may be found in treatises and publicistic writings like B. von Rohr's.

2. An underdeveloped social structure and the absence of many and complexly constituted bodies also had the effect of preventing the police ordinances from being genuinely effective, a point I will argue at greater length in pt. 3 in discussing Russia.

cation, that proved crucial. In those instances where the sovereign succeeded in enlisting the cooperation of lower, preexisting associations, solidarities, or institutions, the police ordinances had the best chances of being effective in their overall purpose of guiding and transforming society.

From the perspective of the national states, it was the centralized monarchy holding sway over a large territory that traditionally has been seen as the dominant force in shaping society. Recent research, however, has shown that the absolute monarchies' achievements were far more modest than had been previously believed, so that contemporary historiography has belittled or even denied the role played by institutions in the transformation of "preindustrial" (or "premodern") society.[3] Yet in fact the record shows not only that the impulses for the transformation of society in a productive and rationally structured direction did come from the political authorities, but it also proves that these endeavors were most notable on the scale of the smaller territories. We shall return to this problem when we consider the human tools and institutional methods available, and we shall try to single out the major dynamic factors in the situation.

As we have just mentioned, at times ordinances were of a general nature and at others very specific in referring to a single, immediate problem. Naturally these circumstances affected the form and manner of publication. As a rule, the ordinance was first "published"—that is, made available to those concerned with its enforcement—as a single document, printed or in manuscript, issued by the competent authority. Ordinances that contained general rules of conduct with respect to broad areas of public life and activity were broadcast as widely as necessary, frequently through several printings of the edict, and publicized locally.[4]

3. This has been the main thrust of the so-called *Annales* school (e.g., P. Goubert) and naturally of its Marxist predecessors and their epigones. Cf. also D. Gerhard, *Ständische Vertretung* (Göttingen: Vandenhoeck & Ruprecht, 1962) and F. L. Carsten, *Princes and Parliaments in Germany* (Oxford: Clarendon Press, 1959) from the perspective of the survival of estate roles.
4. Graphic illustration is provided by the collection of ordinances in the Herzog August library at Wolfenbüttel. Those designed for subordinate authori-

Publication of these ordinances was in the form of reading from the pulpit at regular intervals and of posting at conspicuous places.[5] Ordinances and decrees dealing with a particular administrative problem or social situation were made available only to those immediately concerned with their implementation and enforcement. Such acts remained unknown to the rest of the population or to other institutions; this was especially the case with regulations affecting the modus operandi of princely chanceries, courts, and the like.[6]

Obviously, over a period of time, the accumulation of specific ordinances might become too great for their efficient supervision and execution, while the danger of discrepancies and contradictions between individual ordinances would grow in proportion. This state of affairs led to the compilation of ordinances and their publication in book form. Such compilations were of two kinds: in the first place, official *compendia, Sammlungen,* were put together in the chanceries, with individual ordinances amended, eliminated, or included to make for comprehensive and systematic

---

ties are of small (octavo) format, printed on both sides of the leaf and not suitable for posting. Another group consists of large-format (quarto) sheets, printed on one side of the leaf only, so as to be suitable for posting. There are also bound volumes of collected ordinances published for official use in chanceries, e.g. (under Braunschweig in bibliography) *Sammelband: Landtags- Abschiede, Ordnungen, Mandate—Wolfenbüttel* (Wolfenbüttel: n.d.) or *Dess Herzogthumbs Würtemberg allerhand Ordnungen* (Stuggart, 1670), where individual ordinances are stuck together mechanically with their individual pagination preserved.

5. For example, "Des Durchl. . . . Herrn Augusti . . . algemeine Landesordnung/welche ins künftige auf allen und jeden Landgerichten, wo dieselbigen gehalten werden, öffentlich allemahl verlesen und mit Ernst darüber gehalten soll" (1647), in *Sammelband . . . Wolfenbüttel.* Also *Northausen Policey Ordnung* (1668) and the early order that *Churfürstlicher Pfaltz Fürstenthumbs in Obern Bayern Lands Ordnung* (Amberg: 1590) be read at least once a year in public and relevant extracts prominently displayed for all to see (p. 389).

6. Calenberg ordinance, 1739, in *Chur-Braunschweig . . . Landes Ordnungen . . . .* introduction (no pagination): "Öfters sind gute Gesetze und Verordnungen in vorigen Zeiten publicirt, die Abdrücke aber davon dergestalt vergriffen und abhanden gekommen, dass manchmal selbst in Gerichten, Archiven und Registraturen kein Exemplar davon mehr zu finden ist, wodurch es dann geschieht, dass geschriebene Gesetze auch in eine oft ungewisse Landes Gewohnheit verwandelt werden, und kaum den Gelehrtesten selbst mehr im Lande bekannt sind."

coverage.[7] These compendia had the force of law and served as guides for the courts and government offices. Another kind of compilation was put together for didactic purposes in the universities and institutions that gave professional training to administrative personnel.[8] In this case, professors and scholars (who were frequently also members of territorial administrations) compiled the ordinances relevant or important to their fields (or course of lectures), arranged them in some meaningful and convenient order, and at times annotated them. This kind of compilation displayed a high degree of coherence and analytical synthesis, coming closer to being a code, but only rarely, and unofficially, would such a "code" be used in the judicial and administrative process. For purposes of our study, the differences in manner of publication play a subordinate role and may be disregarded, except in those special instances when some general conclusion can be drawn from the differences.

Some comments on the form and style of the ordinances may be in order at this point, though they involve observations that are also relevant to the final conclusions. The ad hoc, specific ordinances dealing with concrete individual issues normally contained only the briefest statement of purpose and justification. They devoted exclusive attention to the concrete problem they endeavored to deal with, taking for granted that the reader would know the context and background, which were sketched in the barest outline.[9] Usually brief, this type of ordinance displayed little

7. For example, the compendia of Mylius for Prussia and Magdeburg, Kleinschmidt for Hesse, or the huge collections digested by J. J. Moser. For full bibliography of J. J. Moser's voluminous output see now Mack Walker, *Johann Jakob Moser and the Holy Empire of the German Nation* (Chapel Hill: University of North Carolina Press, 1981), especially pp. 350–53. An example of a princely compendium is *Churfürstlicher Pfaltz Fürstenthumbs in Obern Bayern Landrecht* (n.p., 1606), especially the introduction (no pagination).

8. The collections of Bergius, of Freyberg for Bavaria (in topical order), and the several manuscript collections for didactic purposes in the Göttingen library (under Hesse): *Collectiones privato studio factae;* hessian Landesordnungen and Policeyordnung on specific subjects (for example, "Gerichts- und Sportelwesen aus den Jahren 1524 bis 1744," or "Landstreicher und Raubgesindel betreffend," or "Medicinalverordnungen 1616–1699").

9. The Bergius *Sammlung* has many examples. Also the Wolfenbüttel collection of loose ordinances, now repertoried (typescript) by Walter Petersen, "Ver-

effort at rational or logical organization or development. The
ordinances of general purpose, on the other hand, spelled out
more comprehensively the reasons for their promulgation, and
frequently they also gave a full account of all relevant prece-
dents.[10] At times, in an effort to give an international as well as
theoretical underpinning to the policy prescribed, we also find in
the prefaces or preambles of such ordinances references to
similar laws and practices abroad.[11] In the sixteenth and seventeenth centuries, such general ordinances, with the exception of
comprehensive, almost codelike Landesordnungen (especially
those dealing with justice and religion), tended to be disorgan-
ized, making no effort at systematic and logical presentation of
the subject matter: there were frequent repetitions, as well as
sudden returns to topics already covered. Often one has the
impression that topics and issues have been thrown together
helter-skelter, with no attempt to put the norms and rules
involved in generalized form. With the passage of time, however,
and it is clearly the case by the early eighteenth century, the
ordinances become more concise, precise, more logical, and much
clearer in style and organization.[12] The ordinance's general

zeichnis der Einblattdruck." Cf. also single ordinances issued in one volume in
Gotha in the 1650s (see bibliography) and *Augusti Braunschwyg . . . Hofgerichts
Ordnung* (Wolfenbüttel: 1663) (edict of 31. XII. 1643 on roads, or ibid., p. 352,
Tax Ordnung).

10. *Des Ernewerten Ritter Raths gantzen Franckischen Craisses / Verfasste Satzungen
und Ordnungen . . . .* (n.p., 1590), p. 2; *Hildesheimb . . . Policey Ordnung* (1665), pp.
4–5; "Braunschweig Verordnung," 22.XI.1768, in Bergius, *Sammlung*, 4:183–86.

11. See the introduction in Bergius, *Sammlung*, vol. 1: "Und hier muss man
nicht in seinem eigenen Vaterland stehen bleiben, sondern man muss sich
zugleich die Gesetze anderer Länder . . . bekannt machen." And the introduction
(no pagination) of the Ordnungen für Chursachsen of 1583 in *Ordnungen Herzog
Ernsten . . . Fürsten zu Sachsen . . . .* (Dresden, 1583) is an early model that was
much imitated: "Unsere lieben Vorfahren milder Gedächtniss und wir, von dieser
und jetzigen Zeit viel notwendiger und nützlicher Satzungen und Ordnungen
gemacht und in offenen Druck ausgehen lassen, so zu Beförderung unserer
wahrhaftigen Christlichen Religion Gottseligen Wandels, und Wesens, fortsetzung
gleichmässigen Rechtens und der Iustitien, auch zu Erhaltung guter Policey wohl
erwogen dienstlich und hochnötig . . . Articeln so darinne begriffen, und wie
dieselbigen von Zeiten zu Zeiten nach Gelegenheit und Erfordung der Leuffte
vermehrt und verbessert und verendert worden."

12. See Bergius, and Mylius (under Prussia), *Novum corpus constitutionum . . . .*
(Berlin, 1755) for eighteenth-century models.

purpose and justification are clearly set forth at the outset or in a preamble; if helpful or needed, concrete illustration is given of the kind of problem the ordinance aims at settling, and the new rules are set forth analytically, in logical sequence, and stated in generalized terms. Not surprisingly, the Prussian ordinances of the reign of Frederick II provide outstanding examples of coherent, clear, logical, and well-reasoned presentation of legislative norms and administrative practices. Put in another way, in the sixteenth and early seventeenth centuries the legislation was primarily, even exclusively, negative. Note was taken of unsatisfactory conditions and violations of existing laws, and regulations were issued to correct these defects so as to stop the decline (*Verfall*) and bring back the "gute Policey"—that is, restore things to their proper and normal order. In the course of the seventeenth century, and with accelerated, dynamic force, the legislation acquired a positive cast; its aims no longer were to restore and correct abuses and defects but rather to create new conditions, to bring about changes and introduce innovations. Hence also the ordinances' greater rationality and their better presentation and more coherent structure. The justification now came to include such phrases as *Aufhebung* (lifting and transcendence), "Förderung des gemeinen Nutzen" (promotion of the common weal), and as time went on we read more and more frequently of the *gemeine Beste* (common best state) that is to be promoted.[13]

One of the most striking features of this legislative material is its repetitiveness. It is repetitive in several ways: in the first place, most German territories issued very similar (if not outright identical) ordinances, for they had to cope with essentially the same problems and to do so within roughly the same mental and sociopolitical context. Of course there are local differences and variations, and we shall have occasion to return to these, but these

13. For "negative" sixteenth-century examples see preamble to Tiroler Policeyordnung (1573) in *New Reformirte LandesOrdnung* . . . . (1573) and *Churpfaltz Landes Ordnung* (1590), p. 385. Transitional forms in the seventeenth century are illustrated by *Hildesheim Policey Ordnung* (1665), pp. 4–5; *Augusti Braunschwyg . . . Hofgerichts Ordnung* (1663), Tax Ordnung on p. 352; Mylius, *Corpus Constitutionum Marchicarum oder Königl. Preussische* . . . . (hereafter "Mylius"), 5 (3):12 (1620). On the terms *gemeine Beste* and *gemeiner Nutzen*, see n. 205 below.

differences matter only if one has to deal with the details of the specific problems of particular territories. Needless to say, the major difference between the German states was that of religion. But although there are detectable variations in approach and handling of concrete issues on the part of Catholic and Protestant authorities (usually stemming from the particularities of ecclesiastical organization), they did not prove crucial in the long run and did not dramatically affect the most significant aspects of public life. For this reason it seems proper to discuss the ordinances topically rather than geographically; synthetically rather than serially as case studies.

The ordinances are repetitive in another way as well. The same regulations and prescriptions are reiterated constantly and also echoed over long periods of time within the same political jurisdiction (not to speak of the fact that the ordinances may be repeated for different parts or territories of the same political entity—for example, for Brandenburg and Magdeburg in Prussia). The usual explanation given for these repetitions (and at times the explanation is explicitly given in the preamble to an ordinance) is that the original ordinance was not properly obeyed or implemented. Of course, if true, this means that the effort at legislating social or economic change was met with effective resistance of either society or those impersonal forces that allegedly determine the destinies of countries and peoples. There is no denying, of course, that the enforcement of the ordinances, particularly those most innovative in their material and psychological effects on the population, presented serious difficulties. Reiteration was necessary to keep the rules and regulations constantly in the minds of officials and subjects. This was all the more necessary since communication was a serious problem, partly because of widespread illiteracy but also because of the absence of regular channels of communication through the printed word, such as newspapers, to which almost everyone could be expected to have direct or indirect access.[14] The printing of ordinances was too expensive a business to permit indiscriminate distribution of them in the form of separate sheets. The few

14. *Calenberg Ordnung* (1739), preamble.

copies that were printed had to be posted in carefully determined places, under some supervision, to prevent destruction and willful defacing. Finally, until the mid-eighteenth century at any rate, there existed no comprehensive pattern of distribution to official institutions, so that not every official to whom the ordinance might be relevant received a copy or complete set. It was not until the publication of comprehensive codes of law that the basic legal norms became readily available to all institutions and that officials could be expected to know them and base their decisions on their prescriptions. It is, therefore, fair to repeat after Max Weber that no true bureaucracy was possible in Europe until the comprehensive codification of laws had occurred—something that in Western and central Europe took place only in the second half of the eighteenth century, but on ground prepared by preceding police ordinances.

There were further reasons for the frequent repetition of ordinances. The repetition may first be seen as evidence of the transition from an oral to a written culture. The transition was a gradual process, and repetition was necessary to make it stick. There is even internal evidence for the process: the early sixteenth-century ordinances were definitely designed only to be read aloud to the subjects, as demonstrated by the style—for example, frequent repetition or use of several synonymous verbs to make a point: "setzen, ordnen, bestimmen."[15] Such accumulation of synonyms disappeared in the course of the seventeenth century, since ordinances were now intended to be read, and the style became more terse and precise. Another more technical reason has been suggested by Reiner Schulze. He has pointed out that the new ordinances were creating law in a different way and in competiton with the laws previously existing since the Middle Ages. According to the medieval conception of law, in the Germanies at any rate, norms preexist their public expression; judges and officials, in formulating human law, merely seek and find law that is already there in tradition, ethical values, and religious prescriptions. This old law, which sovereigns had only expressed, not created, was now being complemented and at

15. *Tiroler Ordnung* (1573), *Holstein HoffgerichtsOrdnung* (Rinteln: 1640).

times superseded by deliberate acts of will and reason, by a new creation of the sovereign that had to acquire the same power, validity, and moral or legal authority as the old law. Repetition thus aimed at establishing the "normal" and traditional rather than the exceptional and unique character of new legislation.[16]

Another set of reasons for repetition related to what may be termed the premodern mentality of the population to whom the ordinances addressed themselves.[17] For the common people in the seventeenth and eighteenth centuries, time was circular and ever-recurring in the seasons and the calendar of field labors and religious holidays; the ordinary man's memory lasted only for the duration of this natural cycle. A law or regulation that was not repeated regularly (and frequently this assignment was given to the pastor or priest) was deemed to have lapsed. Reiteration was the main weapon against *Verjährung* (superannuation), and frequently this purpose was explicitly stated to justify the reissuing of ordinances whose provisions were no longer obeyed because they had not been kept alive in the memory of the subjects.[18] Naturally the government's failure to repeat an injunction could easily be taken by subjects as a pretext for evasion, but in practically all cases disobedience stemmed from the conviction that a single promulgation, and limited dissemination, of the law was not sufficient to make it known and remembered by all those concerned. Finally, and this too is related to the issue of premodern mentality, many ordinances endeavored to break and change well-established, deeply ingrained patterns of behavior. This could not be accomplished overnight, since it meant restructuring relationships and attitudes.[19] Such an attempt would be resisted in any event, whatever the logic or rationale for doing away with a

16. R. Schulze, *Die Polizeigesetzgebung zu Wirtschaft- und Arbeits-ordnung der Mark Brandenburg* (Aalen: Scientia Verlag, 1978).

17. M. Eliade, *The Myth of the Eternal Return* (New York: Pantheon Books, 1954).

18. In the case of Wolfenbüttel ordinances, we note that the prohibitions are repeated twice at regular intervals. On the question of *Verjährung*, cf. Karl Bosl, *Frühformen der Gesellschaft im Mittelalterlichen Europa* (Munich and Vienna: R. Oldenbourg, 1964).

19. Mylius, *Corpus constitutionum magdeburgicarum*, pt. 3, p. 568.

particular custom or tradition. Repetition thus became part of a process of education, as it is for any child learning a new skill and behavior. It may be noted at this point that the uniformity and permanence of behavioral patterns brought about by repeated police ordinances and bolstered by the economic and social changes for which the ordinances paved the way permitted the emergence of a document-based and unchanging cultural pattern in the rural communities of preindustrial Europe. It is precisely this ordinance-induced pattern that framed the so-called village and folk cultures that became the object of nostalgic populism and brought about the idealization of the "old simple ways" in Europe in the late nineteenth and twentieth centuries.[20]

In view of the general uniformity of socioeconomic and political structures in the Germanies during the period studied, and also of the essentially uniform mental climates in which both rulers and ruled lived, it comes as no surprise that the ordinances in different states dealt with many problems in similar or even stereotyped manner. This was particularly true of those areas that fell under the legislative purview of the overarching sovereign authority of the Empire and of large territorial entities. The first comprehensive police ordinance was issued by the Holy Roman emperor in 1530 (and in revised versions in 1548 and 1570), and the matters it was concerned with—performance of church obligations, prohibition of luxury and begging, supervision of guilds—were treated along the same lines by subsequent territorial and local ordinances.[21] A similar situation occurred after the promulgation of reformed guild ordinances by the emperor in 1660 and 1731. Similarly, the great territorial rulers—for example, those of Saxony, Hesse, and later Prussia—served as models for their counterparts in smaller states, who patterned their ordinances almost word for word on the more comprehensive and theoretically more sophisticated codes and laws of the leading

20. Yves-Marie Bercé, *Fête et révolte: Des mentalités populaires du XVIe au XVIIIe siècles, Essai* (Paris: Hachette, 1976).
21. Cf. Imperial Police ordinances of 1530, 1548, and 1570 in E. A. Koch, *Neue vollständige Sammlung der Reichs-Abschiede,* and for example of specific reference to these ordinances see *Des löblichen Frenckischen Reichskraiss Policey Ordnung* (Nürnberg: 1572), p. i.

states. This circumstance further contributed to the uniformity
and repetitiveness of the ordinances and again justifies our
following a topical rather than chronological or territorial approach in studying them.

But not everything in the ordinances was stereotyped—far
from it. Ordinances dealing with concrete individual issues were
remarkable for their pragmatism and close attention to the
specific conditions that prompted their issuance. Whenever appropriate we shall notice the particular local circumstances and
take into account their impact on the formulation of legislation.
For the present it will suffice to note that there was a significant
difference in approach and form between the ordinances concerning urban conditions and those addressing themselves to
rural circumstances, especially the village and its activities. While
the ordinances relating to urban problems constituted a clear
majority, those aimed at the rural world were perhaps more
interesting from the point of view of their long-term implications
in transforming society.

In studying the ordinances and their impact on society, I have
for the reasons cited, adopted a topical approach transcending
local and chronological boundaries, though taking due cogni-
zance of patterns of development and of those significant de-
viations that help to explain the nature and purposes as well as
impact of this type of legislation. In the seventeenth century, and
in the eighteenth as well (except for the few sophisticated intellectuals in major urban centers) life was dominated and to a large
degree structured by the requirements of faith and religious
rituals. For this reason we shall first take up the ordinances
dealing with religion and church affairs. It is an order of priority
that frequently finds confirmation in the arrangement of compilations and "codes," the Imperial Police Ordinances of 1530 and
1548 being the first exemplars.[22] Next we shall consider the
legislation affecting society as a whole, especially its cultural and
psychological life. The "rational constructionism" (in F. von

22. For example, table of contents of *Pfaltz Landesordnung* (Amberg: 1599),
Northausen Policey Ordnung (1668), and *Anhaltische Gesambte Landes- und Process-
Ordnung* (Dessau, 1777).

Hayek's apt phrase) of seventeenth- and eighteenth-century governments had its most significant impact in this area.[23] We shall then turn to the frequently studied and commented-upon legislation affecting economic activities, with special attention to its role in promoting productivity. This will lead us to a consideration of the extent and nature of the rulers' efforts to promote the material and cultural progress of their societies, with far-reaching implications for the transformation of basic attitudes and values. The nature of these efforts at transformation and the agents used to effect them will be examined next. Particular attention will be given to the creation (or consolidation) of the basic instruments of power and administrative authority, to the routinization of procedures, and to the selection of personnel capable of carrying out the new procedures. This, in turn, raises the question of the possible emergence of a new relationship between ruler and ruled, an issue of central significance in the second half of the eighteenth century. Finally, we shall conclude by remarking on the evolution and changes in state policy, as illustrated in the ordinances, wrought over a period of nearly two centuries, and the implications of this process for the dynamics of evolution of central European society.

2. Religion and Church

In a very real and direct sense, police ordinances came into being as a result of the religious crisis that culminated in the Reformation. As the secular authorities stepped in to fill the gap created by the rejection of traditional ecclesiastic institutions, they issued laws and ordinances intended to help organize the new Protestant church establishment and, in the case of Catholic lands, to counteract the neglect of traditional religious practices. It is no accident that the first comprehensive police ordinance, issued for the Empire in 1530, opened with regulations concerning the observation of Sunday, attendance at worship, and the prosecu-

23. F. A. Hayek, *Law, Legislation and Liberty* (London: Routledge & Kegan Paul, 1973), vol. 1. Cf. G. Abel, *Stoizismus und frühe Neuzeit* . . . . (Berlin and New York: Walter de Gruyter, 1978).

tion of "superstitious" beliefs and practices. The imperial ordinance set a precedent and started a tradition. Most comprehensive Landesordnungen from the late sixteenth century on and throughout the seventeenth century have a first section consisting of general rules and prohibitions relating to church attendance, observation of the sabbath, and expressions of concern for the preservation of orthodoxy (whatever the orthodoxy in the specific instance might be).[24] In the eighteenth century such general statements disappear, by and large, though specific articles continue to emphasize the authorities' responsibility with respect to religion in general and for enforcing proper performance by the population of its ritual obligations. A striking change in the eighteenth-century ordinances consists in their making practically no mention of suppressing superstition, witchcraft, and magical practices, although general theoretical statements against superstitions and "unreasonable beliefs" still occur in other contexts.[25]

Having assumed responsibility for the proper religious behavior of its subjects, the secular power took on the pedagogic role of guiding the people toward their own moral and spiritual welfare. Expatiating on this didactic role, rulers or authorities proclaimed that a belief in God the Creator was the essential foundation of all morality and consequently was also the bricks and mortar that upheld the polity. Naturally, disorders and domestic difficulties were frequently seen as God's punishment for the violation of His laws.[26] It may be worth remarking at this point that in the case of problems that contemporary men could not cope with—especially natural disasters, such as epidemics—reference to God's punishment was not only stronger but persisted much longer. Plague

24. For instance, *Pfaltz Landesordnung* (1599), Sachsen 1580, *Fränckischer Kreis* (1572), *Anhalt Policey und Landes Ordenung* (Dessau: 1572), Magdeburg Ordinance 1652 in *Magdeburg Ordnungen . . . Mandata* (1673), Anhalt-Dessau 1777.

25. *Policey Ordnung Nürnberg* (Bayreuth: 1672), pp. 12–15 (title 5). Calenberg 1739 begins with reference to a Kirchenordnung of 1569, revised in 1615: "unsers Amts mit besonderm Fleiss erinnert, und erwogen, dass för unsern getreuen und lieben Untertanen, nicht allein um zeitlichen Friedens, Ruhe and Einigkeit willen, sondern auch darum von Seiner Göttlichen Allmacht förgesetzt, dass wir bei denselben vor allen anderm, was die rechte Erkenntnis, Anrufung und Dienst Gottes belanget . . . beförderten."

26. *Der Stadt Braunschweig Kleider Ordnung* (1650), introduction.

ordinances in the eighteenth century still referred to the pestilence as the "scourge of God" and enjoined the people, as the first measure, to pray and ask for God's forgiveness and mercy, since only through prayer would the disease be banned. It was added, however, that men would at least try to take precautionary hygienic measures to limit the harm.[27]

It followed from this that the state needed an established religion and that the function of ruler and administrative institutions was to see to the proper organization of the church and of religious life. Obviously atheism could not be permitted, since it would destroy all the norms that bind society and make possible an orderly and lawful way of life.[28] With respect to these fundamental positions, there were variations depending only on the degree of rulers' commitment to their faith and of their moral earnestness and, consequently, differences in the severity of punishment meted out to atheists and unbelievers. Some rulers were extremely pious and believed it to be their duty to insist on a similar commitment on the part of their subjects. Their religious admonitions were verbose, and they were very ready to impose harsh penalties and resort to the secular arm for enforcement and prosecution.[29] In other instances piety and religious uniformity were obviously a matter of political tradition and convenience; in such cases the ordinances merely stated the need for rules that were spelled out in a matter-of-fact and practical way. In the latter

27. Prussian plague ordinances in Mylius, 5 (4), chap. 2. On the specific manner of preaching a plague sermon, cf. Reglement 4.XI.1709.

28. *Pfaltz Landesordnung* (1599), introduction, p. 1. Magdeburgische Policey Ordnung 6.VII.1652, in *Sämptliche Fürstliche Magdeburgische Ordnungen* . . . . (Leipzig: 1673), p. 487. *Policey Ordnung Nürnberg* (1672), introduction and Title 1. And the following eighteenth-century statement of opinion: "Der [Fürst] zu dem Ende vornehmlich dahin zu sehen, dass keine Atheisterey in einem Staat geduldet, und zwar zur Fortpflanzung der christlichen Religion durch vernünftige Mittel Sorge getragen, niemand aber dazu gezwungen werde, als welches nicht nur der christlichen Religion entgegen sondern auch der Aufnahme eines Staats zuwider ist." J. C. Dithmar, *Einleitung in die oeconomische Policey- und Cameral-Wissenschaften* (1731), p. 140. Dithmar was first incumbent of the chair in cameralism instituted by King Frederick William I in Frankfurt/Oder.

29. *Augusti Braunschweig Hofgerichts Ordnung* (1663), p. 283 (29.XI.1646, re "Raufen"); Mylius, 5 (1): 89.

half of our period we encounter more and more frequently what appears to be merely verbal deférence to the state religion and commitment to the regulation of its ritual and institutional life.[30] The tone becomes defensive, and the regulations seemed to be an afterthought expanding a rational argument for the desirability of religion as a socially cohesive force.

In Catholic territories such as Bavaria, the state's regulation of the church consisted primarily in defining the ecclesiastical establishment's fiscal obligations and socioeconomic rights and privileges.[31] Basically the state did not intervene in the internal life of the ecclesiastical institutions, contenting itself with supporting some essential activities and giving its administrative assistance in the clergy's dealings with the population. In short, in Catholic territories the church remained an institution outside the government, though the latter had a voice in controlling its performance and in supervising its relationship with society. Obviously, such was not the case in Protestant states, where the ruler—the nominal head of the church—or the authorities constituted the supreme power that had direct responsibility for supervising and administering ecclesiastical institutions. State and church were not, theoretically, separate but together constituted the two facets of the same establishment. In Protestant states rulers took upon themselves the moral and legal as well as administrative responsibility for the proper performance of all aspects of church life, in the first place ritual. Ordinances enjoined the preservation of decorum in the church at service time, they supervised the acquisition, use, and transmission of pews, and they regulated the order of precedence in receiving communion and the like.[32] These regulations were intended, on the one hand, to preserve the proper and "natural" social hierarchies in which every mem-

30. Mylius 5(4): 298–304, on plague sermons. For separation of the secular and religious spirits with regard to funerals, see Mylius, 5(1), 25.V.1725, royal Reglement.

31. Max Freiherr von Freyberg, *Pragmatische Geschichte der bayerischen Gesetzgebung*, vol. 3, passim.

32. Verordnungen wegen Kirchenstühle, 28.VII.1657, in *Sammelband ... Wolfenbüttel;* Appel and Kleinschmidt, *Sammlung Fürstlich-Hessischer Landesordnungen,* no. 571 (24.XI.1702); Mylius, *Corpus ... Magdeburgicarum* (Kirchenordnung 13.XI.1685).

ber of society had a specific place and function, and, on the other
hand, to eliminate those quarrels and conflicts that might have
undermined the orderly functioning of the community.

The most important—or at least numerous—set of ordinances
pertained to the observation of Sunday. The major emphasis was
on the duty to attend Sunday services and to preserve proper
decorum during them.[33] Ordinances repeatedly prohibited the
carrying on of gainful occupations on Sundays, especially during
the hours of worship. Naturally, essential activities, such as the
feeding of livestock, might be performed but in such a way as not
to interfere with the divine service, at which everyone's attendance was expected.[34] Gradually recognition of the necessity of
economic activity beyond the minimal care of livestock and people
led to the formulation of rules that could satisfy both the
requirements of religion and the maintenance of an active economy even on holidays and Sundays.

One of the major causes for the lack of regular attendance and
proper decorum at services, it was felt, was the congregating of
people outside the church for social intercourse, play, and even
economic transactions. Innumerable ordinances tried to keep
such activities under control, after earlier efforts at banning them
completely had obviously had but limited success. A major
impediment in effectively enforcing attendance and orderly conduct was felt to be the taverns. Not only were alcoholic beverages
sold there, but the taverns also functioned as social centers for the

---

33. In Saxony and Hesse such ordinances date from the mid–sixteenth
century. See also *Anhalt Policey und Landes Ordenung* (1572), no pagination; *Des
Durchlauchtigsten . . . Fürsten . . . Johann Casimirs Pfalzgrafen bei Rhein . . . Christliche
Policey Ordnung* (n.p.: 1579), p. 3; *Northausen Policey Ordnung* (1668); Calenberg
Ordnung 1739 (pp. 416–22, 19.V.1710 Sabbathsordnung, and pp. 422–24,
15.VII.1710 and 14.VIII.1710 restating and implementing it); Wolfenbüttel
2.III.1686 on Sunday decorum; 22.III.1726, enforcement of 1709 blue law, with
elaboration.

34. Calenberg 1739 (declaratio 14.VIII.1710, pp. 423–24 and Sabbath-
ordnung auf dem Harz, 20.VII.1735, pp. 432, 434–37); Bergius, *Sammlung*,
1:25 (Preussische Bauernordnung 30.XII.1764) and 7:161–65, Hessische-Ha-
nauische Sonn-, Bet-, und Feiertags-verordnung 1748 with references to 1678,
1698, and 14.IX.1713 permitting driving out cattle to pasture on Sundays
provided return before first sermon or service).

local communities. The taverns and inns, as well as grocery and dry goods stores, were ordered closed during service time, although they were allowed to open afterward, provided that no gambling, drunkenness, and other riotous behavior took place on their premises on Sundays.[35]

One gains the impression that the Protestant authorities wanted to compartmentalize their subjects' lives. In contrast to medieval (Catholic) intermingling of church and social life, the mixing of economic, cultural, and spiritual activities, an effort was made to separate each sphere. This was done to prevent the contamination of the spiritual side of existence with worldly concerns and also to facilitate the supervision, organization, and disciplining of behavior in each separate sphere of life by keeping them separate and preventing uncontrollable excesses in one from affecting the other. Last, but not least, attendance at church and dutiful participation in ritual served to inculcate in the population a sense of the earnest purposefulness of their activities and obligations and of their role in preserving the *civilitas* of a peaceful and orderly polity.

Closely related was the concern with having the celebration of holidays, and other festivities, stay within bounds so as not to disrupt economic and other necessary activities. In the sixteenth century, ordinances regulating festivities connected with church holidays stressed the prohibition of practices smacking of "paganism" and Roman Catholicism. In the late sixteenth century the ordinances even went so far as to equate some traditional festivities with popish idolatry and pagan superstition.[36] In the course of the seventeenth century such strong terms disappeared almost completely. In their stead there appeared an emphasis on the unsuitability of such festivities and the display accompanying them from the point of view of a productive way of life: holidays interrupted the regular flow of work and business, they induced

35. For example, Bergius *Sammlung*, 1:25, and see section on mores below.
36. Calenberg 1739, p. 430 (edict 17.XII.1734 re "Abstellung von Weihnachts Metten, Pfingst Bier, Johannis Feuer und anderen abergläubischen und ärgerlichen Missbräuche . . . teils abergläubisch teils päpstliche, teils heidnische Misbräuche") and Wolfenbüttel 17.XII.1734 prohibiting similar feasts for the same reasons.

unnecessary expenses, and—perhaps most important of all—they
were not conducive to the promotion of a sober, disciplined
attitude toward one's duties and activities.[37] In many cases, it was
said, the carryings on at holidays might damage health or even
lead to loss of life or limb, and they were therefore particularly
harmful to the community and society at large. For all these
reasons, numerous ordinances eliminated minor holidays and
decreed rigid prohibitions or restrictions on idleness, play, and
drinking during recognized church festivities.[38] From the middle
of the eighteenth century on, the ordinances aimed at internalizing religious feeling (or faith) and at stressing the importance of
inner spiritual experience as opposed to slavish and mechanical
adherence to outward forms.[39] It did not occur to the legislators
that in the process the feeling of community, as well as many
cultural traditions that gave value and meaning to the common
man's existence, might be lost or even willfully destroyed.

37. Appel and Kleinschmidt, *Sammlung*, 3:461 (25.I.1701).

38. *Policey Ordnung . . . Christians . . . Bischofen Minden* (Zelle: 1618), Fastnacht-
ordnung. And for a late statement, but one exemplifying the culmination of the
pattern, Bergius, *Sammlung*, 2:240–43 (Preussische Edict 28.VI.1773, "wegen
Einschränkung der Evangelische Lutherischen Feiertage":

> Was massen Wir erwogen, dass, so löblich auch die Absicht derjenigen
> gewesen ist, welche die Feierung besonderer Feiertage in der christlichen
> Kirche veranlasst haben, doch die Erfahrung gelehrt wie die Menge dieser
> Feiertage dem Endzweck ihrer Einsetzung vielmehr hinderlich geworden ist,
> inmassen die allerwenigsten Menschen diese Tage dem Nachdenken über
> ihre Pflichten und Religion widmen, sondern vielmehr dieselbigen mit
> unchristlichen Müssiggang und öfters in Üppigkeit und Schwelgerei zu-
> bringen. Die öffentliche gottesdienliche Handlungen und deren häufige
> Beiwohnung sind auch an sich selbst noch keine Gottseligkeit, sondern nur
> Mittel die Gemüter dazu zu erwecken, und sie beweisen hauptsächlich ihren
> Nutzen darin wenn die Gottseligkeit sich in den andern Tagen in wirklichen
> Handlungen der Rechtschaffenheit, des arbeitsamen Fleisses, der Menschen-
> liebe, der Treue gegen Gott und gegen Obrigkeit und einer geduldigen
> Ertragung der Beschwerlichkeiten dieses Lebens, äussert (p. 240).

39. For a very late, but Catholic, funeral ordinance, Bistum Fulda 1.IV.1783,
cf. Bergius, *Sammlung*, 9:22–32 and 5:137, Waldeck Verordnung 3.I.1780. Cf.
Freyberg 2, ordinance 1726, restricting pilgrimages, etc., p. 21; Wolfenbüttel
20.XII.1745, prohibiting horseraces at Pentecost and Fastnacht rioting; Calenberg
1739, p. 441 (Ausschreiben 3.IV.1731) prohibiting ministers from making public
rebukes of individuals.

The disciplining role ascribed to the church and to religion could be performed by none but the clergy, whether Catholic priests and monks or Protestant ministers and readers. Territorial sovereigns naturally devoted much attention to proper recruitment, training, and maintenance of members of the cloth. In the Catholic world this role was normally limited to securing for the church a satisfactory economic base. The Catholic Church remaining a recognized, strong, and influential but separate establishment; in Catholic territories the administrations restricted themselves, as earlier, to a negative role: prevention, and punishment if need be, of the grossest derelictions and abuses. The Protestant sovereigns, on the other hand, had a much more direct and positive role, since, as the heads of their churches, they had the latter's institutional organization entirely under their jurisdiction and care. The major instrument of this end was the consistorial visitation. Numerous *Kirchenordnungen* of the seventeenth century (and they continued into the eighteenth) set up rules and provided for periodic visitations by members of the consistory to check on the orthodoxy of the pastors, the congregation's knowledge of the articles of faith, and the proper administration and effectiveness of the schools. The visitations became more and more routine in the course of the second half of the seventeenth and in the early eighteenth centuries, as witnessed by the fact that the reports of them also became more stereotyped. Eventually, carefully set out and detailed questionnaires were provided for reporting according to formula.[40]

The Protestant minister's main functions were to educate the congregation through his sermons, to supervise the behavior and morals of the parishioners, and to teach the children the three R's and the catechism so as to prepare them for their full-fledged membership in the community of the faithful. The pedagogic functions of the clergy, including Catholic priests and monks, underwent a constant expansion during the period we are concerned with. The police ordinances provided for the establishment, upkeep, administration, and supervision of the parish

40. See the handy illustration of the pattern of development of consistorial ordinances in Mylius, 1(1): 433, 447, 513.

schools (or classes).[41] They set the standards for the professional preparation of the ministers and the rules for supervising their activities as schoolmasters and teachers and delegated to the ministers responsibility for enforcing school attendance by the children under their jurisdiction. The ordinances offered rules for the conduct of classes and prescribed the pedagogic orientation and materials to be used in class.[42] Of particular interest was the concern shown by the territorial authorities for the local and social conditions under which pupils had to study and work. Although parents were compelled to send their children to school and to provide support, in money or in kind, for the school and the teacher, the ordinances took into account the fact that the children's labor might be essential to their parents, especially in the countryside in the summer. We read of provisions that allowed classes to be discontinued during harvest time, but at the same time review sessions were to be set up on Sundays, even in the summer.[43] To prevent the children from missing school to herd their parents' cattle, ordinances demanded the hiring of professional shepherds at community expense as a more efficient and desirable way of caring for the livestock.

With the increase in the administrators' concern for more productive and efficient ways of life and the growing realization that such heightening of society's productivity depended on greater technical know-how and understanding of scientific and rational methods, the idea arose (as early as the late seventeenth century, in some cases) that the minister and the schoolmaster, as the most educated persons in the countryside, could play an important role. Ordinances assigned to the minister the role of *Kulturträger* in the rural communities; to this end his education and professional preparation would have to include those subjects

41. *Anhalt Policey und Landes Ordnung* (1572); *Augusti Braunschwyg Hofgerichts Ordnung* (1663), p. 582; Bergius, *Sammlung,* 6:127 (Schleswig Holstein Ordnung 29.I.1768) and 7:129 (Ordnung for Landesschulen des Herzogtums Lauenburg-Ratzeburg, 5.IV.1757). See also below, section 6.

42. *Policey Ordnung Nürnberg* (1672), p. 6, and cf. section 6 below.

43. *Augusti Braunschwyg Hofgerichts Ordnung* (1663), p. 323; *Hildesheimb Policey Ordnung,* (1665), p. 9; Mylius, 1(2): 267.

that could be of value in the endeavor.[44] The training of pastors was expanded by the ordinances to include the basic notions of agronomy, as well as rudiments of medicine and pharmacy. Once installed in his parish, it also became the minister's responsibility to secure the necessary information and literature.[45] The pastor's involvement in agricultural pursuits and the schoolmaster's in some craft were both an advantage and a drawback. The advantage was that minister and teacher could offer practical and concrete models for emulation to their congregation; the drawback consisted in their subordinating pastoral and pedagogic duties to their own economic interests and activities. The balance was hard to strike, and since their training remained basically theological and pastoral, the ministers did not fulfill the legislator's sanguine expectations, failing to become the hoped-for enlightened leaders in agriculture or economic enterprise.[46]

We know that normally teachers and pastors were recruited from among the sons of ministers. While the general ordinances did not deal with the recruitment of the clergy, they did provide for their control and supervision. This was the purpose of the visitations we have referred to earlier and of rules designed to ensure accurate reporting of the future ministers' and teachers' progress in their studies and preservation of their orthodoxy.[47] But an evolution in the tenor of the ordinances can be observed in this respect, too. In sixteenth-century ordinances, those of Saxony and Hesse being the best examples, it was specified that "orthodoxy" was to be defined by adherence to the articles of faith as set by the Peace of Augsburg or similar treaties. In the seventeenth century, orthodoxy was taken for granted, so that it

---

44. Cf. John Michael Stroup, "The Struggle for Identity in the Clerical Estate: Northwest German Protestant Opposition to Absolutist Policy in the Eighteenth Century" (Ph.D. diss., Yale University, 1980).

45. See an early example in *Pfaltz Landesordnung* (1599).

46. Stroup (cf. n. 44) clearly demonstrates the conflict. Note also that Catherine II (and to some extent Peter I) had similar hopes, equally disappointed, for the Russian parish clergy. For examples of early nineteenth-century fulfillments of these policy aims, cf. W. von Kügelgen, *Jugenderinnerungen eines alten Mannes* (Munich: Wilhelm Langeweide-Brandt, 1922).

47. Mylius, 1(1): 401, 429, 431, 559.

was merely mentioned that the orthodox articles of faith had to be taught and known. But in the late seventeenth and early eighteenth centuries, and more particularly in the more progressive and advanced lands of the Prussian monarchy, justification for the church ordinances and consistorial rules were put in rational and tolerant terms; their congruence with ordinary human reason was stressed, though the basic belief in God and his ordained world order was never put in doubt.[48] Because of the variety of denominations in the Germanies and the competition among them, it was felt that the orthodoxy of the clergy (however defined) could be ensured only if prospective pastors received their training in institutions fully controlled by the *Landesherrschaft*. The territorial governments were further confirmed in their attitude in this respect by the economic consideration that training abroad constituted a drain on the country's resources, especially its currency, and provided undue benefits to foreign institutions. Territories with their own universities or academies passed ordinances requiring attendance of prospective ministers at these establishments for at least a limited period (usually two years) to make sure that the students were exposed to and inculcated with their sovereign's values and orthodoxy.[49]

Closely related to the question of orthodoxy was the crucial issue of other denominations, faiths, and religious minority groups in general. Inasmuch as religion was seen as the essential ingredient that held together any society, there could, as already mentioned, be no toleration of atheism, and any suspected manifestation of it was severely punished.[50] But under provision of the Treaty of Westphalia, Catholics, Lutherans, and Calvinists, willy nilly, had to tolerate each other. In territories and towns with sizable minorities of one of these denominations, their members were granted the right to worship and secured in the possession of their places of worship and the appointment of needed pastoral staff. But quite clearly it was mere toleration; there could

48. Sachsen 1583. *Pfaltz Landesordnung* (1599), and Mylius, *Continuatio* 1:75, 325.

49. Wolfenbüttel 9/20.X.1724 and 9.XI.1724, also 30.X.1745; Mylius, 1(2): 229, 247.

50. Cf. n. 28.

be no question of complete juridical and socio-political equality or of absolute freedom of conscience. Even in the increasingly enlightened and secularized eighteenth century, care was taken to see that members of minority denominations stayed within the permitted bounds and did not compete openly with the official state confession.[51] Even the agnostic and sceptical Frederick II of Prussia did not go beyond such benevolent toleration, wary as he was of provoking unnecessary difficulties and opposition.

A somewhat different and more favorable situation obtained in the case of the French Huguenots, who were admitted and settled by the rulers of Hesse and Prussia. The reason for their preferential treatment was quite clearly the economic benefits and social prestige that the Huguenots seemed to confer on the state admitting them. They were guaranteed full freedom and security in maintaining their traditional pastorate and form of worship and in preserving their language, as well as their traditional legal and theological norms. They were even more advantaged than the natives in that they had permission to leave the country without much hindrance and were dispensed from the many constricting obligations pertaining to membership in guilds and the performance of various public servitudes.[52]

The attitudes toward sects and spiritualist groups (for example, Herrenhuter, Bohemian Brethren, Anabaptists, and Pietists) were more complex. It would appear from the ordinances dealing with these sects that the reasons for regulating them—that is keeping them under tight supervision and granting them only what amounted to second-class status—were twofold. First, it was feared that their beliefs and practices, derived as they were from an essentially emotional and inner-directed interpretation of the Christian message, would not be amenable to the kind of control prevailing in the official denomination; and second, that they

51. Calenberg 1739 (25.IV.1713 Verordnung concerning the exercise of Roman Catholicism in Hanover, pp. 1028ff., and the edict on Pietism of 20.II.1703 and 15.III.1703, pp. 1057ff.); Mylius, 1(1): 403 (re Arians) and 413.

52. Calenberg 1739 (Privileges for Huguenots in Hameln, 1.VIII.1690, pp. 1004–22); Appel and Kleinschmidt, *Sammlung* (1688 and 13.X.1700, nos. 437, 439, 531). Mylius reprints various edicts concerning Huguenots under the topical headings he has adopted for the organization of his collection; cf. index.

would introduce an element of discord into the community.[53] In short, the main argument against giving the sectarians complete equality and freedom to worship and practice their beliefs was the fear of introducing an uncontrollable, emotional, psychologically disturbing element into society. No doubt, although the ordinances made no mention of it, economic rivalries and competition aroused suspicion and provoked the opposition of established institutions, and in so doing confirmed (in an act of self-fulfilling prophecy) the authorities in believing that the sects were fomenters of dangerous discord and conflict. As time went on, the regulative and discriminatory legislation against spiritualist sectarians and Anabaptists became less ferocious, while the arguments justifying continued restrictive measures grew increasingly rationalistic and utilitarian. Basing their arguments on the notion of natural religion, the authors of the ordinances viewed the sectarians' practices and beliefs as irrational and contrary to common sense, and consequently as particularly dangerous to the uneducated, psychologically weak, and emotionally unbalanced.[54]

Two minority groups were shown no sympathy whatever by the legislators in our period. These were the Jews and the Gypsies, the latter of whom suffered the most. The Jews were subjected to rigorous, suspicion-laden rules and regulations. In particular, the ordinances tried to keep Jewish traveling merchants and peddlers out of the territories. They were barred with particularly ferocious severity during epidemics, since they were believed to be

---

53. *Pfaltz Landesordnung* (1599), p. 58 ("das die schädliche Sect der Widertäufer . . . gottlob nicht gespürt wird"). Calenberg 1739 (edicts 15.III.1711 and 28.V/8.VI.1734), pp. 1065–66, 1067–72; Appel and Kleinschmidt, *Sammlung*, no. 568, 18.IX.1702; Mylius, 1(1): 413–16 (Verordnung 7.I.1692).

54. Kreitmeyer (under Bavaria), *Sammlung*, Wolfenbüttel 9.XI.1671; Calenberg 1739 (Verordnung 15.V.1711, "die Fanaticos und Separatisten betreffend":

Nun erfordern nicht nur die bekannten Reichs und Landes Constitutiones, sondern auch das von Gott eingesetzte obrigkeitliche Amt, diesem Übel [i.e., "religiöser Fanatismus und verführerischer Dissens"] in Zeiten entgegen zu gehen, und zwar eines Teils keinen Gewissenszwang zu üben, aber doch auch andern Teils denen boshaften oder betörten und dabei halsstarrigen Leuten keines Weges freie Hände zu lassen, leichtgläubige Gemüter zu verwirren und schädliche Unordnungen einzuführen" (p. 1068).

carriers of disease because of their peripatetic lifestyle and association with cattle merchants, rag dealers, and other undesirable contacts. Strict passport requirements and close scrutiny of their credentials were the least of the burdensome and discriminatory practices they had to submit to.[55] But even worse treatment was meted out to the Gypsies. The ordinances insisted that every effort be made to keep them out of the territories and to chase them out if they penetrated. The inhuman tenor of the regulations concerning them is shocking and was maintained even into the eighteenth century. Gypsies were granted the right of passage most grudgingly; they had to submit to very strict checks upon entering and leaving and were under constant supervision. Some ordinances even went so far as to declare them outside the law, *vogelfrei*, that is subject to pursuit and killing on sight by anyone.[56] Only in one respect did a more humanitarian note creep in at the end of our period: while in the seventeenth century the orphaned and abandoned children of Gypsies were virtually enslaved by order of the territorial administration (at times even sold into slavery in the Mediterranean), eighteenth-century ordinances provided that, baptized and given some instruction, these children were to be treated like normal orphans and offered similar opportunities.[57] Evidently it was the adherence to a "normal" style of life that gave an individual or group full legal recognition and the right to participate in the polity without discrimination.

55. Wolfenbüttel 7.I.1680 and 31.VIII.1712, among many others.

56. Freyberg, 2:19 ("Doch sollte gleichwohl nicht jedem erlaubt sein die Zigeuner zu tödten, sondern man sollte trachten ihrer habhaft zu werden, und sie dem Gerichte überliefern") clearly states the problem, and an ordinance of 1726 (Freyberg 2:21) says that Gypsy children under eighteen are to be put in the *Zuchthaus* (house of correction) until capable of earning. Wolfenbüttel July 1711 repeats prohibitions against Gypsies and declares them "vogelfrei." Ibid., 15.IX.1718: Gypsies excluded from the territory as "detestabile vitae genus" and again declared vogelfrei. *Sammelband . . .Wolfenbüttel* has an earlier edict "wider Zigeuner oder Tartarn," 20.VII.1650, pp. 169–70. Also *Augusti Braunschwyg Hofgerichts Ordnung* (1663), pp. 295–97 (20.VII.1650); Mylius, 2(3):141; 5(1):13; 5(4): 358.

57. Freyberg, 2:21, Ordnung 1726, referred to in n. 56.

3. Society

In the seventeenth and eighteenth centuries all German states wanted to secure a sizable, industrious, and productive population. This concern was primarily motivated by the heavy losses suffered during the ravages of the Thirty Years War, which had left some areas with a decimated population and much untilled land.[58] Contemporaries realized that only application of human labor would yield the necessary resources for further economic development and material prosperity for all. Manpower was necessary, first of all, in agriculture, but it was also essential to the development of manufacturing, whose role was growing from day to day. Indeed, the sale of manufactures alone could potentially meet the growing needs of military preparedness and defense, of the court and administration, and also provide reserves in money and material. The example of Holland and of England as well later in the century showed how trading in surplus production, in particular of manufactured goods, could lead to the acquisition of vast wealth. In short, without people there could be no wealth, and even basic survival itself was at stake. It was natural for the German territorial states to adopt energetic "populationist" policies designed to attract settlers and promote the natural increase of population at home.[59]

58. The complicated and still hotly debated question of the economic nature and impact of the Thirty Years War can best be approached through Günther Franz, *Der Dreissigjährige Krieg und das deutsche Volk,* 3d ed. (Stuttgart: G. Fischer, 1961); Henry Kamen, "The Economic Consequences of the Thirty Years War," *Past and Present* 39 (1968):44–61; Franz Lütge, "Die wirtschaftliche Lage in Deutschland vor Ausbruch des 30. jährigen Krieges," *Jahrbuch für Nationalökonomie* 170(1958): 43–99 and "Strukturelle und kunjunkturelle Wandlungen in der deutschen Wirtschaft vor Ausbruch des 30. jährigen Krieges," *Sitzungsberichte—* Bayerische Akademie, Philosophisch-historische Klasse, no. 5 (Munich: Bayerische Akademie, 1958).

59. *Sammelband . . .Wolfenbüttel,* edict 16.VII.1652: "Das beste Mittel erachtet wann nicht allein die Mannschaft durch sonderbare Befreiung ins gemeine wieder herbei zu bringen Fleiss angewendet, sondern auch unsere Städte mit allerhand Arbeits- und Handelsleuten hinwieder besetzt werden mögen." Decree of 24.III.1732 settling veterans in Hesse, "Hessische Militärverordnungen" (1630–1755). And for an early example, *Mecklenburg Policey und Landt Ordnung* (Rostock: 1562), p. 49. Promotion of natural population growth will be taken up in conjunction with health and philanthropy.

We have noted previously an instance of populationist policy at work in connection with the settlement of French Huguenots in Hesse, Prussia, and elsewhere after the Revocation of the Edict of Nantes in 1685.[60] Not only were the Huguenots admitted; they were actively invited to settle in German lands. In Lutheran territories they were given full freedom of worship, including the preservation of their institutional framework of religious life. Even more important in the present context, the Protestant Frenchmen received advantages of a social, legal, and economic nature to foster their active participation in the productive life of their new homeland. For the perfectly good reason that their skills and proficiency were especially valuable, the Huguenots were given privileged status and treatment.[61] Of course, theirs was an exceptional case, though it served as model for the energetic colonization policies of enlightened absolutism in the second half of the eighteenth century.

Of still greater import for the populationist goals of the territorial governments were the many ordinances that aimed at settling new agricultural workers on lands that had been abandoned during the Thirty Years War. The significant measures were of two kinds. The first required landowners (especially noble ones) to ensure the productivity of their domains. To this end they were granted temporary exemptions from taxes and servitudes, while at the same time being threatened with penalties— including confiscation and transfer of ownership—if their lands were not put under cultivation.[62] In a sense, of course, these

60. A curious offer of the right to settle in Muscovy was made by Tsars Ivan and Peter at the request of the Kurfürst of Brandenburg; see *Polnoe Sobranie Zakonov imperii Rossiiskoi* (hereafter PSZ) 1331 (26.I.1689, charter to Prussian ambassador Tschaplitsch) for Russian text, and Mylius 6(1): 581–84 for German and French versions.

61. Appel and Kleinschmidt, *Sammlung*, no. 414, 18.IV.1685, and 3:290–95: chronological list of regulations concerning French *réfugiés* from 24.V.1604 to 8.XII.1702. Calenberg 1739, 1:1004–22, "Déclaration des privilèges" for Huguenots settling in Hameln, 1.VIII.1690 (in two languages in parallel columns). Section 10 reads, for example: "Les Français réfugiés seront traités sans aucune distinction comme Nos anciens sujets et jouiront dans nos états des mêmes privilèges, prérogatives, immunités, charges et fonctions tant militaires que civiles." Mylius reproduces the pertinent legislation in Brandenburg.

62. Freyberg, 2:241 (15.XI.1656); Kreitmeyer, *Sammlung*, pp. 453–56, Man-

ordinances come under the heading of economic measures to
promote productivity, but since such measures would have remained ineffective without an adequate manpower base they also
relate to populationist legislation. The second approach was to
prohibit productive tillers of the land from leaving it. One way of
achieving this was to prohibit transfers of property, forcing those
who left to go without any means for starting a new life.[63] In the
same vein, ordinances endeavored to control, if not stem altogether, the departure of farmers' children to take up service in
towns. Peasants were enjoined to keep children of working age at
home by giving them a share in the property and rewards; at the
same time they were forbidden to hire laborers to make up for
the loss of family members who had moved to town.[64] These
measures for the conservation of manpower had the same purpose and effect as those ordinances aiming to increase manpower
by attracting new settlers. The grandiose, rationally organized
schemes in the eighteenth century in Germany and Russia
(following England's lead in the seventeenth) to settle colonists,
drain marshes, and clear new land are well known and need not
be entered upon here.

In the premodern world, population patterns and the availability of manpower were closely related to family relationships and
family life. Not surprisingly, territorial ordinances had to deal
with this aspect of social relations; in so doing, they influenced the
development of interpersonal relationships, family structures,
and cultural patterns. Since the Reformation had moved the
Church of Rome from its position as the main institutional
regulator of family relations, in Protestant states the temporal
authorities had to take over this function of the Church. The
routine legal issues concerning family relationships (inheritance,
marriage contracts, adoption, and so forth) were left to civil law

---

dat 24.III.1762; *Sammelband . . . Wolfenbüttel,* Allgemeine Landesordnung 1647,
pp. 14–15.

63. *Pfaltz Landesordnung* (1599), p. 145; Wolfenbüttel 19.IX.1692, 28.III.1732
(Gesindeordnung, §27), 21.IV.1734 (giving up right of departure); Calenberg
1739, 4:5–6 (18.V.1708, liberalizing right of departure).

64. Wolfenbüttel, 28.X.1722; *Gesindeordnung Halberstadt* (Halberstadt: 1717),
§§1–2; Bergius, *Sammlung,* 1:29–30 (Preussische Bauernordnung 30.XII.1764).

and handled on the basis of traditional norms by the regular courts, while in the eighteenth century new codes incorporated family law and regularized the procedures for settling conflicts. But territorial police ordinances were issued to take care of special situations, especially those where the legal aspects came into conflict with social and moral norms.

During the span of over a century, from about 1600 to 1750, we observe a growing effort on the part of the authorities to settle difficult family conflicts in a humane fashion. Care was taken not to discriminate unduly against one side; since every subject was an asset to the community and the state, he had to be adequately protected. In matters concerning marital infidelity, we note that the indignant and moralistic tone of late sixteenth-century ordinances yielded later to a sober assessment of guilt and a judicious punishment intended to preserve the social usefulness of each party.[65] Naturally the wife was punished more harshly than the man in case of guilt, but the punishment was no longer demeaning. Only in case of recidivism was the guilty party subjected to corporal punishment and even expulsion from the territory.[66] In all cases care was taken to preserve the economic security of the damaged party as much as possible. Children born of illegitimate unions were to be reintegrated easily into ordinary society without prejudice of their birth. In the case of bastards who were left without protection—for example, orphans and abandoned children—the state tried to take care of them and to pave the way for their eventual integration as productive members of society by giving them useful training without regard to their parentage.[67]

In pursuing this policy, the ordinances were struggling against the exclusions of bastards or children from families engaged in "dishonorable" occupations (*Knaker,* executioner, grave digger)

65. *Pfaltz Landesordnung* (1599), p. 23; Freyberg, 2:176–82 (note changes from decrees of 1636, 1650, and 1737, the latter setting tariffs for matrimonial infidelity); changed rhetoric in Wolfenbüttel, 25.VII.1743.

66. *Fürstlich Anhaltische . . . Landes- und Process Ordnung* (1725 and 1777), pp. 182–88 (Ehemandat 17.VII.1694, especially §9).

67. Wolfenbüttel, 19.VIII.1687 and 24.VIII.1725; Freyberg 2:15; and the late example in Bergius, *Sammlung,* 5:142 (Waldeck Verordnung re child murder, 3.I.1780).

practiced by the guilds, exclusions that prevented many a good
worker from becoming a fully recognized partner in the productive processes of society. By breaking down traditional discriminatory attitudes, the territorial authorities were fostering—perhaps
unwittingly—the formation of a free labor market in which the
individual's competence and skills, not his status and origins, were
the determining factors. An interesting though late example of
this kind of legislation was provided by the *Landrecht* of Hohenlohe in 1738, marking the culmination of the process by
enjoining that women who had given birth to illegitimate children should not be scorned or penalized for it. They were to
be considered as ordinary human beings, since they were the
mothers of potentially useful members of society.[68] Whether
ordinances such as this did in fact change attitudes may be
doubted, but they did make for a degree of legal protection, and
they proclaimed the government's conscious role in transforming
social values and setting guidelines for a new social structure in
which certain traditional norms would no longer have their old
function.

In those centuries, domestic servants were closely tied to the
family and were considered members of the family, in a sense.
This held true of both domestics in urban households and hired
laborers living on peasant homesteads. The numerous ordinances
addressing themselves to this important social group took it for
granted that the interests of the employers had priority. Attempts
were made to give stability to the relationship between domestics
and their employers by restricting the servants' right to leave the
masters' service. In this fashion the ordinances also took care of
another concern of the authorities, namely to prevent vagrancy
and itinerancy among the population. In all fairness, however, it
should be pointed out that the territorial authorities also protected some interests of the domestics. They endeavored to make
sure that the servants' wages were paid properly, that they were
treated decently, and that they enjoyed the status of temporary
members of their employer's family.[69]

---

68. *Der Graffschaft Hohenlohe gemeinsames Landrecht* (Oehringen: 1738), p. 20.
69. Cf. *Gesinde Ordnungung Halberstadt,* and Gesinde Ordnung Hessen in
Collectiones privato studio factae.

It is of course difficult to imagine that such ordinances by themselves were sufficient to ensure fair relations between servants and masters. Yet the fact that the government worked to this end and afforded servants, at least theoretically, the protection of its laws and courts did have an impact in the long run and set the framework for the development of a freer labor market for servants while securing more respectable status for the individual domestic worker. In a related matter, ordinances were issued to make sure that the hiring of domestic servants in the countryside did not diminish the crops available to masters and to society at large. Masters were prohibited from paying the domestics' wages with a share of the crops. Domestic servants had to be remunerated in cash, or, if mutually agreeable, they could be given a small plot of land to cultivate for their own upkeep in partial payment for their work on the homestead.[70] All such measures gave pride of place to the cash nexus in the village economy, and in this manner they undermined relationships based on the family and exchanges evaluated in kind. No doubt in many cases such a development was occurring naturally ("spontaneously," as the Soviets say), yet the fact that political authorities supported it by offering legal sanction and protection helped to consolidate it and to spread it beyond the boundaries of those areas where it had arisen.

With the increase of all types of wealth in the hands of members of society, at least its upper classes, provision had to be made for the orderly transfer and preservation of the property of families. The issue was particularly pressing in the case of escheat in the absence of direct heirs. To promote the subjects' productive activity and to offer its protection to the property they had acquired from their labor, the state relinquished its right of escheat, allowing property to pass on to relatives at normally unacceptable degrees of kinship, even if the heirs were subjects of foreign states and territories. Authorities were beginning to recognize that the pursuit of private interest was of benefit to the entire polity and that this pursuit should have priority over traditional privileges and the claims of the ruler. Formal legislative ratification of this attitude occurred only in the eighteenth

70. Calenberg 1739, pp. 205–10 (edicts 10.VIII.1652 and 10.II.1700).

century, but the ordinances show the increasing willingness of the state to regard as completely separate the spheres of private economic life and the political world[71] with paradoxical results (to be discussed later). The ordinances introduced and confirmed a sharper distinction between *potestas* and *dominium*, the prerequisite for the consolidation of a modern society and economy, and thereby liberated the sphere of individual economic activity from the constraints of customary social and political ties.

For the state to interject itself into the legal aspect of family and servant relationships was natural in this period because of the traditional concept of political authority as the protector of social norms and law. In the seventeenth century, however, the territorial state went beyond this traditional conception of power when it turned its attention to the lifestyle of its subjects. As in most other instances, the impetus was provided by needs arising out of the Reformation. The place of the Church could not readily be filled by local Protestant ecclesiastical establishments, and the ruler assumed responsibility for the defense and maintenance of Christian morals. What had started out as a necessity to fill the void created in the institutional *encadrement* of society gradually developed into a novel and individualized pattern. Defense of traditional Christian values yielded to a rational and production-oriented point of view that treated the individual and his private or public obligations from the perspective of maintaining a coherent, secularized social structure designed to achieve material and cultural goals. As a result, territorial authorities found themselves battling against a host of traditions and customs, battles that were not easily won—hence the frequent repetition of the laws and regulations. We may almost speak of a regular, long-term campaign that eventually ended in the victory of the antitraditionalist rational constructivists and the emergence of new social relationships.

With respect to mores involving the most fundamental events of social or family life—birth, marriage, and death—the legisla-

71. *Hagestolzrecht* (the state's right to claim the estate of bachelors without direct heirs) is given up in the eighteenth century: Wolfenbüttel 21.I.1730 and 18.XI.1730, 18.IX.1731 in agreement with Prussia. Contrast to prohibition of alienating land, ibid., 24.IV.1694. Cf. Calenberg 1739, 2:624–25 (edict 21.XII.1694, re intestate inheritances).

tors endeavored to put an end to practices that seemed irrational
and harmful to the polity. They promulgated rules for schedul-
ing the baptism of infants and for the conditions under which that
ceremony should take place. Similarly they tried to impose
uniform regulations, least disruptive of the normal rhythm of life
and work, on betrothals, weddings, and funerals. A major concern that informed these efforts at systematic regulation and
uniformity was to spare members of the family as much discom-
fort and hazard to their health as possible. Thus ordinances
prohibited too large a crowd at christenings, so that the mother of
the newly born would be spared fatigue and the dangers of
contagion. Other regulations forbade delaying baptism for too
long, so as to make sure the child was baptized, even if it meant
that only a few family members could attend.[72] More obvious still
were health regulations in connection with funerals, since traditional practices increased the danger of contagion from those who
had died of infectious disease. In time of epidemics, in particular,
the dead were to be buried quickly, without undue ceremony and
public display of the corpse.[73] It may be noted in passing that even
in the eighteenth century the death of a child was quite an

72. *Sammelband . . . Wolfenbüttel* (Hochzeits, Kindtaufs . . . Ordnung 1646,
(especially pp. 7–28); ibid., interesting institution of a Commis-Haus for weddings
and feasts (still standing), Commis Ordnung 1645. Bergius, *Sammlung*, 6:140
(Schleswig Holstein Policey Ordnung 29.I.1768); ibid., 7:143–51 (Lauenburg
Verordnung 4.II.1774) and pp. 152–60 (Verordnung Lübeck 1748).
73. Freyberg 2:164 (Trauerordnung 1716); Wolfenbüttel, 13.X.1729; and the
remarkable idea, in *Policey Ordnung Nürnberg* (1672), p. 37, of establishing a system
for renting artificial decorations for funerals:

> Und weiln bis daher gebräuchlich gewesen dass die Gevatter ihren verstor-
> benen Doten und Paten Leichtücher, auch kostbare Kränze und Kreuze
> machen liessen, so soll dergleichen hinfüro gänzlich abgeschafft; hingegen
> bei Kirchen und Gotteshäusern angeordnet, dass von daraus die Leichtücher,
> um eine leidentliche Gebühr, hergeliehen, wie nicht weniger unterschiedliche
> Kränze und Kreuzlein auf die Särge von Draht- und Schmelz- und Blu-
> menwerk, dreierlei Gattungen, zu einem perpetuierlichen Vorrate zur Hand
> geschafft und selbige zu der Verstorbenen Leichbestattung, nach jedes
> Standes und Würde, ebenfalls gegen eine gewisse und wenige Ergötzlichkeit
> . . . um dem Gotteshaus zuverrechnen, gebraucht . . . nach des Amtstaxa
> gerichtet werden.

Bergius, *Sammlung*, 7:336–38 (Heilbronn Verordnung 10.IV.1783), complementing ibid., pp. 331–35 (Heilbronn Verordnung re funerals, 17.IX.1782).

unremarkable event: ordinances prohibited long periods of mourning and elaborate burial ceremonies for children, and in the case of infants who died before baptism public mourning was prohibited altogether.[74]

The regulations and prohibitions pursued a double aim: the first was an effort at restricting the public aspect of these family events. After all, large gatherings at christenings, betrothals, weddings, and funerals, or elaborate display over prolonged periods to mark these occasions (especially in case of mourning), involved society at large directly and indirectly. Traditionally the accepted behavior patterns at these events were designed to involve the whole community, to give public expression to the joy or sorrow experienced by a family and its members. Instead, the state endeavored to privatize the family and endow family events with sober dignity, so as to separate public ceremonies and pageantry from the realm of private experience and emotion. The everyday pattern of life was to become compartmentalized; public and private events were to be kept distinct, and the latter were to involve only those most directly concerned. The effect was to foster the individualization (and privatization) of experiences and emotions. The second goal was to prevent the loss of time spent doing productive work because of interruption of the work routine. Closely related to this concern was the belief that conspicuous public display was a waste of resources in an unproductive manner. Innumerable ordinances endeavored to curtail

---

74. Bergius, *Sammlung*, 9:32–35 (Hamburg Mandate 10.I.1729 and 23.X.1752); ibid., 1:27 (Prussian rescript 18.IV.1769); ibid., 9:22–32 (Trauerverordnung Bistum Fulda, 8.IV.1783). This would seem to qualify Ariès' thesis of the "discovery" of childhood in the late seventeenth and first half of the eighteenth century. True, the prohibitions suggest, very strongly, that such mourning did occur. But I would say that the long period of mourning and elaborate funeral display in the case of children precisely show that the latter were treated like grownups (cf. Ariès' telling point about the clothing of children in the seventeenth century being only the reduced version of adult dress). The fact that the authorities tried to impose a different approach to children shows the change described by Ariès as well as recognition of the high infant mortality rates that made such frequent, long, and ceremonious displays quite costly and economically harmful. (P. Ariès, *Centuries of Childhood: A Social History of Family Life* [New York: Random House, Vintage, 1962].)

luxurious dress and excessive consumption of food and drink at family events and to eliminate the unseemly or riotous behavior that often accompanied them. Ordinances were issued limiting the number of guests that could be entertained at baptisms, marriages, funerals; the number and quality of dishes that could be served; and the kind of foods and beverages that were to be consumed.[75]

These regulations seem to have been dictated by several different considerations, and it is important to make them explicit so as to bring out the contradictions and ambivalences inherent in them. We note first the intent of social disciplining that was clearly present in the efforts at privatization and rigid compartmentalization. There was also the evident desire to prevent unnecessary consumption and waste of material resources and goods, especially of foodstuffs, that could easily become scarce. This might well have been a reflection of the economic difficulties experienced by the "iron century" in contrast to the relative abundance of the late fifteenth and early sixteenth centuries.[76] The authorities were concerned lest labor be deflected from its useful occupations and the productive potential of society not utilized at its maximum capacity at all times; this easily accounts for the limits set on the number of people involved in and the time devoted to family festivities. An unstated and implicit contradiction to be detected in this approach was only temporary and disappeared once technological progress came into its own. On the one hand, there was the fear of wasting scarce and limited resources—hence the prohibition of excessive consumption and display; on the other hand, there was the belief that the productive potential could be maximized by husbanding these resources well and by ensuring the availability of labor to turn the potential

75. For example, Magdeburg Ordnung 1662, in *Sämptliche Fürstliche Magdeburgische Ordnungen. . . .* (1673), p. 835. "Hessische Verordnungen das Zuchthaus betreffend," 1/12.I.1734, sets fees for wedding entertainments and dances. Bergius, *Sammlung*, 1:25 (Preussische Bauernordnung 30.XII.1764 empowers authorities to control spending by peasants at festivities). Mylius, 5(1):83.

76. Henry Kamen, *The Iron Century (Social Change in Europe, 1550–1660)* (London: Weidenfeld & Nicolson, 1971), pointedly summarizes recent research on the question.

into actual production. At any rate, labor was clearly the major scarce resource; it had to be organized and disciplined to ensure its full productivity.

To be sure, an essential consideration present in this kind of ordinance—a consideration that has been unduly stressed in the secondary literature—was the preservation of social hierarchies. In a *société d'ordres,* hierarchies are manifested and displayed through visible means. The ordinances regulating public behavior at family festivities carefully discriminated among the orders of society as reflected in manner of dress and consumption of edibles. Naturally the nobility was subjected to the least constraints, though even in their case limits on consumption were occasionally set. The various groups of the urban population were limited as to the number of participants at festivities, the amount and kind of food and drink to be consumed there, and the elaborateness of decor and materials displayed.[77] Lastly, for the peasantry the ordinances emphatically set very strict limits on the level and manner of feasting at family and village gatherings.[78] In this case the frequent admonitions to consume less stemmed only in part from the fear of wasting much-needed reserves and from a desire to protect the peasant from the ever-present threats of starvation and ruin. The very necessity of issuing and repeating such ordinances suggests that in many instances food and drink was available in abundance. Obviously the peasantry preferred to consume what was available in a conspicuous manner at traditional occasions rather than hoard it under most precarious conditions of security and preservation. It might also be argued, of course, that conspicuous consumption on the part of the upper classes affected only the expendable surplus and that this, in turn, generated new demands for manufactured and agricultural goods and in so doing stimulated production.

77. Freyberg, 2:154–62; Wolfenbüttel, 5.V.1690; *Der Stadt Braunschweig Kleider Ordnung* (1650). On clothing ordinances see the useful monograph by L. C. Eisenbart, *Kleiderordnungen der deutschen Städte zwischen 1350–1700* (Göttingen: Vandenhoeck & Ruprecht, 1962).

78. Pfaltz, 1599. "Hessische Verordnungen das Zuchthaus betreffend"; Policey Ordnung Christians ... Minden (1618). Freyberg 2:147–54. Wolfenbüttel, 27.X.1740. *Stadt Braunschweig Edictum das Gevatter Brod betreffend* (Braunschweig: 1649).

It was to be expected that the territorial sovereignties would wish to preserve the existing hierarchical order of society.[79] In their view, not only did such an order secure law and domestic peace; it also corresponded to the prevailing and still useful structuring of man's world. Yet the structure itself contained the seed of a basic contradiction: rigid social hierarchies were not readily compatible with the individualism implicit in the stress on the productive worth of each person. Furthermore, if society were to be organized rationally in a universe of expanding possibilities, traditional hierarchical barriers would surely become an impediment. The legislators' pragmatism precluded their facing the issue squarely. But in later ordinances, and they still occurred in the second half of the eighteenth century, we note that the regulation of consumption became less detailed and the prohibitions less severe.[80] On the other hand, we also encounter instances where the traditional rationale was completely abandoned and display and consumption were made to depend on the available resources and means in each particular case. Eventually the authorities gave up the notion that it was their task to control such things for the protection of society and of its future, and they gave free rein to decisions taken by the individual, who also had to bear the consequences. The development ended in the triumph of a new approach to society and government: that of the statutory separation between the private, the public (socio-economic), and the political realms. Judging from the didactic style and form of their ordinances, the governments of the seventeenth and eighteenth centuries did not simply acquiesce in and ratify a process and a state of affairs that had arisen

---

79. *Pfaltz Landesordnung* (1599). "Hessische Policey Verordnungen Sittlichkeit, Luxus, Spielen und Lotterie betreffend" (1526–1744), pp. 46ff., no date, gives simple formulation of rationale:

Demnach vieler Orten . . . übermas in Kleidung und anderm so gar gesteigert und überhand nimmt, und weder Edel noch Bürgersleut bey ihrem Stand bleiben noch mit seiner Standeskleidung sich begnügen lassen . . . dass dahero man öftermals keinen Unterschied zwischen adeligen und denen nicht von Adel und zwischen niedrigen und hohen, Herr und Knecht, Magd und Frau machen kann . . . weil kein Stand in seinem Stande bleiben will sondern der Hochmut bei allen überhand nimmt.

80. Freyberg, 2:163 (14.V.1700).

spontaneously outside the influence of the administrators' actions; rather, a deliberate choice was made and an intention declared.

After what has been said, there is no need to go into the details of the ordinances regulating social and civic events. They displayed the same concerns, purposes, and resorted to similar means as those dealing with family events. It may, however, be noted that conspicuous display and consumption were deemed an essential aspect of authority and power. The powerful of this earth were to manifest their status and role; this was their obligation and duty, as well as their privilege. It behooved the rulers, the highest functionaries, and in general the members of the elites (including the academic) to "show off." Ordinances and regulations provided for the norms and practices of public display, and treatises rationalized them.[81] Public display was given legitimacy as an expression of prestige, authority, and ultimately of power, and for this reason it became the monopoly of the official establishment—the monarch and his officers. Since luxury and extravagance, pomp and circumstance, were banned from the realm of private events and individual public activity, they were flaunted with increasing elaborateness by sovereigns, governments, and public institutions. In the Catholic territories, where the state shared the functions of moral and spiritual leadership with the Church, the latter not only retained but even intensified its ceremonial displays and increased their artistic and luxurious character. In the Protestant territories, where secular and ecclesiastical authority were merged into one, we observe a division of function: the church became the advocate and guardian of the private, sober, and restrained style of life, while the state monopolized ceremonial pomp to assert its authority in the public sphere.

Regulating traditional customs and public festivities constituted a significant object of police ordinances. Originally there had been two major motives for so doing. The first has been suggested earlier—to do away with manifestations of so-called popish idolatry in religious feasts and practices. The second motive, closely

81. Bergius, *Sammlung,* 4:209–11 (Hessen Darmstadt Verordnung 29. VI.1751). *Stadt Braunschweig Kleider Ordnung* 26.XI.1650.

related to the first, involved the safeguarding of order, decorum, and peace that might be disturbed by the riotous excesses induced by some popular customs. Outside the domain of religious festivities, the situations that seemed to require administrative intervention and control occurred in connection with the public and professional functions of guilds and corporations. Here, as in the situations considered previously, the legislators' main concern was to restrain conspicuous consumption and to reduce the burden of public activities to be borne by members of the guilds or corporations. In addition, some ordinances were intended to control guild festivities and customs in order to limit their impact on the productive routine and normal work patterns. Such concerns were particularly prevalent in the second half of the seventeenth century as ordinance upon ordinance enjoined guilds to prevent their festivities from degenerating into rowdyism and from incapacitating their members for work the next day, the so-called blue Monday. No effort was spared to circumscribe the effects of these blue Mondays and to reduce the number of occasions for external and exuberant celebrations.[82]

As time went on, the ordinances dealt less and less with problems created by corporations and guild festivities, for both types of organizations were obviously on the decline. In contrast to earlier ordinances, the Imperial Ordinance on the Guilds of 1731, extended to and enforced in practically all the German territorial sovereignties, did not address this aspect of guild life to any significant extent. On the other hand, ordinances continued to be issued frequently to curb traditional festivities in the countryside. These measures were justified and rationalized on the ground that such feasts were superfluous survivals of pagan beliefs and idol worship and, in addition, presented great dangers to the participants' safety.[83] The reasoned arguments and the

---

82. Saxen Policey ... Gesind Tagelöhner und Handwerks Ordnung" 22. VI.1668, in *Corpus Iuris Saxonici* (Dresden: 1672). Appel and Kleinschmidt, *Sammlung*, no. 397 (21.V.1683). Wolfenbüttel, "Verordnung und Reglement wegen Einrichtung der Aempter und Gilden," Hanover 1692. *Policey Ordnung Nürnberg* (1672), p. 88.

83. *Pfaltz Landesordnung* (1599); Magdeburg Verordnung, in *Sämptliche Fürstliche ... Mandate. ...* (1673), p. 510; Wolfenbüttel, 10.VIII.1705 (fire threat), 18.VIII.1735 (student behavior a hazard in Göttingen), 23.VIII.1745, 20.

priority given to the safeguarding of health obviously illustrated an important shift: the legislators no longer perceived the significance of festive customs for promoting the cultural and social cohesion of village communities. What was perceived—and feared—was the "irrational," that is emotional and presumably threatening aspect of uncontrolled and exuberant behavior. Clearly the well-meaning and rationalistic legislators no longer had any understanding of rural "primitive" culture; instead they relentlessly pushed for a uniform way of life to be shared by all members of society. And it was a way of life that put primary emphasis on the physical well-being and preservation of active and productive populations, whether in towns or in villages. Public manifestations of most traditional customs were to be banned (at any rate discouraged), since they set bad examples and helped to preserve foolish and childish ways.

It is difficult to separate the ordinances directed at certain traditional beliefs from those concerned with customary behavior on specific occasions, but the didacticism of many ordinances—especially from the late seventeenth century on—clearly aimed at changing beliefs. In most cases the motive for wishing to change beliefs arose in connection with giving technical advice or promoting innovations in agriculture or manufacturing. The introduction of the modernized and improved calender after 1700 is one illustration. Pragmatic considerations, however, allowed for modifications in application of this ordinance. Certain traditional dates set aside on the old calendar for seasonal rural activities (hunting season, and so forth) were to be retained.[84] The rational, didactic tone of the ordinances and their ridiculing of traditional beliefs as superstitious or primitive were instrumental in inculcating new beliefs and ideas, as well as undermining old ones.

As the eighteenth century wore on, ordinances prohibiting luxury became less frequent, less strident in tone, and less sweeping in their prohibitions. This indicates, I believe, that the state, perhaps feeling that its task of reeducation was accom-

20.XII.1745 (health hazards of horseraces at Pentecost). Nürnberg Bayreuth 1672, pp. 60–61; *Mecklenburg Policey und Landt Ordnung* (1562) for very early prohibition but without rational argumentation.

84. Wolfenbüttel, 16.X.1711; Calenberg 1739, 3:374 (edict 21.II.1701).

plished, was withdrawing from the sector of private life in this area too, leaving it up to the individual's taste and capacity to set his own level of expenditures. With respect to the rural population, however, the state's paternalistic supervision lingered on for much longer.[85] The legislators' restrictions on luxury in the villages clearly show that, in their view, the peasants were less mature or more childish than city dwellers (how reminiscent of Karl Marx's view in the matter!). Thus we have the amusing prohibition of or restrictions on the consumption of coffee in the countryside, rationalized partly by considerations of economy (since it was an expensive imported article), partly by reasons of health.[86]

What were the implications of these efforts at controlling and transforming, or redirecting, established behavior and norms? To see in the flow of ordinances only a manifestation of the government's police functions, in the restrictive modern sense of *police,* would be taking a narrow and distorted view. Considering the many difficulties faced by the governments in regulating and controlling festivities, family and social events, dress and display, and life-style, we can identify another underlying motive for this legislation. It would seem that an essential aim of these ordinances in the area of social life was to undermine, constrict, and eventually to eliminate what may be called traditional (premodern) patterns of social behavior. Traditional popular notions had it that social cohesion and human relationships were best manifested through extensive and frequent celebrations, display, and the extravagant consumption of one's wealth, since the latter validated one's place in society. Almost any pretext or occasion, whether familial or religious, was appropriate. Implicit was the belief that work or labor was but the means for making the festivities possible. In short, man worked in order to celebrate, and in the absence of public occasions for celebration there was no point in laboring beyond the production of the bare necessities for physical survival. The more extended the periods of celebra-

85. Cf. discussion of Bauernordnung from Mylius below.
86. Bergius, *Sammlung,* 3:68–70 (Prussian declaration re coffee consumption, 19.VI.1778) and ibid., pp. 74–83 (Hessen Darmstadt 12.IX.1766, Hildesheim 4.I.1768, Hessen Darmstadt 11.II.1775).

tion, the greater the expenditures lavished upon them, the more successful the economic and social structures were deemed to be and the more manifest the prestige of those who could afford such displays for such a long time. With the territorial sovereignties' monopolization of authority, competitive displays by private individuals or groups could not be allowed. Police enforcement occurred within the broader context of a struggle against a whole attitude toward life. In this sense, and in this sense only, may we say that the ordinances endeavored to secularize—or rationalize and deprive of traditional and effective symbolization—the people's way of life and assert the supremacy of the political establishment, resorting to religion only as a means of social control and disciplining.

The ordinances on social behavior had still another facet. Anthropologists and sociocultural historians have observed that because the traditional (medieval or premodern) pattern of life was so constricted by religious institutions and norms as well as by the limitations of an economy of scarcity, people needed occasional release from accumulated tensions and insecurities. These releases were provided by festivities, especially those in which the world could be turned upside down, as in carnivals. During such celebrations, the normal hierarchies and values were flaunted and the instinctual forces in man given symbolic and stylized recognition. The physical or animal side of man was given free rein to express itself in the inverted world of the carnival, the *kermesse,* or the feast. At such moments, too, man's basic play instincts could find temporary release in a free, yet formalized, and hence acceptable manner.[87] But members of the elite, with their evergrowing rationalism, viewed this instinctive, childish, "inverted" emotional behavior as an impediment to an efficient structuring of society for functional purposes through rational constructivism. This behavior was also felt to be antagonistic to the goals of a society organized for productive purposes, a society that husbanded the surplus of production for further production in the future instead of squandering it in a wild throwaway. Naturally

87. Discussion largely inspired by the works of M. Bakhtin, E. Leroy-Ladurie, R. Mandrou, K. Thomas, and J. Huizinga.

such motivations and goals were neither comprehensible nor acceptable to the ordinary people. They resisted not so much by any overt acts as by passive disregard of the prohibitions and by carrying on their folkways and celebrations as of old. In the long run, reinforced by the gradual transformation of economic life and social organization that the ordinances promoted, the prohibitions did stick; the old "wasteful" folkways disappeared giving way to the sober and on the whole dull and drab festivities organized under the aegis of the temporal authorities. Since play, pomp, and gaudiness were now provided by the monarch and the state, the people turned into passive spectators. Their potential for emotional outbursts had been tamed.[88]

We have seen that the aim of disciplining society constituted the truly innovative aspect of the ordinances in the area of social life. Gerhard Oestreich identified the notion of "disciplining" in the political thought and practice of the seventeenth century. When it is applied to the cultural and social realms, the meaning or implication of disciplining needs to be altered. In Oestreich's use of the term, disciplining suggests controls that the centralized absolutist state forced on the political body and upon estates that challenged its monopoly of power and authority.[89] In his view, this was done to provide the modern state with the cohesive and effective military establishment it needed in order to pursue its foreign policy goals and to compel the population to pay it taxes and perform services. Certainly these were major aspects of *Disziplinierung*. But they were only a part of it, and our review of the ordinances has enabled us to see the much broader context— that is, the aim of adapting the population to the performance and attainment of the new economic and productive goals set by the state.

In a sense, this disciplining aimed at instilling a new attitude,

---

88. W. Nahrstedt, *Die Entstehung der Freizeit* (Göttingen: Vandenhoeck & Ruprecht, 1972), and the studies of M. Ozouf, R. Agulhon, and J. Bercé on festivities in the ancien régime and revolutionary France.

89. G. Oestreich, *Geist und Gestalt des frühmodernen Staates* and *Verfassungsgeschichte von dem Ende des Mittelalters bis zum Ende des alten Reiches* (Minden: Deutscher Taschenverlag, paperback ed., 1974). Vol. II of *Gebhardt: Handbuch der deutschen Geschichte*, edited by Herbert Grundmann.

Gesinnung, toward the *vita activa,* to dethrone the respect paid
formerly to the *vita contemplativa* as man's highest achievement on
this earth.[90] The new attitude was to be fostered, in the opinion of
the legislators, by establishing a closer connection between the
moral realm and the life-style of the population. The moral
notions to be inculcated by the religious, political, as well as
pedagogic establishments were those of sobriety and purposefulness, the voluntary and stoic acceptance of the duties of earthly
existence for its own sake. It was imperative that the same norms
and values inform every activity of the individual and group. The
neo-Stoic morality and world view defined man's place in a
rational world order that rested on Natural Law and the laws of
nature, and in that world man's activities were to be carried on
within the same lawful and orderly framework, eschewing both
the irrational (that is, unreasonable and emotional) and the
unnatural. This was deemed possible by relying on man's ability,
by an act of will and determination, to shape his destiny within the
boundaries set by nature. Man asserted his being and proclaimed
his autonomy only in an active, creative, and productive existence.
What Professor Hirschman, on the evidence of theoretical trac-
tates, has described as putting the passions to use for the purpose
of productive interest was also the goal pursued by the ordinances.[91] The latter endeavored to actualize and implement the
transformation that was taking place in the conception of man's
nature (in fact his psychology) and of his place in the world. Is it
to be wondered that from its very inception the dominant
modern economic ideology carried a strong moralistic undercurrent and by implication rejected the traditional notions of man's
relationships to his fellows and to nature?

This aspect of the process of disciplining also found expression
in numerous efforts at controlling, if not eliminating outright, the
"superfluous" purposeless, unstructured, and fickle elements of
society. The plethora of ordinances against begging and vagrancy
that are usually adduced as evidence of poor economic conditions

90. *Stadt Braunschweig Begräbnisordnung* (Braunschweig: 1650).
91. Albert O. Hirschmann, *The Passions and the Interests* (Princeton, N.J.:
Princeton University Press, 1977).

(which certainly did prevail most of the time in the seventeenth and first half of the eighteenth century) and of the government's desire to control the lawless and footloose who threatened peace and order had another purpose as well. But before dealing with it, it may not be amiss to observe the notable evolution of the ordinances on begging that took place between the sixteenth and early eighteenth centuries. In the sixteenth century, and starting with the Imperial Police Ordinances of 1548, beggars and vagrants were banned as a threat to domestic peace, law, and order. In the latter part of the sixteenth and in the first half of the seventeenth centuries the economic hardships created by the beggars and their associates became the primary concern. This brought about the distinction between local, domestic, and outside poor. The local poor were to be taken care of in some way or other, while the foreign ones were to be expelled so as not to burden the community. At the end of the seventeenth century, however, and quite definitely so in the early eighteenth century, there was a further shift in the direction of making use of this element of society. The distinction between foreign and domestic poor was maintained, though the foreign beggar might not only be expelled but also imprisoned and put to work. The local poor, unless obviously incapable of working, were now put into workhouses of various sorts (even in poorhouses the residents were required to be as useful as possible).[92] Furthermore, there was also a change in attitude, though less marked, with respect to the truly foreign elements among the footloose and poor—for example, the beggar Jews and the Gypsies. In all cases, and throughout the period, efforts were made to keep them out of the territory,

92. The evolution makes two things clear: the increasing involvement of society in dealing with the problem of poverty (i.e., decline of the narrow police aspects) and the less moralistic tone of the ordinances, the stress on rational and pragmatic coping with problems in the most efficient manner possible. Freiburg i. Breisgau Poor Ordinance of 1781 (Bergius, *Sammlung*, 5:1–23). Also, Armencassa ordinance, ibid., 6:133–35 (Schleswig Holstein Policeyordnung 29.I.1768). Concerning putting the poor to work, see Bergius, *Sammlung*, 7:319–30 (Preussische Reglement für Spinnschulen, 6.XII.1764); Calenberg 1739, 1:943 (Armenordnung 6.XII.1702, 4.XII.1700); *Sammlung Anhalt-Dessau Verordnung*, no. 70 (8.II.1772, pp. 139–41), no. 76 (25.II.1773, pp. 150–56). Good picture of the evolution of Prussian legislation in Mylius, 5:31ff.

and we have seen the barbaric measures taken with regard to Gypsies. But in the eighteenth century, more particularly in the Prussian lands, there occurred a change in the ordinances in that the Gypsies were lumped together with other beggars and vagrants, though still singled out by name. Eventually they were subjected to the same treatment as the vagrants, at least the women, children, and those men among them who seemed amenable to work. They were to be put to work in workhouses and efforts were to be made to provide some training in useful occupations for the children.[93]

But to return to the basic purpose of the ordinances on begging and vagrancy—the purpose was to capture and *encadrer* individuals (and groups) who might be put to productive use under supervision. Hence the efforts to put all vagrants and beggars into poor- or work-houses under parish control where they would be engaged in productive labor at cheap rates.[94] It was a way to exploit unfree labor within the context and possibilities of European society. If we are to follow up the argumentation of Michel Foucault, the structured productive society had to put everybody into a rigid institutional setting, not only to control them but also to preclude the possibility of their becoming dangerous models for others. The direct connection that existed between the beggar and the vagrant, on the one hand, and the economic conditions of society on the other was not always recognized or admitted. Only the "deserving poor," that is the innocent victims of the natural working of the economy or of natural disasters and accident were to be helped to get back on their feet. This was more easily done in rural settings, provided the land remained fertile, the climate favorable, and the people able to work. But the malingerers, those

93. Mylius, 5(5):55–64.
94. Freyberg, 2:13. *Sammlung Anhalt-Dessau Verordnung*, no. 32 (25.VI.1764, pp. 54–58, setting up Arbeit- und Armen-Haus in Dessau) *Allgemeine Verordnung des lünebergischen Zucht- und Werck-Hauses* (1702), 1.VIII.1702, gives a most comprehensive and typical statement of the rationale. Calenberg 1739, vol. 1 as in 92 above. Calenberg 1739, 2:696–98 (28.II.1717 replacing physical punishment by term in the Zuchthaus at labor) and detailed Anordnung für Zucht- und Toll-haus in Zelle, 2.XII.1732 (pp. 717–72). *Sammelband . . . Wolfenbüttel* (Hospital und Armenordnung 1660) for an earlier, more moralistic, religious rationale and less involvement by society in running it.

unwilling to do their share, were to be treated without pity—punished and put to work. Naturally the moral distinction drawn between the deserving and the culpable poor resulted in discriminatory legislation: the local poor, those who were known and whose condition could be proved to have been produced against their will, were to be supported and helped.[95] Even such assistance had to be given in an orderly, organized fashion so as to make use of whatever productive potential was still available in the local poor and in such a manner as to spread the burden fairly among the whole community. On the other hand, the status of the outsiders could not be ascertained and the reasons for their miserable condition could not easily be checked; these people were to be treated as parasites, threats to the social order, and expelled or harshly punished as evil trespassers. Such ordinances were telling illustration of the increasing isolation and self-contained selfishness of the territorial sovereignties.

To put the poor and vagrants in work- or poorhouses or the insane and criminals into hospitals served a twofold purpose. For one thing, it helped to reinforce the notion that unwillingness to work was a moral defect, and consequently a crime, and that it had to be punished. In the second place, it strongly made the point that an unstructured and anarchical way of life, itinerancy and natural freedom, were intolerable in a well-organized, rationally structured polity. At the same time the ordinances exemplified the new outlook on man's ability to be the captain of his fate; they reinforced the view that to be a normal and productive member of society was a deliberate act of will based on an implicit understanding of the law-regulated structure of the universe. A man's failure to make that act of will could be nothing else than an act of willful violation of the basic order of things—proof of a criminal and immoral inclination.

---

95. *Policey Ordnung Christians . . . Minden* (1618) makes special provision for poor foreign students; Freyberg 2:46ff. (Bettelmandat 5.I.1655, pp. 47–48); *Sammlung Anhalt-Dessau Verordnung,* no. 18 (26.VII.1755, Armenverpflegung, p. 30), nos. 67–68 (25.XI.1771, 10.I.1772, re foreign beggars); Wolfenbüttel, 9.XI.1671, 3.X.1698, 29.VII.1709; *Sammelband . . . Wolfenbüttel,* pp. 16, 18, 26 (Hospital and Armen Ordnung, 1660) and "Fürstliche Privilegia, Statuta . . . der Heinrichstadt" (1602) §36.

In conclusion, the aim of the ordinances was not the mere regulation of outward behavior but the disciplining of attitudes. This aim explains the close connection the ordinances tried to establish between morality, a rational world view, and productive work. It was yet another way of struggling against traditions, passions, and against recognized forms of manifesting irrational and unproductive enjoyment—in short, yet another method for disciplining society and culture.

4. Economy

We have seen in the preceding section that a major purpose of the police ordinances was to instill and encourage active, rational, and production-oriented attitudes in society. We must now consider in what way the ordinances directly endeavored to structure and develop economic patterns involved in this transformation. For clarity's sake we shall consider (seriatim) the documents relating to trade, manufacturing, agriculture, and fiscal affairs, although the separation between these sectors of economic life was obviously never watertight. In some areas they were closely interrelated, especially in terms of the personnel involved, for the latter was still far from being specialized and professionalized.[96]

It is usually and quite correctly asserted that mercantilism, by whatever definition, inspired the economic theory and practice of cameralism and that government ordinances gave this economic theory administrative and political expression. While policies and regulations pertaining to trade should be viewed within a mercantilist framework, mercantilism did not provide quite as clear and comprehensive a framework for government regulation of manufacturing; although many practices prescribed or countenanced by the ordinances were derived from mercantilist attitudes, other considerations were also operative. Strictly speaking, mercantilist governments did not concern themselves directly with agriculture, though they recognized and promoted it as an essential

96. For the several definitions of mercantilism and an up-to-date discussion and bibliographical aid, see D. C. Coleman, ed., *Revisions in Mercantilism* (London: Methuen, 1969).

foundation and precondition for the prosperity of societies actively engaged in manufacturing and commerce. Physiocracy, on the other hand, although intellectually the heir of earlier attitudes, put agriculture and the marketing of its products at the center of its program for economic and social prosperity. It will be interesting to note that seventeenth-century ordinances presaged physiocratic attitudes, advocating practices and policies that aimed at expanding agriculture and making it the dominant economic activity long before the theorists of physiocracy published their views. The early efforts at creating (in today's jargon) statistical and economic data banks were closely related to the development of modern economic policies but will be treated later in connection with the formation of bureaucratic techniques and attitudes.

In the area of trade, international commerce need not detain us long. "International," in our context of course, meant primarily trade between the various German sovereignties and between any one of them and a country outside the Holy Roman Empire. Basically the ordinances aimed at establishing proper control at border points where duty would be levied and collected. In characteristic mercantilist fashion, they also encouraged the export of manufactured goods and discouraged the importation of those that could be duplicated at home. Trade in raw materials and staples was to be limited by the needs, real or putative, of local consumption and the monopoly of some items—for example copper, iron, or other minerals detained by the treasury (*Fiskus*).[97] The export had to yield tax revenue, so that there were duties on exports as well as tariffs on imports.[98] To secure normal food supplies, the commerce in foodstuffs, preeminently grain, was subject to regulations that controlled and restricted this kind of trade to ensure adequate supplies at home in case of crop failure. However, with the beginning of the eighteenth century, as a

97. Wolfenbüttel, 6.II.1674, 26.VI.1688, 18.II.1708; Bergius, *Sammlung* 1:45–137 (Preussische Bergordnung für Schlesien und Glatz, 5.VI.1769). In the eighteenth century, the monopoly claims were more frequently relinquished; see Calenberg 1739, pp. 326–27 (Patent 31.III.1728).

98. Freyberg 2:132–33, 315 (with reference to Reichstagsausschuss, 21. I.1666); ibid., pp. 330–31 expressed the basic principles of policy for ca. 1720.

result of better yields and of the acceptance of a degree of freedom in trade, these regulations began to weaken. We encounter then only temporary export prohibitions on grain, while its domestic trade was to remain free; in any event, as soon as harvest predictions improved or the foreseen shortage did not materialize, the free exportation of grain was permitted again.[99]

The trade ordinances were mainly concerned with domestic trade. We may distinguish two major aspects: interurban or interregional, and exchanges between town and nearby countryside. With respect to the former, the ordinances endeavored to put interurban and interregional trade on as regular a basis as possible and to ensure the safety of merchants and the orderliness of transactions. Ordinances provided that taverns, inns, postal relays, and roads be properly maintained and that the personnel working in them refrain from asking excessive prices for their services, so that high costs would not prevent smooth traffic.[100] To bring about order and regularity in the collection of duties and tolls, the territorial chanceries compiled systematic and detailed lists, which were steadily improved, of articles and materials that had to be declared upon entering the district or town limits. The ordinances were concerned with the authority and rights of officials, with procedures for controlling and investigating those suspected of fraud, and with the keeping of accurate records of goods and the tolls and duties imposed on them.[101]

99. Freyberg, 2:98–100 (re vagaries of policy in this respect conditioned by the war and foreign occupation) and p. 280 (resolution by Geheimer Rat, 12. III.1694); Wolfenbüttel 2.IX.1684, 28.IV.1685, 20.IX.1697, and also 1.VI. 1709 and 8.VII.1709, showing how policy depended on existing or expected conditions.

100. Freyberg, 2:345–47 (decree of 17.XII.1731) and 1730 opinion of Commerz Collegium, "Es möge zur Erleichterung des Handelsverkehrs, so wie um Verzollungsanständen abzuhelfen ein Generalmandat erlassen werden, dass nach Verlauf von 3 Monaten nach geschehener Publikation desselben, bei Strafe von 3 Rthl. auf allen Schrammen in den Kürfürstl. Landen nur nach dem Münchener Getreidemass verkauft werden dürfe."

101. Freyberg, 2:330–31, 356: "Man solle aber auch überhaupt die Handelsleute mehr in Achtung und Würde halten, ihnen mehr freie Hand in ihrer Handtierung lassen, und sich nicht immer in ihre Angelegenheiten mischen.

Regulating the transactions and keeping peace at the markets held periodically were major topics in the ordinances dealing with domestic interurban trade. The ruler's officials, or the elected or appointed competent townsmen (guild and council members), were entrusted with the opening, closing, and supervising of the markets, the latter of which duties also included examining the price and quality of the merchandise offered for sale.[102] A major concern expressed by the ordinances was that the goods not be sold outside the market, to avoid their being bought up by intermediaries at unfair prices and to prevent their hoarding, so that craftsmen could acquire needed raw materials at regular prices. These measures were always justified by the paternalistic consideration of preventing "monopoly," the cornering of all supplies by a few who would then inflate prices.[103] To this end the ordinances required that duties in kind be levied inside the town walls, at specified places and by specially appointed competent collectors only. Furthermore, no commercial transaction was allowed to take place outside the town gates or away from the market (except in special cases). Since markets and fairs were important sources of revenue for the towns and the territorial sovereigns, they were frequently established to compensate for damages suffered through fire or some natural calamity.[104] Thus

Unvermöglichen wäre jedoch unter die Arme zu greifen, gegen die Fahrlässigen und Verschwenderischen aber soll die Obrigkeit einschreiten und die Magistrate verständige Leute anordnen die über die Dinge wachen, und von Zeit zu Zeit Relation abstatten." Wolfenbüttel, 1735 extract, gives a clear summary by categories of goods and actions, taxes and penalties. Ibid., 3.VIII.1737, Zoll und Accis Rolle in alphabetical order and the same in 30.VII.1740. Appel and Kleinschmidt, *Sammlung,* no. 383, 5.XII.1681, instruction for examiners and custom clerks.

102. "Hessische Policey Verordnungen Marktsachen betreffend" (1631–1745); Wolfenbüttel, 11.XII.1724, 3.VIII.1733 (tolls to be collected only at packing house and scales, 10.VII.1730 (Messeverordnung, based on opinions of merchants as well); 4.VI.1740 (prohibition against advance sale); Calenberg 1739, 3:76–78 (16.IX.1704) and 3:88–89 (5.X.1720 and 24.II.1721 prohibiting advance sale of specific items).

103. A good summary of the cultural context of the fear of monopoly is given in E. P. Thompson, "The Moral Economy of the English Crowd in the Eighteenth Century," *Past and Present* 50 (1971): 76–136.

104. Wolfenbüttel 9.X.1722 (establishing cattle fair at Vecheld); 13.XII.1732 (the same in village of Grene).

direct interference and control by the political authorities were fully accepted and duly enforced as a recognized practice throughout the period. The hour of free and unfettered exchanges between localities had not yet struck.

On the other hand, recognizing the value and necessity of bringing goods to market, the ordinances provided protection and special fiscal dispensations to merchants going to and coming from the markets. Of crucial importance was the duration of the privileged periods during which the merchants might travel to and from a fair or market without having to pay normal tolls and transit dues on bridges, town gates, and roads.[105] A serious effort was made to define the free periods as comprehensively as possible and to extend their duration to the maximum. Even foreign merchants were freed from paying transit duties when journeying to a regularly held fair. Some articles, however, were excluded from these advantages, and ordinances were issued to provide for close watch over traders so that they did not smuggle these articles in in defiance of the rules, all of which were standard measures in those times. The same problem might have arisen when some types of traders were banned or subjected to special discriminatory regulations (for example, Jews and peddlers).[106]

A difficult problem was presented by the peddlers, whose activities involved the ill-defined areas between the regulations affecting interurban and interregional trade and those involving commerce between town and countryside. The peddlers were a problem for two reasons: in the first place, they could not, of necessity, be limited to plying their trade at markets or at fairs (although efforts were made to reorient their activities exclusively in that direction). Since they came themselves to offer their wares to individual purchasers at home, they were less amenable to supervision and control. Secondly, they dealt in a variety of articles, including prohibited or closely supervised ones such as tobacco products or books, and in so doing undermined the

---

105. Mylius, chap. 9, 5(2):563.
106. Most frequently when government *Regale* (state monopoly) was involved—e.g., tobacco: Wolfenbüttel 5.VIII.1698.

rights and privileges of specialized traders (or the state). Many ordinances endeavored to bring peddlers within some stable and rigid framework, but the problem of enforcement was well beyond the capacities of the administration and society of those days.[107] Eventually the situation took care of itself when the modernization of transportation and a vastly expanded consumer market put the peddlers out of business. The ordinances regulating the peddlers were also concerned with restraining itinerancy and free movement by individuals. Moreover, it was claimed that peddlers were a threat to public health, since by their comings and goings they could carry contagious disease from one region into another. They also presented a political and cultural threat, for they might peddle forbidden literature (and ideas) and articles of luxury in defiance of the law. Lastly, they provided a personal mode of communication, on an informal level, among the communities; they therefore aroused the suspicion of the authorities as potential political messengers and fomenters of subversion and dissidence.[108] Still, as one of the main connecting links between the economies of town and countryside, the peddlers could not be eliminated or prohibited altogether. And their own security was at issue, too, since they were easy targets of attack by highwaymen, increasing the problem of policing roads and taverns.

Of major interest to the authorities was the desire to regulate exchanges between town and countryside for their mutual benefit so as to eliminate ruinous competition and unfair exploitation of the villagers. Ordinances were passed to allow peasants to market their produce in town only at officially sanctioned times and in recognized marketplaces. Efforts were made to protect the peasants from those buyers who took advantage of their straitened circumstances before harvest time to purchase their grain at low prices and resell it to them at planting and sowing time for much more. The practice of advancing money before harvest and of

107. See beginnings in sixteenth century, *Pfaltz Landesordnung* (1599), p. 278; Wolfenbüttel, 27.IV.1719, 1.X.1738, and 16.IV.1740; Calenberg 1739, 3:360–62, 367–68 (edicts of 31.X.1701, 2.IV.1721, 27.VI.1724). Mylius, *Continuatio*, 1:27–30 (27.III.1737).

108. Wolfenbüttel 9.X.1727 (re book peddling).

purchasing grain in the field (on the stalk—as was and is Soviet practice) was equally detrimental to the peasants, for it indentured them and their crops in advance. Another way in which the peasants were put at disadvantage and cheated was when second-rate manufactured goods were brought to the villages and sold at exorbitant prices, taking advantage of the villagers gullibility and limited access to alternative sources of supply. The ordinances tried to legislate for all these situations so as to protect the interests of the peasants (which was felt to correspond to the sovereign's interests as well). It would appear from the economic evolution of central Europe over the long term that the success of these measures was not overwhelming.[109]

On the other hand, the townspeople too could be cheated and taken advantage of by the peasants. For this reason ordinances tried to ensure that the produce and wares brought to the towns from the country be of uniform quality. In line with the paternalistic tradition of direct involvement, prices were controlled as well, so that the peasants would not take undue advantage of temporary demand. Last, but not least, ordinances prohibited the peasants from trading in those goods that they produced in competition with and against the exclusive rights of the towns. Thus, the countryside *(Dorf)* was not to sell the beer it brewed at home or the cloth spun or woven in the villages in violation of the privileges granted to urban manufacturers. As domestic industry and the "putting out" system expanded in the period of protoindustrialization, the legislator's concern in this area increased too.[110]

Quite clearly, with respect to trade policies the ordinances were conservative. They aimed at preserving the separate activities and functions of town and country, of producer and consumer.[111]

109. Wolfenbüttel 26.VI.1710; *Magdeburgische Ordnungen* (Leipzig: 1673), p. 582 (with exception for Notdurft); "Hessische Cameral-Ordnungen die Serviten betreffend" (1630–1740), 16.II.1733, 27.VII.1738, 12.XI.1734.

110. Mylius, 5(2): 25. Cf. also C. Brauns, *Die kurhessische Gewerbepolitik im 17. und 18. Jahrhundert,* Schmoller Staats und Sozialwissen-schaftliche Forschungen, no. 156 (Leipzig, 1911 and P. Kriedte, H. Medick, and J. Schlumbohm, *Industrialisierung vor der Industrialisierung* (Göttingen: Vandenhoeck & Ruprecht, 1977).

111. Mylius, *Corpus . . . Magdeburgicarum,* 3:9.

They were equally conservative in their approach, for they gave only negative protection (displaying mere paternalistic concern) to the peasant, while endeavoring to provide positive encouragement to the urban sector. One may ponder the implicit contradiction manifested by the ordinances as they tried to transform the norms and behavior of the country people while at the same time discouraging parallel transformation in the productive process. This discordance between differentiation between town and country and laissez-faire, on the one hand, and active interventionism or even *dirigisme,* on the other, characterized the cameralist approach, making it difficult to define the direction and assess the effectiveness of the well-ordered police state's economic policies. It should perhaps also be noted that the lack of a clear direction illustrated the cautious, gradualist approach taken by cameralist legislation—possibly an outcome of the legislators' realization that the malleability of human nature had limits and that it was not the legislator's function to substitute for God. With respect to new industries and enterprises, however, (man-made creations), these cameralists felt that these should indeed be introduced by acts of will and given proper guidance. Such was the thrust and purpose of the legislation concerning new manufactures, particularly in Prussia. The same might be said for the didactic rules concerning the handling of certain materials and specific regulations of certain industries that were to be introduced or developed. It was their novelty that made it possible to legislate positively and to plan for better use and more efficient methods.

The most effective means of controlling and fostering specific commercial policies were fiscal measures—taxes and duties. Naturally trade was taxed in a variety of ways for revenue purposes, and it was a major item in the budgets of both territorial and local authorities. The right to levy tolls and duties, however, implied a degree of autonomy and self-government on the part of the individual regions, towns, and communities. In addition, differential toll and duty rates could be used by administrators to encourage, promote, or prohibit trading in specified commodities from certain sources. The specific economic implications of such policies have to be examined on a case-by-case basis, taking into account complex local circumstances, but that would take us beyond the purpose of the present essay. Suffice it to note that to the extent that the territorial authorities were able to enforce quality controls and levy tolls and duties they were also able to influence appreciably the pattern and direction of society's economic development. In so doing the German rulers were consciously trying to emulate the example of Holland (and later of England), which had shown that with limited natural resources but sufficient industriousness and population, commerce could become the mainstay of great prosperity and power. Mercantilist notions provided additional theoretical underpinning for the great faith the political elites put in commerce.[112]

The ordinances concerning trade reflected these general principles, even though they did not make statements of purpose. They did, however, introduce concrete and practical measures to bring about more effective and reliable trade patterns. We have mentioned the special provisions made for the encouragement and protection of merchants traveling to markets and fairs. Given the limitations of technology, reliance had to be put on the energy, initiative, and resourcefulness of local military and police authorities, thus strengthening their role in economic life. The territorial administration directly intervened and managed the maintenance, improvement, and extension of the basic means of transportation, such as the network of roads, bridges, and canals. A notable aspect of the ordinances dealing with these matters was their increasingly "scientific" approach: roads to be built or rebuilt should be laid out in a straight line wherever possible; modern techniques should be resorted to for the improvement of bridges, canals, and market halls; care is to be taken to bar devices harmful to the preservation of these facilities (such as iron-bound wheels on cobblestone roads). Technologization and scientific planning were quite evidently on the march.[113]

Another factor in promoting the exchange of goods and ideas

112. But see also C. Wilson, "The Other Face of Mercantilism," *Transactions of the Royal Historical Society,* 5th series, no. 9 (London, 1959).

113. Fürstl. Hess. Polizei Ordnungen Landstrassen u. Wasserbau, 1543–1743. *Sammelband* . . . *Wolfenbüttel,* 10.IV.1657 (prohibition of iron-bound wheels); Wolfenbüttel Jagdordnung 1603, re forest roads; Wolfenbüttel, 1.XII.1742 edict to cart stones for road building; Bergius, 2:208–15 (7.III.1767, Churbayerische

was better communication. Territorial authorities took an active interest in establishing better postal service to enable people and letters (or other messages) to travel quickly and safely. Of course, for "international" mail (that is, mail transported within the boundaries of the Empire), the Empire was served by the monopoly granted the princes of Thurn and Taxis by the emperor in the sixteenth century. On this model, territorial rulers established messenger services and coach routes to forward letters and parcels within their domains. The postal service also enabled rulers and their functionaries (as well as armies) to communicate with the outlying communities of their realms. Postal service was therefore taken care of at first by those who had horses at their disposal. Curiously enough, in Würtemburg at any rate, the first postal relays were the responsibility of the butchers, who were supposed to hold horses at the disposal of the monarch's couriers. Their duties, however, were limited to forwarding the material received to the next relay.[114] Later, as for example in the case of Wolfenbüttel-Braunschweig, the postal service was granted as a lien to a prominent member of the sovereign's entourage, who administered it as an office *(Amt)*.[115] Finally the postal service became the ruler's or state's exclusive prerogative. Once that had happened, it was important to break away from relationships with private individuals. For this reason the ordinances of Prussia prohibited private arrangements with the postal service, whether it be for forwarding of packages, letters, or receiving preferential seating on the basis of rank and status, as well as for having mail picked up or dropped outside the regularly established postal stations.[116] Finally, increasing routinization and bureaucratization

Generalverordnung zur Herstellung neuer Chaussée und Strassen); 3:358–60 (18.V.1754, upkeep of Heerstrassen); Bergius, 9:1–18 (Wegeordnung Schleswig, 28.X.1784, very technical and specific); Calenberg 1739, 3:939–47 (Wegeordnung 2.III.1691); 961–62 (23.X.1737, extending side roads); 962–88 (17/18.III.1738, renovating and updating 1691 ordinance); Mylius, 4(1):995.

114. *Dess . . . Würtemberg allerhand Ordnungen* (Stuttgart:1670), Post und Metzger Ordnungen, 26.VI.1622.

115. "Fürstl. Braunschw. Lüneburg. revidierte und erneuerte Post Ordnung," 1682 (Wolfenbüttel Ordnung) conferring hereditary office of General Post Amt on Franz von Plater.

116. Mylius 4(2):913–1022 (Neue Post Ordnung 10.VIII.1712, prohibiting mixing of private and official dealings in the postal system).

meant that good records had to be kept of all transactions, as well as security given for the materials and letters forwarded. The ordinances of the eighteenth century provided for registers and their accurate updating of all needed information; under the provision of these ordinances, intact delivery of money and valuables could be assured only if they were properly declared, registered, and paid for at the postmaster's. Ordinances also endeavored to see to it that postal coaches ran regularly and safely and that the passengers' social status was not allowed to interfere with efficient operation; thus seat reservations were to be made on a first-come, first-served basis and uniform tariffs imposed.[117] Only privileged institutions such as the universities were allowed to maintain their own messenger services and, on occasion, accept deliveries for nonmembers.[118]

Related to the improvement of communication was the creation of exchanges and the promotion of insurance of goods. The exchanges were to provide convenient meeting places for traders and producers and to serve as clearing houses and information centers. Insurance, besides offering greater security for transactions, was also to contribute to the development of a tighter and more efficient network of communication between the members of the economic community.[119]

Since manufacturing was starting on its rapid and victorious progress in Europe, a progress that within a little over a century was to transform it into large-scale industry, it too was bound to become a foremost concern of the authorities issuing ordinances. The budding manufacturing sector, it was believed, had to be regulated, protected, and assisted, and the ordinance was consciously used as a vehicle for all three purposes. The spread of manufacturing involved the increased standardization of operations and procedures (partly in imitation of foreign models). It became more and more necessary to be able to rely on the

117. Bergius, *Sammlung*, 10:103–191 (Erneuerte Postordnung Preussen, 26. XII.1782); Fürstliche Postordnung, 1682 (Braunschweig); and Mylius, 4(1), as in n. 116 above.

118. Wolfenbüttel, Postordnung 1682 and "Fürstl. Braunschw. Lüneb. . . . Post Ordnung," as in n. 115 above.

119. Wolfenbüttel, 16.XI.1706 (Commissionsstube in expectation of establishment of a convenient exchange, or Börse.)

unimpeded and regular delivery of the right raw materials and instruments. In the historical literature, the detailed and at times petty technical regulations of various manufacturing processes have been explained by fiscal needs and the economic policies of mercantilism. No doubt these played a major role, for in the event of successful manufacturing operations the sovereign and the administration were to reap large benefits. But this was not the only cause. The detailed technical specifications had a double purpose. Significantly, they appeared in the second half of the seventeenth century and were related to new techniques and imported innovations. They had, first, the didactic purpose of spreading knowledge and the use of new, better, and more profitable techniques. In the second place, but equally important, was their effort (however timid and inadequate by later standards) to bring about uniform manufacturing methods, so as to obtain standard products that could be used in many places and in various ways; and standardized uniformity, in turn, broadened the impact and expanded the range of technological progress.[120]

It was to be expected that the regulation of manufacturing would take the guild system as its point of departure. After all, the known manufacturing processes were carried on at first within the framework of the traditional guilds and corporations. In the legislation and regulations affecting the guilds and their productive activities, the ambivalence and conservative pragmatism of the cameralists found their fullest expression. The ordinances regulated, but also protected, the existing guild structure, yet in so doing they also introduced new notions and practices, as always happens when traditions are systematized and contradictory customs eliminated (*"Erneuerung ist selektive Tradition,"* as one of my German colleagues put it).

Ever since the Imperial Police Ordinances of 1530 and 1548, whose main provisions were emphatically reiterated in the emperor's guild ordinance of 1660,[121] a major concern had been the policing of the guilds' membership, especially the apprentices. We

120. Mylius, 4(2) has collection of ordinances on saltpeter, iron, glass, copper, etc.; and Mylius, *Corpus . . . Magdeburgicarum,* 3:433 has collection of ordinances on minting and manufacturing of gold, silver, tin, copper, and brass objects. Note similarities with Petrine legislation in Russia.

121. See Imperial Guild Ordinances of 1660 and 1731.

have mentioned some features of this policing in connection with the authorities' efforts to transform mores. In the present context we should point out the regulatory role of the ordinances— setting limits to wage levels, controlling the movement and travel of journeymen and apprentices, and prohibiting associations for the purpose of making economic demands. There was a systematic policy of keeping down wage labor; it was seen as an unreliable and potentially dangerous element of society, largely because it was breaking through the traditional framework of guild and family structures.[122]

On the other hand, ordinances contained provisions designed to secure full application of guild rules and, if necessary, to liberalize them so as to facilitate access to mastership by apprentices and journeymen. In particular, we detect a note of innovation and modernization in the efforts made to keep the "masterpiece"—the single most important requirement for mastership status—on a modest scale; masterpieces should be objects of use and not of fancy, not intended for luxury or display, and their fabrication (and exhibition) should not be unduly costly to the candidates.[123] In the ordinances' language one may detect (modernizing a bit perhaps) the emergence of the notion that in manufacturing the important thing is the technique used to make the ordinary object produced for "mass" consumption rather than individual imagination and conspicuous display of inventive talent. The masterpiece need be but one of a series, made in order to demonstrate technical competence rather than artistic genius or creativity. The ordinances argued and justified the new standards by pointing to the need to lower the cost of the master's "diploma" so as to facilitate its acquisition by a greater number of

122. *Magdeburgische Ordnungen* (1673), pp. 502ff. (Policey Ordnung 6.VII. 1652); *Würtemberg allerhand Ordnungen* (1670), p. 104 (Bauordnung 1655, pt. 2); Wolfenbüttel 12.X.1682; Hanover 1692 Verordnung und Reglement wegen ... Aempter und Gilden; Wolfenbüttel, 5.VIII.1723 (prohibiting associations of Handwerker); *Sammelband ... Wolfenbüttel,* Mandat 24.IV.1656; *Des ... Herrn Augusti ... Tax Ordnung* (1645), title 31 (Von den Handwerkern, §2); Calenberg 1739, 4(6), 22.VII.1698 (with reference to miners).

123. A particularly early example outside German lands, *Ordonnance du Roy sur le faict de la police générale* (Paris: 1578), 2.XI.1577, p. 55; Mylius, 5(2):645; 5(2):755–56.

candidates. It was but another aspect of the opening up of the guilds, paving the way for their members' transformation into a protoindustrial labor force of workers hired to perform technical tasks routinely. It helped to undermine artisanal craft in favor of manufacturing industry.

The tenor of the ordinances indicates that new attitudes were being fostered, attitudes that viewed the activity of guild members in strictly technical and economic terms, rather than as a complex social and cultural behavior. It involved stressing routine and "bureaucratically" controllable forms of behavior, rather than perpetuating behavior that was, though formalized, freer and more individualized. This was particularly noticeable in the policy of imposing administrative control and uniform procedure for the hiring and firing of journeymen and apprentices and for their traditional journeys. At the same time the governments were undermining the guild pattern by gradually making it easier for new elements of the population to be admitted to the useful trades. Thus at the end of the seventeenth century we find ordinances enabling former prisoners who had received training in prison or the poorhouse to be entered onto the guild rolls; the same was done for orphans. Obviously, the guilds' traditional right to admit only the "ehrbare"—that is, those born of legitimate unions and barring those whose parents exercised "dishonorable" trades—was consciously eroded by the governments to increase the pool of industrial manpower.[124]

While ordinances frequently served to remove the apprentice or journeyman from the arbitrary or unfair wage arrangements imposed by local custom or the master's whim, they also destroyed personal bonds and imposed a uniform, socially determined wage scale not subject to negotiation by either party. Not unexpectedly, the wage levels set by the authorities were low, and it is interesting to note that some ordinances permitted paying below the standard level but specifically forbade exceeding it.[125] In short, with respect to the guild establishment, the legislator's major concern was to preserve peace and avoid disorderly behavior or disruptive

124. Mylius 5(2):641, 647–48 (2/12.III.1691), 663–66 (28.VIII.1710).
125. Des . . . Herrn Augusti . . . Tax Ordnung (1645), especially Titlen 31, 49.

conflicts. The cultural and social results were secondary and easily sacrificed for the sake of economic efficiency, defined exclusively in terms of lower prices charged for ordinary wares.

Preoccupation with controls to safeguard the interests of the polity led the territorial administrations to interfere in the productive process itself. In the ordinances issued in this domain, one can detect a general purpose and a broad perspective with respect to the future interests and development of society. As perceived by the legislator, these interests went counter not only to established practices but also to the narrow, selfish advantages sought by particular crafts or guilds. A series of ordinances restricted or mandated certain manufacturing operations, such as the soaking of flax, and tanning, so as to safeguard public health or the environment; today we would label it "ecological concern."[126] Because of the rather primitive technologies then prevailing, such ordinances were most frequently disregarded, since alternative techniques were not readily available. But constant reiteration, and, on occasion, forcible removal of objectionable activities from a public location to a more removed locale did have their effect, not to speak of the fact that blatant disregard of the ordinances might eventually lead the authorities to resort to drastic measures such as closing down the objectionable operations entirely.[127] The end effect was to stimulate a global approach to economic life, especially in the manufacturing sector, and a regional, even national, policy to maintain a balance between the existing environment and traditional patterns on the one hand and the new techniques and their effects on the other.

In a variety of ways the ordinances promoted the modernization of manufacturing, whether it was in the hands of guilds or not. In the first place, the administrators endeavored to develop a cash nexus between supplier and producer by restricting and eventually eliminating transactions based on barter and exchanges in kind. Ordinances forbade payment in kind by either supplier or producer, so as to eliminate the personal, uncontrollable, and hence easily abused and exploited aspects of such trans-

126. Wolfenbüttel 29.IV.1692, among many others.
127. *Sammelband . . . Wolfenbüttel*, 18.IX.1651 (edict on flax).

actions.[128] In yet another way the administration endeavored to secure uniformity in standards of production and to ensure that the country's merchandise and matériel stay under its fiscal supervision and quality control. The brandmarking of products with officially designed seals, stamps, or other distinguishing marks was required of most items, in particular those of special importance to the territory's economy (which meant also to the ruler's treasury).[129] To promote energetic entrepreneurial and explorative activities, ordinances granted freedom to prospect for new mineral deposits and to open new manufacturing establishments. In all the ordinances dealing with these matters, the tone and form clearly indicated the belief or hope that such enterprise and innovative energy would yield an increase in the productive potential of the country, benefiting not only the state but society as a whole.[130]

Expansion of the economic potential depended on the availability of skilled labor, as was duly recognized by the rulers. Special schools and institutions for training in specific industrial skills and techniques were set up. These establishments served the additional purpose of making sure that groups and individuals able to work could acquire a valuable skill and be occupied.[131] In line with similar considerations, the ordinances fostered functional specialization as the more efficient ways of organizing, expanding, and

---

128. Wolfenbüttel, 2.VIII.1699 (miller paid in cash); indirect evidence, Wolfenbüttel, 5.XII.1722 (reconfirming that some services were to be performed in kind and not replaced by cash payments); Calenberg 1739, 3:205–208 (10.VIII.1652, on paying wages to rural laborers).

129. Calenberg 1739, 3:250–51 (Ausschreiben 13.IX.1720); Wolfenbüttel, 6.II.1674, 4.X.1704; *Sammelband . . . Wolfenbüttel* (edict 24.II.1653).

130. Freyberg, 2:261 (3.II.1691, with reference to mining): "Um den in Bayern sonst stark im Gange gewesenen Bergbau wieder zu heben, wird derselbe für Bayern sowohl als für die Oberpfalz frei gegeben, so dass In- als Ausländer aller Orten auf Gold, Silber, Quecksilber, Zinn, Kupfer und Blei enschlagen, suchen und schürfen darf, ohne hierin von jemandem, insonderheit von den Grundherren und Besitzern der Güter, auf deren Grund und Boden nach Erz eingeschlagen wird, gehindert werden zu können."

131. Bergius, *Sammlung*, 3:443–44 (16.X.1765 Preuss. Zirkularschreiben), 6:319–30 (6.XII.1764, Silesian Reglement); cf. also the section dealing with schools, below.

innovating productive activity. To promote innovation, ordinances were issued to establish or support specific new types of activities and new areas of manufacturing or enterprise. The policy of protection and restriction was designed to offset the competitive advantages deemed to be enjoyed by foreign or "unfairly" situated enterprises at the expense of new, local ones. These protective measures included discriminatory tariffs, monopolies, and excises, as well as special regulations of the labor supply and work discipline.[132]

A most sensitive area with respect to manufacturing was the relationship between town and countryside. It was here that the cautious conservatism of the ordinances became particularly apparent, and it was in this domain, too, that the paradox of the "well-ordered police state" mentality found its clear expression as well. On the one hand, the authors of the ordinances staunchly believed in a balanced and functionally organized society, a society resting on the apportioning of labor and responsibilities among the principal groups (estates) of the population. They clung to the notion that manufacturing and commerce were the business of the towns, while the countryside—villages and large landholders—had to take care of the production of food and of some agricultural raw materials. In line with this traditional conception, as suggested earlier, the authorities legislated to keep certain manufacturing activities out of the hands of the rural population—for example, the brewing of beer for sale or the making of textiles.[133] On the other hand, to prevent the urban sector from getting involved in rural activities, they prohibited

---

132. This question has been fully dealt with in the secondary literature on mercantilism and the economic histories of Europe.

133. Early example in Saxony, *Ordnungen Hertzog Ernsten . . . Chur und Fürsten zu Sachsen* (Dresden: 1583), Ausschreiben 1550, p. 83, *Magdeburgische Ordnungen* (1673), p. 489 (Policey Ordnung 6.VII.1652; prohibition also applied to clergy and nobility); Freyberg, 2:116 (21.IV.1675): "Es könne der Landes- und Polizeyordnung . . . nicht gemäss befunden werden, dass der geistliche Stand und die Landsassen in den Städten und Märkten Bräuergerechtigkeiten an sich bringe; auch würde solches sowohl für den bürgerlichen Stand, als für die übrigen Stände Nachteil nach sich ziehen und sey demnach abzustellen." Wolfenbüttel, 27.XI.1722; *Sammlung Anhalt-Dessau*, no. 109, 21.VII.1781, makes exceptions for necessary crafts, but these exceptions have to be reported.

townspeople, noble officials, and other urban dwellers from exploiting estates and agricultural enterprises.[134] A major difficulty in separating the two spheres lay in the fact that, economically speaking, there was no sharp cleavage between town and countryside before the complete triumph of industrialization (if even then).[135]

An additional difficulty stemmed from the fact that some activities—for example, textile production (flax and hemp) or milling and brewing—involved both sectors of society and brought countryside and town into rather close relationship. It was readily apparent, too, that the population in the countryside was not effectively employed throughout the year, so that it could be used advantageously in manufacturing. This situation was brought home more and more forcefully in the course of the eighteenth century as the putting out system and the setting up of manufactures in the countryside broke down the supposed functional separation. Since these new developments clearly furthered the economic interests of individual territories, the ordinances restricted, supervised, or prohibited only such "trespass" as seemed to threaten social peace and order; they intervened only in those instances when trouble seemed likely to occur. In short, to the degree that the promotion of manufacturing and the modernization of the economy were bearing fruit, the administrators tended to treat strictly economic activities with benign neglect, retaining only a concern for their political implications. Clearly, administrative efforts to maintain geographic separation of functions along traditional lines were failing, and the political authorities were beginning to withdraw from this particular sector of the polity's life.

One may be emboldened to the sweeping generalization that the ordinances helped to break down the compartmentalization between town and countryside by imposing administrative, moral, and cultural uniformity, by providing for standard operat-

134. Early example in *Anhalt Policey und Landes Ordenung* (1572), §29. Freyberg, 2:80–81 (reference to principle expressed in 1616 and maintained throughout century); Bergius, *Sammlung*, 2:381–82 (Preuss. Zirkolarschreiben 5.X.1763, against urban professionals buying up plowland).

135. See n. 133 and general remarks in Brauns, *Kurhessische Gewerbepolitik*.

ing procedures and accounting methods, and by promoting the
expansion of economic life in general and of commerce and
manufacturing in particular. In this respect the very success of
the ordinances' policies brought about an end to the functional
separateness that had been their original point of departure and
methodological basis. The territorial sovereignties pragmatically
took this development in stride and easily adjusted to the changed
circumstances that they themselves had helped to bring about.
They turned from a defense of the traditional division of functions to the advocacy and promotion of generalized efficiency and
productivity, on the condition that peace, order, and security
were preserved.

The ordinances' general thrust with respect to manufacturing
found coherent and fuller expression in the regulations and
statutes pertaining to mining. Mining was an old occupation and
had long been strongly promoted by the authorities and supervised by the state; moreover, in our own period it was undergoing
rapid technological and organizational modernization. The trend
to be observed in the mining ordinances reflected quite clearly,
and not unexpectedly so, an increasing preoccupation with new
technological and scientific knowledge and a refusal to take any of
the traditional methods for granted. In addition, the mining
ordinances set up routinized procedures that sooner or later
would serve as standard models for further development and
export to other places. In this connection it is interesting to note
that it was realized that routinization implied public knowledge.
Skills, as well as the specific knowledge of concrete conditions in a
given area or mine, were to be shared, so that later generations
could continue the work and also so that fresh initiatives and
innovation would continue to appear. The transmission of knowledge by tradition and by word of mouth had resulted in stultify-
ing and harmful monopolies. Because of their long-standing and
juridically sanctioned involvement, the territorial administrations
were in a particularly favorable position to devise comprehensive
policies and procedures for the operation of mines, and to a very
high time horizon.[136]

136. Wolfenbüttel, Bergfreiheit 1716 and 1718; Bergius, *Sammlung*, 1:45–137
(Preussische Bergordnung Schlesien 5.VI.1769); 3:47–49 (8.I.1778, Preussisches

Whatever the efforts of territorial governments to promote manufacturing and to modernize the economy along the lines of an industrial, or rather protoindustrial, model, agriculture remained the basic activity of German society in the period we are studying. Although customary methods and attitudes continued to prevail strongly in the agrarian domain, a significant number of ordinances addressed themselves to rural problems, and this with growing intensity and comprehensiveness from the late seventeenth century on. In this case, too, legislators faced a basic ambiguity in the situation: on the one hand, agriculture was the most traditional occupation, its methods hallowed by customs accumulated over generations and circumscribed by the relatively inflexible limitations of the physical environment. It was therefore an area where administrative interference was most difficult to enforce and where such interference also might easily result in failures, with disastrous effects on the supply of essential products. On the other hand, precisely in order to obviate or reduce the likelihood of such disasters as well as to increase the country's productive potential, agriculture seemed to require the most persistent efforts at innovation and modernization. The latter conclusion was reached with particular clarity early in the eighteenth century when accumulated scientific knowledge, as well as the experiences of such dynamic agrarian societies as Holland and England, pointed to the direction that administrative efforts should take. For this reason it is particularly difficult to identify clear and rigid patterns of policy developed by the ordinances. It is even more difficult to assess their effectiveness, the more so since implementation, as we shall see, was frequently delegated to those constituted bodies and institutions in the villages that were most resistant to change. This explains the fact that the economic provisions of the many *Bauernordnungen* dealt mainly with *Gesinde und Schäfer* (domestics and shepherds)—that is, with only that sector of the village population that was easily amenable to and in need of government supervision—the landless rural laborers and

Publicandum); Mylius 4(2):15; Mylius, *Corpus . . . Magdeburgicarum,* 5:274. For a very comprehensive treatise that set forth the basic outlook and policies followed in the seventeenth century, see Georg Engelhard Löhneyss, *Bericht vom Bergwerck* [Remlingen]: n.d., seventeenth c.).

their families. It may also be noted that these ordinances often appeared to be archaic in that they were primarily negative in tone, ennumerating prohibitions rather than making specific positive recommendations. The trend that emerges clearly in them, however, was that of a growing concern for the labor supply for agriculture (which, as we know, always seemed to be inadequate), and this in turn meant paying greater attention to providing more humane treatment and better economic security for the landless rural laborers. But only comparatively speaking did the ordinances have a positive character; the strong undercurrent of suspicion and fearful scorn for the uncouth *campagnard* never disappeared. This was also the reason why at no point did the authorities intend the basic social relationships in the villages to be abandoned or weakened, which, in turn, meant preserving intact the authority of the lord or of the sovereign's representative. In a sense, all the *Bauern, Gesinde,* and *Schäfer* ordinances were the extension of the *Bauernschutz* measures that had been initiated in the seventeenth century to repair the damages of the Thirty Years War.[137]

A primary concern of any government was to ensure a proper supply of agricultural produce to feed the population. Quite naturally, ordinances were issued to protect the rural sector from having its productive capacities undermined. This meant, first of all, protection of those who worked the land by controlling the latter's mobility through sale or exchange. In the second place, it involved the protection of the inhabitants of these productive lands, which meant essentially the peasants' right to remain on the land they worked, even if they failed to fulfill all of their obligations properly. A number of ordinances, especially in the seventeenth century, provided the peasants with means of avoiding expulsion from the land and of fulfilling their obligations and paying arrears on dues, taxes, leases, and the like. Further protection was afforded by limiting the right of seizure of

137. Collection of Gesinde, etc., Ordnungen in Mylius, 5(3) gives panoramic picture of trend. Also, Mylius, *Novum Corpus Constitutionum* . . . , 1:147–58 (Dorfordnung 22.IX.1751, with reference to need to improve 1723 ordinances); Mylius, *Corpus . . . Magdeburgicarum,* 3:191ff.

livestock, movables, and equipment for the nonfulfillment of obligations.[138]

Basically the authorities treated the peasants like minor children, exaggerating the extent of their ignorance and lack of capacity to absorb novelty and adapt to circumstances and afraid of their "irrational" traditions and uncouth ways. It was believed that like children they had to be protected from doing harm to themselves through ignorance, stupidity, or "laziness." Thus ordinances were issued to regulate and preserve arable land and cattle, establish and maintain proper water control where needed, and to secure peasant houses against fire hazard by following modern and scientific building techniques. This concern extended to prescribing better methods for the proper performance of such basic tasks as harvesting, threshing, upkeep of barns—in short, the ordinances aimed at limiting or eliminating altogether wasteful and customary patterns of operation believed to be contrary to efficiency and higher productivity.[139]

Of greater historical significance than these negative ordinances were those that actively promoted change in an effort to secure greater efficiency and higher yields in agricultural production. Such regulations suggested—at times commanded—the in-

138. *Magdeburgische Ordnungen* (1673) (Policey Ordnung 1652, pp. 508ff. and Schäfer Ordnung 1651, pp. 634ff.). There is an early example with rationale spelled out in *Anhalt Policey und Landes Ordenung* (1572), §16. Freyberg 2:85 (25.IV.1614) and change in tone, ibid., p. 247 (17.VI.1706); Wolfenbüttel 15.VIII.1707; *Sammelband . . . Wolfenbüttel* (Allgemeine Landesordnungen, 1647, p. 13); Bergius, *Sammlung*, 1:20–24 (19.XI.1773 Hesse, forbidding splintering of estates) and ibid., pp. 24–31, Preussische Bauernordnung 1764; *Fürstlich Anhalti-sche . . . Landes- und Process-Ordnung. . . .*, (1777) (§17, p. 50). The broader implications for the evolution of agrarian policies and conditions, into which I am not entering, are set forth in the classic works of W. Abel, *Agrarpolitik* (Göttingen: Vandenhoeck & Ruprecht, 1951), *Agrarkrisen und Agrarkonjunktur in Mitteleuropa vom 13. bis zum 19. Jahrhundert* (Berlin: P. Parey, 1935), *Geschichte der deutschen Landwirtschaft vom frühen Mittelalter bis zum 19. Jahrhundert* (Stuttgart: E. Ulmer, 1962), and of Franz Lütge, *Geschichte der deutschen Agrarverfassung* (Stuttgart: E. Ulmer, 1963; 2d ed. 1967), *Die mitteldeutsche Grundherrschaft und ihre Auflösung* (Jena: 1934; 2d ed., Stuttgart: G. Fischer, 1957).

139. *Pfaltz Landesordnung* (1599); *Sammlung Anhalt-Dessau*, no. 63 (14.VI.1771); Wolfenbüttel, 6.V.1744; Bergius, *Sammlung*, 2:201–206 (23.XII.1764) and 3:26–27, 43–44 (1765 Prussia).

troduction of better and more modern techniques and tools. Ordinances prescribed the use of scythes instead of sickles, the pruning of trees, and more hygienic care for cattle.[140] This type of legislation offered an entire program of technical improvement and innovation, and such legislation was produced at an increasingly faster and more insistent pace as the eighteenth century wore on (though little regard was paid to the financial requirements involved). The ordinances were accompanied by injunctions and advice for the prospecting of new resources, mostly through better knowledge and care of the soil and the observation of climatic conditions, or more frequently through the introduction of new crops and plants. The state was prepared to help out by training or by temporarily alleviating fixed obligations, though the extent of the latter relief was not always clearly stated. The creation of establishments for training and experimenting in these innovations was also sometimes suggested, but in most cases we do not know with what success.[141]

The authorities' efforts to improve the environment, as well as to provide additional income and productive capacity, was particularly evident. Measures were taken to encourage the planting of trees, especially fruit trees, not only for the sake of their crops but also for beautification and soil conservation. Bounties were promised to those who followed the advice, and extensive arguments were presented in favor of the benefits that would accrue from planting useful as well as beautiful shrubs and trees. In some instances the ordinances resorted to compulsion, and we read of rules for the obligatory planting of trees and crops under well-defined conditions and strict supervision by the local authori-

140. Bergius, *Sammlung,* 1:1 (20.VI.1766, in imitation of English models); 1:225 (4.VI.1773, Hesse); 2:233 (12.VII.1764, Prussia introduced scythes); 2:250–52 (3.IV.1763, growing of Spanish clover); 4:202–205 (26.VIII.1765, Braunschweig).

141. The Pfaltz 1599 ordinance established *Feldschauer* (*Pfaltz Landesordnung,* p. 267). Kreitmeyer, no. 25, pp. 471–74 (Mandat 9.XI.1770, to promote gardening). Rich material on that in "Hessische Policey Verordnungen die Hude, Gärten und Plantagen betreffend" (1647–1745). Note the curious policy of Baden Durlach of paying bounties on sparrows' heads to protect trees and crops, Bergius, *Sammlung,* 1:6, 11.

ties.[142] Even with respect to traditional crops, ordinances introduced compulsory schedules of sowing and planting. We may
wonder whether such an approach was not counterproductive,
since it forced innovation onto a well-structured traditional
pattern and used compulsion to promote individual enterprise
and creative initiative.[143]

In agriculture, as in manufacturing—and we may note the
similarity of approach as indicative of the uniform, rational, and
efficient attitude that informed the ordinances—the legislators
realized that innovations of techniques and improvement in
production hinged on the availability of a proper labor force. We
have mentioned the measure to protect the social and legal status
of the peasantry, as well as the efforts at transforming behavior
and ways of life. Equally significant in shaping a proper labor
force was education. Leaving aside for a later section the ordinances dealing specifically with schools and education, we should
take note here of several initiatives to provide technical knowledge and training for selected members of the peasantry. This
was to be accomplished partly through special establishments,
partly through the dissemination of new information that might
be helpful in raising productivity.[144] Individuals and communities
were encouraged to take such steps on their own. At first, in the
seventeenth century, government concern focused on the mere
return to and preservation of the level of agrarian production
that had been attained before the ravages of the Thirty Years

142. *Augusti Braunschwyg Hofgerichts Ordnung* (1663), p. 337; Mylius,
5(3):367ff.; 5(1):567; and a very early example, *Churfürstl. Pfaltz . . . Landes
Ordnung* (1590), p. 235.

143. *Magdeburgische Ordnungen* (1673), Policey Ordnung 1652, p. 509, and
Amts Giebichstein Ordnung 1656, p. 993; *Sammlung Anhalt-Dessau*, no. 54
(25.I.1769); "Hessische Policey Verordnung die Hude," op. cit., in n. 141 above;
Bergius, *Sammlung*, 1:35 (Prussian edict 7.VI.1765 for planting fruit trees and
other trees); 5:245–48 (Hessen Cassel, 10.X.1764, for planting oaks); Calenberg
1739, 4:223, 228 (27.IX.1667 and 7.XII.1681, regarding goats).

144. Bergius, *Sammlung*, 3:6–8 (29.V.1765); 4:32–35 (Braunschweig 10.X.1765,
re beekeeping, with reference to *Hannoversche Gelehrten Anzeige*, 1750, 1762);
6:163–81 (Wied-Runkel principality offering bounties on sparrows); Calenberg
1739, 3:841 ff. (technical and didactic treatise-ordinance on epizootics), and pp.
1046–58 (18.XI.1737, concerning elimination of weeds).

War. But once this goal had been attained, governments turned to active and didactic encouragement of all methods that could increase, rationalize, and modernize the cultivation of the land.

What mining was in the context of manufacturing, forestry was in the context of agriculture. The ordinances provided the first comprehensive reforestation plans and policies, as well as codes for the upkeep of forests and their constant replenishment. In the legislation on forestry there may be observed an evolutionary pattern similar to that seen in the case of other areas noted in this study. In the late sixteenth and early seventeenth centuries the ordinances were negative and aimed only at protecting the rulers' forests from damage by interlopers or peasants and safeguarding the wild game for seigneurial hunts. The foresters and their assistants (appointed officials of the sovereigns) were to prevent specified practices destructive of trees and game, as well as unauthorized trespass. It was only in the second half of the seventeenth century that we have systematic reference to the need to protect the forests for the future—to make sure that felled trees were properly replaced, that new areas were planted, and that the forest resources were properly exploited with an eye to future lumber resources. The specific prohibition of harmful practices and the "thoughtless" behavior of the peasantry (thoughtless in the eyes of the authorities, of course) were presented more comprehensively and cogently and related to positive measures for enhancing the value and potential growth of the forests. Finally, in the eighteenth century, we have a more or less "scientific" approach as the ordinances prescribed methods of building up the future lumber and forest reserves of the territory. The role of the foresters underwent a shift as well; it became more positive. No longer would the foresters merely guard and protect; they also had to initiate and supervise the methodical and rational building up of future fuel and lumber resources. Such policies also resulted in greater bureaucratization of the forestry service, involving use of elaborate registers and records and the issuing of specific technical operating instructions. As a consequence, too, the foresters were isolated and further removed from the peasantry and from effective social and cultural contact with the population; they had become genuine officials. If the protection of the lord's hunting rights and interests had been one of the original stimuli for *Forstordnungen,* this concern receded in the eighteenth century. In the second half of that century it was limited to ordinances enjoining the pursuit of wolves as generally damaging to cattle and men.[145]

We observe again a mingling of the traditional and the modern, a reliance upon old customs and personnel along with an effort at instilling new goals, new attitudes and practices. Unlike the situation with the mines, however, the ultimate objective of the forestry regulations was the preservation and conservation of energy resources and environmental quality (to use modern notions) rather than the maximization of production. The ordinances' concern for energy (fuel), however, pointed to another paradox that we see looming on the horizon: on the one hand, the productive potential was deemed to be well-nigh inexhaustible, requiring only proper handling to maximize the yield. On the other hand, it was realized that some potential resources might be finite and require close husbanding. At the end of the seventeenth century, it was often felt that lumber or wood (charcoal) would be the first resource to be limited in supply and finite. Hence the efforts at conservation, efforts that then as now implied a limitation of production, illustrating a basic and perennial paradox of the modern economic predicament. It might be of some amusement to contemporary sceptics to note that the same half-baked measures, the same panicky fears and dire predictions, and the unexpected discoveries of new possibilities (some of them only half perceived, others wildly imagined) were abroad then as they are now when we face another energy crisis and contemplate the necessity of conserving a specific form of fuel while searching for alternative solutions.[146]

145. Wald Ordnung Ober ChurBayern 1594 (cf. Freyberg 2:251–53 and n. 146 below). For a comprehensive discussion of approaches to and legislation on forestry in France in the seventeenth century (which served largely as a model elsewhere), see Michel Devèze, *La grande réformation des forêts sous Colbert (1661–1683)* (Paris: Presses Universitaires de France, 1954).

146. *Würtemberg allerhand Ordnungen* (1670), Erneuerte Forstordnung 1614, especially pp. 41ff.; Wolfenbüttel, 20.X.1699, 3.XI.1719; Bergius, *Sammlung,* 2:315–16 (Prussian circular 21.III.1763, on conservation of timber); Calenberg

A last, but not least, and vital aspect of economic life remains to be touched upon, although very briefly because of the technical complexity of the subject and my lack of expertise in it. This was the realm of fiscal policy. The general problem of taxation, and its implication for the policy of development, has been dealt with magisterially by G. Ardant.[147] In the present context it may suffice to note that the promotion of production and the fostering of technical innovations were accompanied by fiscal measures that aimed at facilitating the acceptance and implementation of the new techniques. These measures could be, as noted earlier, relaxations of tolls and duties; they could also involve granting specific bounties and establishing a system of state excises and monopolies to increase fiscal revenue while furthering innovative production and cultural transformation that required relatively heavy investments at first.

A problem of major consequence for many territories was the variety of coinage and the ease with which debased coins could be used and circulated. It made possible harmful speculation and frequently constituted an additional drain on the limited resources of a country. To control these manifestations, ordinances prohibited (or restricted) the importing of foreign specie or at any rate ordered their compulsory exchange at fixed rates in specified localities. The same type of measures served to combat flight of better coinage abroad.[148] All this made for extensive controls and the erection of additional barriers to the exchange of goods. By the same token it compelled many territories to remain self-contained and in so doing limited their capacity for expansion and production. A further broadening of scope would have been possible only if the economic area had been enlarged, so that many restrictions on currency and commercial transactions could

---

1739, 4:268–75 (forms to be used in reporting timber damage, 16.II.1715); *Sammelband . . . Wolfenbüttel* (Mandat 28.II.1645 and 1.III.1647, pp. 138ff. and 165ff., on waste of timber).

147. G. Ardant, *Historie de l'impôt,* 2 vols. (Paris: A. Fayard, 1972).

148. An early example is *Ordonnance du Roy sur le faict de la police,* p. 3. Wolfenbüttel, 29.XI.1678 (table of acceptable coins) and numerous decrees in Herzog August Bibliothek collection demonstrate the perenniality of the problem. Mylius, *Corpus . . . Magdeburgicarum,* and Mylius, 5.

be lifted too. The time was not yet ripe for such a policy, for either technical or political reasons.

In the meantime, occasional efforts were made to alleviate the problem by establishing better banking and credit facilities. While these played an important role in the numerous proposals and schemes for economic development drafted by scholars, publicists, or even administrators, they did not find much of an echo in the realm of practice as reflected in the ordinances of territorial governments.[149] Indeed, the horizon of territorial sovereignties was narrow and parochial, while the larger entities, Empire and Kreise, were still inchoate confederations, so that only the larger states (such as Prussia) could pursue active, innovative policies despite the conditions prevailing elsewhere in the Germanies.

To conclude, it is worth reiterating that in the economic domain the ordinances permitted and encouraged rapid and significant strides toward productive progress. But it was precisely in this realm, too, that the technical limitations and contradictions of the well-ordered police approach became most glaringly apparent. In the final analysis, however, bolstered by the measures taken in the social, cultural, and administrative realms and following the lead of Holland, the economic ordinances of cameralist governments, by showing the way to increased productivity and by fostering the development of a protoindustrial society, constituted a significant motor force for the modernization of the central European economy.

5. Material Progress

The social policies expressed in the ordinances were designed to promote material progress. Such progress was not conceived in a narrow sense and naturally included not only an improvement in the material conditions of life and their productive base but also

149. Tax Ordnung . . . Friedrichen Ulrichen . . . 1622, (Wolfenbüttel). Bergius, *Sammlung,* 9–10:238–56 (Leibordnung Göttingen 1731) and pp. 256–64 (Verordnung Creditcasse für Dänemark, 16.VIII.1786) as a very late example. See the useful survey and bibliographic introduction to cameralist literature on this topic (among others) in Joseph A. Schumpeter, *History of Economic Analysis* (London: Allen & Unwin, 1954).

important changes in cultural and intellectual life. While the strictly material changes are in a sense inseparable from the cultural and intellectual changes that accompanied them, for the sake of clarity the material changes will be discussed in this section and the cultural and intellectual changes in section 6.[150]

An essential precondition of progress was an improvement in the conditions of life; this meant, in the first place, securing the population from the dangers of disease and epidemics. As long as life expectancy remained very short and the hazards to health both innumerable and inescapable, no genuine sense of progress could be developed, and men could not be persuaded to plan for the future (another cause for the low time horizon discussed by A. Gerschenkron[151]). The medical ordinances of those times appear pathetic indeed, since they tried hard to deal with insuperable problems of poor hygiene, disease, and high mortality rates with medical theories that were not only inadequate but also erroneous. From a different perspective, however, these ordinances may be seen as a noble commitment to a fundamentally optimistic belief that proper knowledge will help overcome the most inexorable aspect of human existence, its fragility in the face of nature. In this light, the ordinances paved the way for the universal belief in the beneficence of science and in its ability to improve the quality of life.

The main focus of medical ordinances was the fight against contagious disease, primarily the plague, which was still the scourge for all of Europe throughout most of our period. Since plague and similar diseases were hardly amenable to effective control or prevention by the means available at the time, the ordinances concerning them retained a religious cast much longer than other ordinances. However, in the course of the

150. The definition and problems of modernization have given rise to a vast body of literature in recent decades. For present heuristic purposes, I would say that modernization is that attitude of mind and that form of conduct that aim at maximizing and making full use of the potential resources of a society for an ongoing increase (whether it be considered an improvement or not) of its material and cultural creativity, promoted both for the benefit of its members and for the creativity's own sake.

151. Cf. A. Gerschenkron's essays, cited in n. 26 to pt. 1, above.

seventeenth century a trend did emerge, and as the late George
Rosen has pointed out the ordinances on the plague prepared the
way for medical police in the modern sense.[152] Given the limited
medical knowledge of the time and the realization that disease
was spread through contact, the measures of control naturally
consisted almost entirely of quarantines of persons and cattle and
the fumigation of wares from infested regions. Throughout most
of the seventeenth century the plague ordinances, issued when
the disease broke out in a neighborhood, merely set up barriers to
the movement of goods and people from infected areas and
prescribed the manner of dealing with infected corpses, houses,
and household goods. Emphasis was on those measures that could
prevent human greed (and economic interest) from undermining
the effective implementation of the regulations. But at the end of
the seventeenth century, and increasingly so in the eighteenth, in
addition to repeating these prohibitions and protective measures,
rules and injunctions about actively treating the disease and
preventing its spread through medical and pharmaceutical intervention were issued. Naturally, since the real cause of the disease
remained unknown, these measures too proved ineffective. But it
is important to realize that they witnessed an intention of taking
active steps and of relying on the scientific, medical knowledge of
the day to do so effectively.[153]

152. G. Rosen, "Cameralism and the Concept of Medical Police," *Bulletin of the History of Medicine* 27(1953):21–42 (I owe the reference to the kindness of Professor J. T. Alexander of the University of Kansas). For an up-to-date and convenient bibliographic introduction to the area of medical legislation and police in early modern times, see now John T. Alexander, *Bubonic Plague in Early Modern Russia (Public Health and Urban Disaster)* (Baltimore: Johns Hopkins University Press, 1980).

153. The ordinances are not very interesting in themselves, repeating stereo-typed injunctions; they declined in number simply as the diseases themselves retreated. Mylius, chap. 2, 5(4):279ff., gives a handy chronological survey for Prussia. We should note the increasingly rational, scientific, and pragmatic formulations of the ordinances as the centuries progress. For example, in "Hessische Policey Ordnungen Pestanstalten betreffend," the one for 28.IX.1719 includes provision for distributing medical information and instruction to local officials and school teachers (but not, curiously enough, to pastors, apparently). Previous decrees did not specify such a wide pattern of distribution. *Sammlung Anhalt-Dessau,* no. 105, 7.IV.1781, a late edict, attempted to control rabies and mad

A by-product of epidemic control legislation was the gradually increasing interest in preventive measures, more particularly in the area of public hygiene.[154] As the realization grew that poor environmental conditions promote disease, measures were taken to fight them. A similar awareness informed didactic ordinances and regulations issued to assist the population in taking care of accidents and injuries. Eventually, at the very end of our period, planned campaigns were undertaken to introduce preventive measures, such as the ones culminating in the inoculation programs against smallpox. The pedagogic, long-range educational role of these ordinances turned out to have far-reaching implica-

---

dogs by requiring every dog to be registered and tagged. Most quarantine edicts also included direct mention of Gypsies and *Betteljuden* (beggar Jews) or "plain Jews" as main objects of the quarantine measure, since they constituted the majority of the footloose in society. Wolfenbüttel 23.IX.1680, 20.X.1719; a 1739 injunction for polite behavior on part of quarantine personnel; 29.VIII.1744 strictly enforces a Medicinal Ordnung, with implication that government knows what is best. Similarly, for animal diseases, such as epizootics affecting especially cattle, ordinances follow the pattern set by plague legislation: Mylius, *Continuatio,* 3:9ff. and *Novum Corpus,* pp. 227ff.; Wolfenbüttel 2.VIII.1714 (Entwurf einiger bewarten Mittel).

154. Freyberg, 2:70 (26.III.1631, Mandat on public baths). For a late instruction with didactic intent, see *Sammlung Anhalt-Dessau,* no. 80, 15.I.1774, providing for free medical and pharmaceutical assistance to the needy. Its philanthropic tone deserves quotation:

Welcher gestalt wir aus Landesväterlicher Gnade und Mitleid gegen die armen Kranken, oder unglücklich Beschädigten . . . die Verfügung gemacht, dass dieselbigen die menschliche Hülfe nicht entstehen mögen . . . die Besorgung des Arztes und die nöthigen Arzneien unentgeltlich geniessen haben können[,] . . . [but since doctors should be compensated] so sollen die Einwohner des [entfernten] Ortes wo der Kranke sich befindet, welche Pferde haben, schuldig und gehalten sein, nach der Reihe ein Pferd zur Abholung und Zurückbringung des Medici oder Chirurgi, so oft diese den Besuch des Kranken nöthig finden unentgeltlich zu geben und herzuleihen. . . . Da nun diese die Menschlichkeit gegen die kranken arme Mit-Einwohner jeden Orts erfordert, so habe die Richter solches jedesmahl gebührend zu veranstalten und hat ein jeder sich danach zu achten.

Bergius, *Sammlung,* 1:271 (18.IV.1769) gives brief instructions how to behave and what to do in the absence of a doctor in case of smallpox; ibid., 2:400–402 (Baden Durlach, 2.III.1770, gives instructions for curing sheep disease and proposes remedies to be obtained abroad). Wolfenbüttel 1717–18(?) (27.VII.1718 lists medical advice concerning dysentery).

tions, for in many instances they impinged on hallowed beliefs and customs, for example pilgrimages, gatherings for worship, and traditional festivities.

Hygienic and medical measures had but limited effect in the absence of an impact on the physical environment as well. There could be no question of trying to transform the environment in the country-side (with the exception of swamp drainage and land reclamation programs initiated in the seventeenth century but not seriously undertaken in the Germanies before the middle of the eighteenth century), so that such ordinances as there were concerned in the main the urban environment. Two paths of approach were possible: negatively, to eliminate harmful conditions, especially with respect to cleanliness and orderly management of public areas and street traffic. The second approach was more direct and positive, consisting in constructing, either *ab ovo* or by rebuilding old structures, a desirable urban environment through rational planning: *urbanism*, we would call it today.

The negative approach, embodied in the *Gassenordnungen*, consisted of legislation compelling the municipalities to dispose properly of refuse, to clean the streets, regulate traffic, and to maintain buildings in proper repair to prevent them from becoming health and fire hazards. An evolution may be observed in this case, too. At first the ordinances were only concerned with the removal of accumulated refuse; then regular systems were set up for periodic collection and for compelling the population (the homeowners) to abide by it. Of particular significance in this connection was the fact that some individuals, classes, and estates claimed exemption from these obligations by virtue of their legal status and traditional privileges. The ordinances had to make it clear that in this matter the rules applied to everyone, marking the beginning of treating all urban inhabitants in uniform and equal manner for the sake of general benefit and breaking down traditionally privileged groups.[155] Finally, positive measures were taken to ensure better lighting, peace, and order. To implement

155. Wolfenbüttel, 27.VII.1699, 26.V.1703, 22.V.1717 (stressing responsibility of privileged classes; special record book to be kept). The most comprehensive street maintenance ordinances were in Prussia, Policey Avertissement for Berlin, 28.VII.1777 (Bergius, *Sammlung*, 3:321–22) and the earlier Gassen Ordnung, 3.V.1707 and Gassen Reglement 3.IX.1735.

these regulations, all inhabitants were put under the jurisdiction
of a *Polizeimeister,* usually an appointed official, who was to be
assisted by selected members of the population in each urban
section. In time more matters came under the jurisdiction of the
urban police—for example, the proper provisioning of the town.
In this respect the German ordinances at times antedated the
famous statement of police functions in the widely known *Traité de
police* by de La Mare, though not necessarily the actual practices of
the *lieutenant de police* of Paris.[156] Along the same line we find
ordinances concerned with the proper flow of urban traffic: they
prohibit the building or rebuilding of structures that would
impede circulation in the streets. Some regulations even went so
far as to require adjustment or demolition of standing buildings
to make way for traffic and to straighten out crooked and curved
streets.[157] In an effort at relieving the congestion of streets and
the unhygienic conditions that resulted from it, convenient public
transportation was introduced or promoted.[158]

Health and cleanliness were not the only considerations in-
forming the police legislation. Aesthetic requirements were high
in the period, and they found reflection in the approach to urban
building: an admiration of proportion and symmetry was expressed, as well as a desire to highlight the majesty of the princely
residence. There may also have been the implicit purpose of
opening up broad avenues to make it easier to control mobs,
though it would seem that this did not become a conscious
element in town planning before the revolutionary ferment at the
end of the eighteenth century. The ordinances dealing with
building codes and architecture provided for the planning and

156. Nicolas de La Mare, *Traité de police* (Paris: 1722; 2d ed., expanded,
Amsterdam, 1729).
157. *Würtemberg allerhand Ordnungen* (1670), Bau Ordnung 1655, revising and
updating the ordinance of 1568, especially pp. 24–26; Wolfenbüttel, 29.III.1703,
18.XII.1713 (tax relief for useful and not extravagant buildings); Bergius,
Sammlung, 9:101–111 (Hessen Cassel Bau Ordnung 9.I.1784 summarizes practices and establishes institutions for supervision). Cf. also Mylius, *Corpus . . .
Magdeburgicarum,* 3:513ff.; Mylius, V-1, p. 313; VI-1, p. 539; *Continuatio,* 2:51, 57.
Slüter and Stisser, eds., 3:45–47 (Wolfenbüttel Gassen Verordnung 22.V.1717
repeats earlier provisions).
158. "Hessische Policeyordnungen über verschiedene Gegenstände" (11.
VIII.1731); Wolfenbüttel, 25.I.1725 and 13.XII.1714.

rebuilding of towns to create spacious perspectives, clear shapes, and harmonious groupings. Of course not all of the urban plans were on the scale and comprehensiveness of such completely novel creations as St. Petersburg, in Russia, but we do detect similar considerations in the modest programs and regulations issued for the small princely residences and commercial centers in German territories.[159]

Elaborate building codes combining practical needs and aesthetic considerations were drafted and introduced in many towns. The prime concern, naturally, and one that extended to building regulations for the countryside, was safety from fire. This perennial scourge was hard to control in view of the crowded layout of towns, the overwhelming prevalence of wooden structures, and the nearly total absence of functional distinction among buildings (for example, a bakery or smokehouse might be built into the wall of residential quarters or barns). From the late sixteenth century, and increasingly as the seventeenth century wore on, the efforts grew more systematic: fireplaces, chimneys, roofs had to be built, or if necessary rebuilt, in a prescribed manner. Regulations required that they be built of stone or brick and that all lumber, straw, and other flammable materials be removed from roofs and garrets. New buildings had to be properly spaced to reduce the danger of spreading a fire, which, incidentally, also contributed to promoting the aesthetic aims we have just mentioned. These rules were most forcefully insisted upon in those cases where rebuilding of towns damaged by fire or war and the construction of new buildings were involved. In any event, such regulations put an end to the indiscriminate adding on of wings, service structures, and so forth to existing town houses without regard to the open space available.[160] The chaotic and anarchic building pattern of an earlier period, the owners' complete freedom to decide on how, what, and where to build, were coming to an end under the impact of rational urban planning inaugurated by these ordinances.

159. For contemporary opinion and emphasis on the aesthetic element, see Christian Herold, *Historischer und politischer Tractat* (1683), pp. 30–31.

160. Wolfenbüttel, 5.X.1685, 7.VI.1725 (smoking pipes to be provided with metal covers); 7.I.1729 (chimney to be built under control of Baumeister Binneweiss only); 11.XI.1733 (re burning torches); 8.X.1744 (chimneys built of ma-

Nor should we forget the social aspect of the building codes and fire regulations. Fire fighting was organized according to standardized and rational procedures, with the same obligations imposed on every householder regardless of social and legal status. The primary role given to skilled fire fighters, drawn mainly from among the personnel in the building trade, the universal obligations of all citizens to assist, according to prescribed manner, in fighting a fire—all pointed to the standardized and professionalized patterns of a later time and showed an awareness of the need of technical skills and apparatus to attain the desired end.[161]

The high social cost of fire damage and a realization of the limited resources available locally and individually to make good such losses without seriously impairing the potential for material and cultural progress helped to spread the notion of collective cost sharing through insurance. Eighteenth-century ordinances, all very pedagogic in tone, suggested and at times required the setting up of insurance agreements to enable the owners to rebuild houses destroyed by fire without either facing ruin or making excessive demands on the ruler's benevolence and treasury. These insurance agreements were held out as a new departure to put an end to the traditional reliance on aid from the ruler. Sovereigns thereby relinquished their moral burden on plausible economic grounds, for they wanted to end the

---

sonry). Bergius, *Sammlung*, 1:201–22 (Prussian regulation re fire prevention in countryside, 18.I.1772, with summary of previous one); ibid., 3:26–27 (n.d., re baking ovens in villages). Mylius 5(1):218ff.

161. Fire ordinances displayed a similar pattern and trend, from purely negative measures (such as orders to remove objects and conditions that are fire hazards), to the regular organization of fire fighting (towns divided into sections, with one person responsible, readiness of equipment, etc.), to positive injunctions to build and maintain streets and structures so as to keep fire hazards at a minimum. *Ernsten Hertzogen zu Sachsen . . . gemeine Fewer Ordnung . . .* (Gotha: 1651); Wolfenbüttel, Feuer Ordnung 1661, reproduced in Slüter and Stisser, eds., vol. 3 (1738), very detailed and well organized; Freyberg, 2:37ff. (starts with ordinance of 1600). *Sammlung Anhalt-Dessau,* no. 23 (10.IV.1761, to help fight fires even beyond territorial frontiers); ibid., nos. 35 and 36 (the ordinances of 1661 and 1764 give a picture of evolution in technological and social assumptions). Wolfenbüttel, 3.VII.1745 (extending rules to villages). *Policey Ordnung Nürnberg* (1672) permanent administration, preservation of archives. *Policey Ordnung . . . Christians . . . Minden* (1618), one of the earliest making provision for maintenance of fire-fighting equipment, pp. 65–66. Mylius, 5(1):191, 241ff.

patriarchal view of power and authority that this obligation implied. The burden and responsibility for preserving the general welfare were shifted to society as a whole. These features of the evolving new situation required the didactic tone and insistence characteristic of the ordinances.[162] It was not only a question of overcoming distrust and making clear the material advantages inherent in the insurance scheme; it meant proposing a completely new outlook on society and on the role of political authority.

In the process the ordinances were helping to bring about two contradictory consequences. On the one hand, insurance schemes furthered the atomization and individualization of the population. Indeed, participation in the plans was based on a set formula of compensation for damages, and in this respect all participants and their property were treated on an equal footing without regard to social hierarchies. On the other hand, the insurance plans fostered local, urban, or regional coherence and provided experience in independent management of common affairs in a specified area of material interests, thereby also transcending traditional status categories and hierarchies. Was it not a sign of compartmentalization, as well as of growing "mass" organization? True, in several instances—especially in the countryside—the leadership role in these insurance schemes was reserved not only to the rich or to a supervisor nominated by the authorities but also to socially prominent participants.[163] All in all, new patterns of social loyalties and a modern structuring of social action were making their appearance under the prompting aegis of the ordinances. The insurance plans proved quite successful, so that some were introduced by ordinance at the request of various groups of the population. The notion of providing insurance was extended to other things, such as crops and business transactions.

---

162. Freyberg, 2:39 (first trace of discussion of insurance scheme in Bavaria, 1726). *Sammlung Anhalt-Dessau*, nos. 26 (19.IV.1762), 39 (13.II.1765), 45 (1.X. 1765). Bergius, *Sammlung*, 3:10–18 (Braunschweig 16/27.III.1750 and 18.V. 1754); 4:37–60 (Hessen Darmstadt Brand Assecuränz Ordnung, 1.VIII. 1777); ibid., 61–66 (Hildesheim 12.XII.1765), 9:117–30 (Mainz 15.VII. 1780). Mylius, 5(1):173.

163. Bergius, *Sammlung*, 1:172–90 (Churmärkische Feuersocietät auf dem platten Lande, 7.IX.1765).

The trend was clearly in the direction of estimating the worth of objects on the basis of a single, uniform, and quantitative standard and of abandoning qualitative evaluations.[164]

Last, we should not overlook the fact that the insurance schemes enhanced the sense of security, in a material as well as psychological sense, a consequence advocated and promised by the ordinances' didactic preambles. The feeling of security was an essential prerequisite for a more aggressive, enterprising, risk-taking mentality, a cast of mind that lay at the root of modern Europe's economic and cultural expansion and its faith in progress. What had been invented by the Venetians as a mechanism for the protection of naval and colonial enterprises (and further developed for the same purpose by the English and the Dutch in the seventeenth century) was now extended to other areas, and by strengthening a psychology of stability, it further opened the way to ongoing material progress.

Since society was being atomized to enhance its creative and productive activities, and since to this end the traditional leadership based on status and privilege was being modernized or eliminated altogether, a new elite, that of professionals, had to be shaped. Professionalization of many important social functions was an implicit, at times even explicit, aim of the policies pursued by the territorial sovereignties, policies that, starting early in the seventeenth century, the ordinances served to implement, regulate, and also to entrench. Naturally the administration's first concern was with the competence of its own personnel: for this reason the legal and administrative realms were to become professionalized first. It may be worth taking note of the evolution of the requirements for legal staff: in the beginning, that is in the late sixteenth and early seventeenth centuries, the only

164. Insurance plans and schemes were developed for pensioned officials and their widows and other select groups of society. "Hessische Verordnung der Witwencassen und Civilbedienten" (1751); Bergius 4:259–69 (Hildesheim, Witwenkasse 25.III.1770); Mylius, 1(2):209–14 (Evangelischer Reformierter Prediger Witwen und Waisen Cassa in Churmark, 1716); Wolfenbüttel, 3/14.III.1738 (modified crop insurance); Bergius, *Sammlung*, 1:105 (miners, Preussische Bergordnung 5.VI.1769) and Reglement referred to in n. 163 above; ibid., 1:191–200 (7.XI.1772 for Altona Kreis); ibid., 3:21–25 (24.X.1765, cattle insurance).

requirements were good birth and (theoretically) good moral character; some familiarity with the law was deemed desirable but not essential.[165] By the late seventeenth century, and certainly in the eighteenth, knowledge of the law was a prerequisite, knowledge attested to by examinations, certification, and proof of attendance at a university or similar establishment. Mere practical know-how, knowledge acquired by doing in an apprenticeship situation, definitely came second after formal education.[166] Since this technical knowledge had to be acquired primarily in institutions of higher learning, the professional status of the academic world was enhanced as well and the role of the universities strengthened.

But not only the top leadership of the administration was to receive professional training. As the amount of paperwork grew (and much of it resulted from the policies of urbanization, fire protection, and insurance that have just been mentioned) and the need for accurate information and records was increasingly felt, it became evident that the lower echelons of the bureaucracy, the scriveners who performed routine office duties, also had to be given proper training. Early in the eighteenth century, ordinances endeavored to support existing bureaucratic training centers by making attendance at them a prerequisite for steady employment. As a consequence, the number of such institutions, run by professional academics, also experienced a rapid increase.[167]

A similar trend can be observed in the domain of legal procedure in connection with private business and entrepreneurial activities. Lawyers and solicitors had to be professionalized and their training, standards, and practices regulated and supervised.

---

165. Chur Pfalz Oberbayer (1606), p. 2; Hofger. Ordnung Würtemberg (1669), p. 15; *Augusti Braunschwyg Hofgerichts Ordnung* (1663), p. 14; "Allgem. königl. . . . Justizbediente," in Halberstadt (1723), pp. 2, 11; Otto . . . Holstein Schaumburg Hofgerichts Ordnung (1540), p. 8; Mylius, 2(1): 252, 357ff., 392; Mylius, *Corpus . . . Magdeburgicarum*, 1686, p. 31.

166. *Hohenlohe . . . gemeinsames Landrecht* (1738), introduction. Cf. section 7, below.

167. Calenberg (1739), 3:458–59 (declaratio 20.VIII.1731, re registration and certification of medical personnel). See also J. J. Moser, *Wiederholte Nachricht von einer Staats- und Canzley Academie* (1749).

A number of territorial ordinances in the seventeenth century set up the rules for the private practice of law, regulating and controlling it so that hopefully lawyers would serve society and not exclusively selfish private interests. The existence of a corps of lawyers and solicitors doubtless helped the development and spread of what we usually call capitalistic forms of economic relations, which depend so much on legal and written formalism.[168] The fiscal interests of the state, incidentally, were safeguarded by the requirement that stamped paper be used for all public and legal transactions carried out with the assistance of lawyers.[169] The interests of both clients and the public were to be protected by the requirement that all actions involving a lawyer or solicitor be properly witnessed, signed, and certified, so that in case of doubt or appeal the responsible advisor could be readily identified and brought to account. Professionalization turned out to be not only a means of securing the autonomy of practitioners but also a way for the state to supervise economic and legal transactions.

The professionalization of such fields as mining, forestry, and building went hand in hand with the expansion of scientific knowledge. Similarly, another activity of great social utility that received official legal status and was subjected to administrative controls was medical practice. Doctors, of course, had been professionalized during the Renaissance, but now their numbers were expanded and controlled, while their training in the universities was improved and supervised by the authorities. Of still greater significance proved to be the emergence of trained paramedical personnel and the supervision of public health by boards of medical professionals. This development took place in the eighteenth century, although some important steps in this direction had been taken in the seventeenth. Medical boards were

168. Protection was also sought against harm to the economic interests of clients and against introduction of informal practices into courts and administration. Mylius, *Continuatio*, 1:101; *Corpus . . . Magdeburgicarum*, 2:1, 215ff.

169. An early expression is in *Anhalt Policey und Landes Ordenung* (1572), §7. Cf. also Chr. A. Beck, *Versuch einer Staatspraxis* (1754) and the very comprehensive pedagogic handbook, Spaethe (Kaspar von Stielen), *Der Teutsche Advocat . . .* (1678), with citations from ordinances.

set up and were entrusted with several important new functions
in the professionalization of health care. In the first place, the
boards helped to supervise medical training, and they also set the
scales of medical fees; more important, they made for stricter
delimitation of the areas of competence of the medical practitioners, differentiating the duties and responsibilities of doctors,
surgeons, barbers, midwives, and pharmacists while assigning to
the medical doctor a privileged status and leading role. Naturally
the doctors on the boards were given a determining voice in the
certification of fellow doctors as well as the authority to supervise
and control all medical activities so as to prevent malpractice and
abuses (such authority, in the eighteenth century, included specific recommendations on treatment and the administering of
drugs). The boards' opinion was sought and required in drafting
legislation and regulations concerning public health, the fighting
of epidemics, and the like.[170]

More important still, medical boards or individual medical
officers supervised the training of midwives and kept an eye on
their practice. When we remember the hazards accompanying
childbirth in the eighteenth century and recall the many superstitions and prejudices surrounding this event, the formation and
training of a reliable and properly instructed corps of midwives
appears as a major milestone in Europe's progress to prosperity
and security. The training of midwives was put on a modern,
solid, scientific footing, with a remarkable stress on practical
experience and knowledge.[171] Ordinances set up training institu-

---

170. *Des Durchlaucht. . . . Ernsten Hertzogen zu Sachsen . . . Patent und Mandat die
. . . Landt Medicos, Wundärtzte . . . betreffend* (Gotha: 1657) 9.X.1657, tariffs for
separate categories of practitioners. Freyberg, 2:71ff. (from 1599, on certification
requirements; 25.VIII.1708, additional certification for priests *ratione baptismi*);
Wolfenbüttel 26.VI.1719, 29.VIII.1744; Bergius, *Sammlung*, 5:63–93 (Hildesheim
Medicinal Ordnung 1782 establishes medical collegium with wide competence);
ibid., 6:247–78 (Würtemberg Medicinal Ordnung 16.X.1755) and pp. 205–207
(2.IV.1782, concilio medico in Bavaria) and pp. 197–201 (Hessen Hanau tariffs
for doctors, 1772); Calenberg 1739, 3:454–58 (1.V.1731, edict requiring official
examination and competition for licensing); Mylius 5(4): 9, and *Corpus . . .
Magdeburgicarum*, chap. 25, pp. 97ff.

171. Bergius, *Sammlung*, 3:164–66 (Braunschweig ordinance re midwives,
22.IX.1778); 5:24–44 (Herzogtum Holstein, 18.II.1765, very comprehensive
midwives' ordinance); 8:317–65 (Augsburg 1750); Mylius, 5(4): 9ff., 219.

tions for midwives under the supervision of regular doctors and medical faculties. The legislation was also remarkable for its language, which stressed not only the utilitarian and scientific aspects but the social and psychological dimensions of a midwife's duties. Pharmacists, too, were put under control of the medical profession, and ordinances set high standards of scientific competence and professional achievement for them.[172] These measures made for stricter separation of functions and a greater degree of specialization. This, in turn, encouraged respect for professionalism in general and reliance on the technical know-how of a trained elite. The reign of the expert intellectual was about to dawn in Europe.

Personnel in other fields were slower to become professionalized, since there was less awareness of the significance of their work for the community, and their training requirements were not as elaborate. However, as time went on technicians and professionals were increasingly called upon in a variety of areas, more particularly, as indicated earlier, in building, forestry, mining, and the like. The ordinances encouraged reliance on these professionals, discouraged recourse to the amateur generalist, and endeavored to undermine the status of traditional social elites in all domains where specialized knowledge was becoming necessary.[173] Even with respect to the humble forester and shepherd, the ordinances prescribed that their services were to be called upon, rather than those of ordinary peasants and villagers.

172. Pharmacists were very important, since they often provided, as they still do in Europe today, the most direct and frequent contact the population at large had with things medical. Ordinances concerning pharmacists underwent an evolution similar to those concerning doctors; they were at first negative, to prevent poisons from being administered, but culminated in requiring regular professional standards and forbidding the involvement of outsiders. Bergius, *Sammlung,* 8:91–121 (Augsburg 1761); 6:247–78 (Würtemberg 16.X.1755); Mylius, *Corpus . . . Magdeburgicarum,* Process Ordnung 15.III.1686; Early example, *Churpfürstliche Pfalz in Obern Bayern Landes Ordnung* (1590), p. 286.

173. *Würtemberg allerhand Ordnungen* (1670), Erneuerte Forstordnung 1614, p. 4; Wolfenbüttel, 13.VI.1716 (certified slaughterers, not ex-soldiers, to be employed exclusively); Bergius, *Sammlung,* 3:47 (Prussian publicandum 8.I.1778, re Hüttenbedienung); Calenberg 1739, 3 (24.IV.1710, re training of masons and carpenters); Mylius, *Corpus . . . Magdeburgicarum,* 2:216.

Last but not least, the profession that was the most essential foundation or prerequisite in modernizing society, namely that of the teacher on the elementary level, received its official formulation too. Ordinances enforced uniform standards of achievement on the part of teachers, although local conditions frequently precluded their being attained. Combining the function of teacher with the exercise of trades that might interfere with the primary pedagogic duties was prohibited, though here again the ordinances had to allow exceptions and compromises. As we know from literary evidence, most village schoolmasters had to combine teaching with other trades (especially sedentary ones like shoemaking and tailoring,) yet the drive for professionalization was strong—witness the preference given to those teachers who prepared for the ministry or helped out in church.[174]

Concomitant with this effort to promote professional competence and specialization was the introduction of uniform and scientifically recognized tools, data, or principles. This drive for scientific (or rational) standards and uniformity manifested itself in ordinances requiring uniform weights and measures to facilitate commercial and administrative transactions over wide areas and to make for a common language of communication. Once again we may discern a clear trend in this type of ordinance. It started with the prohibition of inaccurate, false, or foreign measures and subsequently imposed greater accuracy and stricter standards by means of the labeling and stamping of measuring devices. Of course, this meant that the units of specific localities would be taken as the standard and enforced both locally and more widely on a regional basis. Often the standard was the measure of the capital city, but not necessarily so. Finally, uniform measures based on scientific grounds were introduced and imposed, with appropriate instructions on the methods to be used to conform to them. Closely related to the efforts to impose accurate and standard measurements was the introduction of a more

---

174. Karl Ernst Moritz, *Anton Reiser* (Munich: Wilhelm Goldman Verlag, 1961), and the autobiography of Jung-Stilling (Johann Heinrich Jung), *Lebensgeschichte* (Munich: Rowohlt, 1969); Bergius, *Sammlung*, 7:128 (5.IV.1757, school ordinance, Lauenburg-Ratzeburg examination and certification requirement); *Fürsten . . . zu Anhalt . . . Landes- und Process Ordnungen* (Cöthen: 1666).

correct, scientific calendar. It is interesting to note in this connection that the introduction of the new calendar was justified by reference to rational "enlightenment." In the same vein, prohibitions of the sale and import of other calendars not based on the new dating was justified not only because the state derived income from a tax on the printing of calendars but also because traditional calendars of the almanac type were thought to include inaccurate information and superstitions.[175] On the Continent, as is well known, the trend culminated in the introduction of the metric system at the time of the French Revolution. From this point of view the Revolution and the reign of Napoleon may be viewed as a culmination of an evolution initiated by the well-ordered police state.

The effort at systematizing and furthering the material progress of German society found its repercussion in and provided a stimulus for legislation that promoted cultural and intellectual progress in central Europe. No doubt to a significant extent it was an organic outcome of trends rooted in Renaissance Humanism, the educational policies of the Reformation and Counter-Reformation, and a response to the scientific revolution of the early seventeenth century. Yet it clearly was also the result of conscious

175. Mylius, 6(2): 3ff. (Patent 10.V.1710):

Nachdem aus Landes-Väterlicher Vörsorge will allezeit dahin bedacht gewesen, wie in Unsern Churfürstentum und Landen nicht nur die Handlung und Gewerbe, sondern auch nützlicher Künste und Wissenschaften zum Besten des gemeinen Wesens und derer Einwohner, mehr und mehr gepflanzt und in Aufnehmen gebracht werden möchten, Wir auch zu solchem Ende, so wohl in dem einen oder andern verschiedene nützliche établissements zu stiften, keine Gelegenheit vorbeigelassen . . . auch sonsten in Mathematis, mechanicis und dergleichen nützlichen Künsten und Wissenschaften anzurichten, und mit gelehrten Gliedern, guten Gesetzen, benötigten Gebäuden und anderen erforderten Bequemlichkeiten zu versehen und beneficiren . . . damit die bishero so häufig im Schwange den Lügen, Historien, nichtigen Weissagungen auch schandbaren Gesprächen . . . angefüllten Calender. . . .

Freyberg, 2:345ff. Sammlung Anhalt-Dessau, no. 8 (11.XI.1738, standard measures in building trade); Bergius, Sammlung, 4:122–27 (Braunschweig 29.XI.1765); 6:141 (Schleswig Holstein Policey Ordnung 29.I.1768); Calenberg 1739 3:225–39 (Reglement 22.XII.1713 with reference to models in Hoya und Lüneburg); Mylius, 5, chap. 8.

efforts by territorial administration to change society through ordinances.

6. Progress in Education and Culture

We are accustomed to gauge cultural progress by the share humanitarian considerations have in a society's way of life. That is why, since the eighteenth century, the humanizing of justice, especially criminal justice, has been considered a fair measure of cultural advance. In this respect the German police ordinances of the seventeenth and eighteenth centuries give the picture of a significant and on the whole positive evolution. In the first place, the range of criminal cases, while remaining extraordinarily broad by our contemporary standards, was narrowed down with respect to misdemeanors and crimes of a religious nature. More significant still was the decline of appeals to religious feelings and to reliance on church penances for anything but a few obvious crimes against religion. We note, furthermore, a definite trend toward "civilizing" criminal processes—that is, the transformation of a criminal delict and prosecution into a civil action or a case in equity.[176]

Last but not least, efforts were made to transform convicted criminals into useful members of society, either through reeducation or more frequently by forcing them to make a contribution to society through their labor. What we have noted in connection with vagrants and beggars also applies to criminals. To the extent that the misdeed was not so heinous or recidivous as to warrant the drastic step of eliminating the criminals from all contact with society, the ordinances prescribed putting them to work under supervision. Such an outlook and policy contributed to the establishment of workhouses as punitive centers or prisons where inmates worked under harsh discipline for very low "wages."[177] Such houses were supposed to yield social and economic benefits as well. This, at least, is what the governments believed, and they

176. For an early instance, *Ordnungen . . . Sachsen* (1583), Ausschreiben 1550, p. 52; *Sammlung Anhalt-Dessau,* no. 6 (9.VIII.1710); Calenberg 1739, 4 (19.X.1719).
177. Cf. section 3.

hoped to reap the additional advantage that work in these establishments could be combined with pedagogic efforts to rehabilitate criminals into permanently useful members of society. Since criminal behavior was ascribed to heredity, and also because it was necessary to provide for the offspring of male criminals and their female companions, similar arrangements combining punishment, useful work, and educational treatment were made in caring for their children and for juvenile delinquents.[178]

The implementation of seventeenth-century judiciary ordinances also led to a transformation in methods of prosecution. It is noteworthy that even before the well-known pamphlet of Thomasius and the later treatise of Beccaria on the abolition of torture, a number of territorial sovereignties were limiting (and in practice even discarding altogether) the use of torture in exacting confessions, in taking evidence, and in punishing. Even when recourse was made to torture, ordinances provided that it be done under more stringent controls to safeguard the victims from death or permanent maiming. Youngsters, old men, and women were to be free from torture altogether.[179]

Respect for the human person and greater faith in a man's testimony and word, as well as considerations of health, paved the way for a fairer treatment of the suspected criminal. Obtaining

178. More humane treatment of mothers guilty of child murder was advocated: Mylius, *Continuatio*, 1:371.
179. *Ordonnance pour l'administration de la justice* (1707), titre 10 (under Lorraine); Wolfenbüttel, 4.V.1744; Calenberg 1739, 2:696–98 (28.XII.1717) and 796–884 (30.IV/11.V.1736), especially 868-77, chap. 11; Mylius, 2(3): 3, 57, 61; 2(1): 597–604 (19.III.1717). Similarly, witch trials, while not abolished altogether, were being discouraged as lacking solid evidence. On the matter of torture, see the very suggestive study by John H. Langbein, *Torture and the Law of Proof: Europe and England in the Ancien Régime* (Chicago: University of Chicago Press, 1977), which puts the question in a different, more convincing, pragmatic and juridical light. Frederick III of Prussia ordered a woman child murderess beheaded, instead of having her buried alive. At the same time we may note a regression from the more enlightened and tolerant ordinances of earlier years. A similar trend may be observed in the legislation of Anton Ulrich in Braunschweig. Can this regression perhaps explain the greater virulence and energy of the "enlightened" counterattack in the later decades of the first half of the eighteenth century?

adequate evidence and proper recording of court proceedings as well as establishing the accuracy of statements of fact became absolute prerequisites that resulted in greater uniformity and regularity of the judicial process. The codifications and reforms of procedure that took place in the "enlightened" eighteenth century were but the last step in a trend that had developed fully in practice in the Germanies and elsewhere in the course of the second half of the seventeenth century. This development promoted greater reliance on professionalism by requiring lawyers to defend the accused and see to it that procedures and records corresponded to established norms. The concept of the lawyer as a defender of the client's interests was replacing the traditional view of the lawyer as a mere scrivener performing routine procedural acts who was not allowed to plead in favor of the criminal once the fact of crime had been established.[180] As a result, the administration of justice was turning into a genuine adversary procedure, restricting the scope of administrative and executive tyranny.[181]

Whatever the immediate effects of judicial practices on cultural progress, it was quite evident that in the long run progress could be secured only by an effective educational system. In this regard the pattern had been set in the sixteenth century when as a result of the Reformation the ability to read and understand the Scriptures had become a primary requirement for all Christians. The goal of limited literacy, subsequently also pursued by the Catholic Counter-Reformation, although less consistently and aggressively, was broadened in the late seventeenth and early eighteenth centuries to become virtually a policy for general education. The police ordinances enable us to follow the progress of this trend. In the first place, leaving out the universities for the time being, the curricula of both primary and more advanced schools became progressively broader to include not only the basics of reading, learning the catechism, writing, and counting but also some elementary notions of history and natural science as

180. *Magdeburgische Ordnungen* (1673), Process Ordnung 6.VII.1652, especially p. 894; Würtemberg Ordnung (Hofgerichtsordnung 1654, p. 17); *Halberstadtische Canzley Ordnung* (Northausen: 1652), pp. 16–17.
181. Cf. Langbein, *Torture and the Law of Proof.*

well as a more solid grounding in grammar, logic, and mathematics. Throughout the period improved knowledge of German was emphasized, though Latin remained the sine qua non of scholarly and sophisticated intellectual intercourse. The study of German stressed the skills of good reasoning and hence better analytical and synthetic thinking. An ever-expanding number of subjects was added to provide comprehensive basic knowledge of the physical environment as well as a smattering of classical and historical culture.[182]

A shift may also be noticed in pedagogic methods. While the ordinances did not mention it specifically, the shift doubtlessly took place under the influence of such pioneers of modern education as Comenius, Weigel, and Weise in the seventeenth century and Locke in the eighteenth. Although still strictly held to their studies and impressed with the earnestness of the enterprise, pupils were beginning to be treated with understanding, gentleness, and kindness—like children, and not like small adults. Firmness, even occasional harsh disciplining, were not to be allowed to become ends in themselves but were to be resorted to only as means for enhancing the child's awareness of the importance of study. Attention was increasingly paid to differences in levels of maturity and development of children, so that teaching methods as well as subject matter became better adapted to the age of the pupils.[183] Naturally there could be no question of a

182. *Magdeburgische Ordnungen* (1673), Visitations Decret 1656 and Schul Ordnung 1658, pp. 241–43, 272; Kreitmeyer, no. 27, Mandat 1730, pp. 475ff. In Wolfenbüttel, "Des . . . Herrn Augusti . . . Schulordnung . . ." (1651) (especially for second and third groups of schools). Cf. A. B. Rautner, *Anführung zur Teutschen Staats Kunst* (1672), pp. 29, 39–40; C. A. Beck, *Versuch einer Staatspraxis* (1754), p. 8; D. Nettelbladt, *Sammlung kleiner juristischen Abhandlungen* (1792), in particular "Politische Vorschläge zur Verbesserung der jurist. Vorlesungen" and "Von der Kenntnis der Rechtsgelehrten"; Chr. Weise, *Politische Fragen* (1708); Spaeth, *Der Teutsche Advocat*, pp. 133ff. In Protestant schools, even on the secondary level, the stress was on what we would call the natural sciences, in contrast to Catholic schools, which tended to favor the classical, philosophical, and philological aspects of the humanities. In both school systems, we note the indubitable influence of Jesuit pedagogic conceptions and models.

183. *Des Herrn . . . Augusti . . . Schulordnung* (1651). Bergius, *Sammlung*, 7:127–43 (Ordnung für die Landschulen . . . Lauenburg-Ratzeburg 5.IV.1757, pp. 130ff.

uniform pattern of schooling for all classes of society. The peasantry and the lower urban classes were to be given only the necessary rudiments, while the children of better-situated parents and of the elites were to obtain as advanced an education as possible. On the lowest level, the emphasis was to be on perception and experience at the expense of mere book learning—quite obviously the lesson derived from the writings of Comenius, Weigel, and Locke. Not surprisingly, therefore, on the level of primary and secondary education we note a definite bias toward the practical, on occasion even on manual skills, and firm opposition to strictly theoretical and rote learning associated with scholastic pedantry.[184] The latter was deemed to be superfluous and perhaps even positively harmful for the future of the ordinary subject.

The educational system was designed to produce members of society who were not only disciplined and shared broad social and cultural values but who would also be active and productive citizens. The pragmatic bias of the ordinances on education was universal. This was one of the reasons why the ordinances did not deal much with approaches to the education of the upper classes, especially the aristocracy. But the authorities' concern in this domain was evidenced by the establishment of special schools for the education and training of the noble elites. These schools were closely supervised by the ruler, and their aim was to educate the sons of the nobility to become active, productive, useful officers and the cultural as well as economic leaders of their countries.[185]

in particular). Although quite late, *Schulen Ordnung* (1774) of Bavaria gives a good summation of trend. Cf. Erhard Weigel, *Kurtzer Entwurff der freudigen Kunst- und Tugend-Lehre vor Trivial und Kinder-Schulen* (1682) and *Aretologistica* (1687).

184. *Des ... Herrn ... Augusti ... Schulordnung* (1651); *Schulen Ordnung* of Bavaria (1774); Calenberg 1739, 1:1009–10 (re Huguenot schools).

185. *Magdeburgische Ordnungen* (1673), Erneuerte Stipendiaten Ordnung 1671. Freyberg, 3:251ff. (passim, various Bavarian ordinances establishing special schools and awarding ranks to teachers). "Hessische Verordnung in Consistorial and Kirchensachen" (1627–1745), 26.IX.1720 *Collegium illustre* established in Cassel for natural sciences and mathematics as intermediary level between schools and university faculties. Wolfenbüttel 1.II.1688 (Ordonnances et privilèges à l'érection de l'Académie de Volfenbüttel), 9/20.X and 9.XI.1724. Naturally, the presence of a university presented police problems of special kind; cf. numerous

The importance of education for a leadership role was relentlessly stressed, and its successful acquisition was turned into a
prerequisite for any public career.

No doubt an overemphasis on education and schooling might
also have undesirable effects, effects that came to the attention of
authorities early in the eighteenth century; to counteract them a
new feature made its appearance in the ordinances dealing with
schools in that century. It was realized that under the circumstances of the time schooling beyond the minimum level tended to
enhance the intellectual and scholarly abilities of the pupils, who
were then attracted to the professions (law, medicine, administration) and repelled from much-needed manual and artisanal or
manufacturing activities. We even find isolated expressions of
fear concerning the emergence of an intellectual proletariat or of
a class of semitrained, semiprofessionalized individuals incapable
of playing the productive role they had been trained for. The
obvious answer to such fears was to restrict schooling to children
of parents already members of the professional elites and to
discourage those coming from the laboring and peasant classes.[186]

Wolfenbüttel ordinances concerning dueling, rowdy conduct, etc., in Helmstedt
(e.g., 18.VII.1735) and similar legislation after the founding of Göttingen
University. *Policey Ordnung . . . Nürnberg* (1672), p. 4, establishing *gymnasium illustre*
in Bayreuth. But note the concern expressed by Prussia a propos of gymnasia and
universities: Mylius (30.IX.1718), 1(2):229–35.

186. Mylíus, Patent 25.VIII.1708, 1(2):173–74, deserves quoting in full:

Nachdem Se. Königl. Maj. in Preussen . . . Unser allergnädigster Herr
erwogen, wasgestalt bereits von vielen hergeklagt worden, dass die Studia in
allen Facultäten dadurch in Abgang und fast in Verachtung geraten, weiln ein
jeder bis auf Handwerker und Bauern seine Söhne ohne Unterschied der
Ingeniorum und Capacität studieren und auf Universität- und hohen Schu-
sumptibus publicis unterhalten lassen will, da doch dem Publico und gemeinen Wesen vielmehr daran gelegen, wann dergleichen zu deren studiis
unfähige ingenia bei Manufakturen, Handwerken und der Miliz, ja gar bei
Ackerbau nach eines jeden condition und naturlicher Zuneigung angewendet, und sie dergestalt ihres Lebens-Unterhalt zu verdienen unterwiesen
würden. Als seind Se. Königl. Maj. aus Landes-Väterlicher treuer Vorsorge
veranlasset worden dahin bedacht zu sein, welchergestalt solcher Inconve-
nienzen remediret, die studia in vorigen Wert gebracht und das commodum
publicum befördert werden möge, zu welchern Ende Se. Königl. Maj. hiermit
und Kraft dieses verordnen, auch zugleich allen und jeden Magistraten in

Class discrimination in access to educational opportunities went hand in hand with a stress on education for leadership functions. The end result was the demand of democratic access to all educational opportunities, the notion that all careers should be open to talent that was to be the battle cry of late eighteenth-century progressives and radicals who themselves, as R. Darnton has suggested, were often semiskilled, unsuccessful professionals or intellectual proletarians.[187]

The number and types of schools established by territorial authorities or by private individuals underwent an appreciable increase in the period we are concerned with. First came serious efforts at expanding the network of primary schools, especially in the countryside, and numerous ordinances indicated the methods and regulations to be followed as well as providing the means for their operation.[188] Secondly, a number of specialized technical establishments were founded and ordinances issued to make sure that they were launched on their proper courses and maintained

---

Städten und führnehmlich denenjenigen, sowohl geistlichen als weltlichen, welchen die Aufsicht der Schulen anvertraut ist, allergnädigst und ernstlich anbefehlen, auf die Jugend in selbigen fleissig Acht zu haben, solche selbsten zum öfteren zu visitiren unter denen ingeniis welche zu den Studien sich wohl anlassen, und von ihrer Fähigkeit gut Probe geben, einen selectum zu machen, und diesen zwar in ihrem Zweck beförderlich sein, diejenigen aber welche entweder wegen Stupidität, Trägheit oder Mangel des Lustes und Triebes oder auch anderen Ursachen zum studieren unfähig seind in Zeiten davon ab- und zu Erlernen einer Manufaktur, Handwerks oder anderer redlichen Profession anzuweisen, selbige auch nicht weiter als fürnemlich in dem wahren Christentum und Fundament der Gottesfurcht, dann auch im Lesen, Schreiben und Rechnen, unterweisen und informieren zu lassen, damit nicht, wie es sich wohl zuträgt, Schüler von 20 bis 30 Jahren dem Publico und ihnen selbst zu Last und denen Informatoren zur Verkleinerung erfunden werden mögen. Hieran geschiet Unser ernster Wille und Meinung. Charlottenburg den 25 Augusti 1708 / signatur / Friedrich Graf v. Wartenburg.

Bergius, *Sammlung*, 3:443–44 (Circular 6.X.1765) reproduces similar ideas in the more cogent and terse formulation of Frederick II.

187. Robert Darnton, "Reading, Writing, and Publishing in Eighteenth Century France: A Case Study in the Sociology of Literature," *Daedalus* winter (1971):214–56.

188. *Pfaltz Landesordnung* (1599), pp. 37, 86; Bergius, *Sammlung*, 7 (Ordnung für Landschulen Lauenburg-Ratzeburg 1757).

at an acceptable level. Finally, and this was the truly significant innovation, education for girls became a significant concern and desideratum. In Bavaria, and following its example elsewhere, schools for girls of the nobility and upper classes were established under the patronage of the ruler's wife.[189] In the eighteenth century girls schools were frequently included in the regular educational system, albeit on a restricted and simplified level.

To ensure that the educational system played its assigned role, ordinances from the seventeenth century on provided for compulsory school attendance both in the villages and in the towns. To enable peasant children, especially the poorer ones, to attend, special arrangements were made releasing them from school during harvest time and prohibiting their use in the fields or for tending cattle during the normal school year. We also read of efforts to set up schools close enough to the villages and farms so that all children, even the small ones, could walk to school in all seasons.[190] To make the expanded school system work, the first prerequisite was an adequate teaching staff. Earlier we mentioned some measures taken to ensure the availability of teachers; in addition, constant efforts were made to encourage the profession, and care was taken to employ only qualified persons. The teachers' qualifications were to be evaluated not only on the basis of their factual knowledge but also on that of their pedagogic ability and possession of the psychological traits needed to ensure effective teaching and a positive influence on their charges.[191]

To modernize education, books were needed, and on books, too, depended the progress and spread of knowledge. Thus the publication and circulation of books was of concern to administrators, and a number of ordinances dealt with this quintessentially

189. Freyberg, 3:283–84; also *Ordnungen Sachsen* (1583), Ausschreiben 1550, p. 57; *Fürstlich Anhaltische Landes-Ordnung* (1777), Titel 3, p. 12.

190. *Magdeburgische Ordnungen* (1673), Visitations Decret 1656, p. 246; *Policey Ordnung Nürnberg* (1672), p. 6; Bergius, *Sammlung,* 7: (Ordnung Landeschulen Lauenburg-Ratzeburg 1757, p. 131); Calenberg 1739, 1:912–18 (Consistorial Ausschreiben 31.VIII.1736).

191. Kreitmeyer, §27, Mandat 1730 Schulwesen; *Des . . . Herrn . . . Augusti . . . Schul Ordnung* (1651), p. 5; Bergius, *Sammlung,* 8: (Landeschulen Lauenburg-Ratzeburg), p. 129.

modern activity. These ordinances pursued two related purposes in connection with the book trade. In the first place, care was to be taken that no "harmful" literature be published and circulated. Censorship was taken over by the lay authorities, largely to fill the void left by the Catholic Church or to counteract the Index of Rome. Censorship focused on defending religious orthodoxy and morality. With respect to the former, only books of a philosophic or theological nature were of concern, while with regard to the latter belles lettres, too, were an object of censorship.[192] The censorship was essentially negative and most frequently ex post facto as well, dealing with the circulation rather than the printing of books. The second purpose, especially in some territories, as for example Saxony, was to regulate the book trade. Specifically the aim was to safeguard "copyright" and to protect the interests of the publishers, in the first place, and those of the authors in the second place. The ordinances regulating the book fair at Leipzig provided an early and comprehensive statement of the need to protect publishers and to guard against plagiarism.[198] In view of the importance of the Leipzig book fair, these ordinances had more than local significance and set a pattern for subsequent legislation elsewhere. The prohibitions against distribution through peddlers and unauthorized merchants have already been touched upon. That this injunction was not intended to preclude the development of a reading public may be inferred from an ordinance instituting book auctions at the newly established University of Göttingen.[194] Such measures doubtless helped to account for the rather widespread pattern of private libraries in North Germany, even in relatively isolated localities and among the less sophisticated classes of society.[195]

192. Freyberg, 2:196 (7.IV.1728); Kreitmeyer, §§28–29, pp. 479–83 (1.VIII and 28.XI.1769); Mylius, 1(1):553; note also the "Enlightenment" aim in Mylius, 6(2):5.

193. Wolfenbüttel 20.VII.1709, 24.V.1745; from Wolfenbüttel, *Tax Ordnung . . . Friedrichen Ulrichen* (1622), §19; *Des . . . Herrn Augusti . . . Tax Ordnung* (1645), Titlen 47–49; Bergius, *Sammlung*, 7:282–86 (Chursächsische Mandat 18.XII.1773, re book trade); ibid., 9:225–38 (Strassburg ordinance re the printing trade, 1786).

194. Calenberg 1739, 1:781–83 (3.IV.1737, re book auctions).

195. Professor Harms, now of Munich, has launched an investigation of village libraries in northwestern Germany.

Travel was a major means of spreading knowledge, the arts, and cultural progress in general. Naturally ordinances did not concern themselves much with travel, since it was a private, individual matter and accessible only to the high and mighty. In this regard we need only remember that all measures taken to facilitate transportation and communication, such as the postal service, stage coaches, improved roads, and policed inns, also benefited individual travel.[196] A subsidiary aspect of travel that the ordinances did address was the danger that extensive travel and residence abroad would be financially onerous for the country by producing an outflow of specie and socially harmful by accustoming members of the elite to wasteful, luxurious, and alien ways. Despite these undesirable and dangerous consequences, governments looked favorably upon travel for education and enlightenment. This positive attitude found expression not so much in specific ordinances as in treatises and publicistic writings sponsored and approved by territorial sovereigns.[197]

All these endeavors in the cultural realm helped to foster a new view of man's condition and nature, a secular attitude that judged individuals by their worth as productive members of society. In pursuing this aim, some ordinances took a negative approach—that is, they discouraged the manifestations of those human traits that were deemed harmful and undesirable in a productive society. Their purpose was to eliminate from society all those who would not contribute positively to its material progress. This explains the virulent and tenacious struggle against idleness in all its aspects, whether real or imaginary. We have already mentioned the campaign against beggars as part of the transformation of a traditional point of view (Christian charity: poverty necessary to enable alms giving) in favor of a "modern" normative attitude that stressed production-oriented activity.[198] But all other

196. Mylius, 4:963ff.
197. *Die rechte Reisekunst* (1674) is an example of many guides to cultured travel. Mylius 6(2):7ff; Mylius, *Corpus ... Magdeburgicarum*, 3:500–502 (Mandat wegen Reisen ausserhalb Deutschland, 8.VII.1700); Mylius, *Novum Corpus ...*, pp. 97–98 (edict 19.VI.1751).
198. Cf. the apt remarks of B. Groethuysen, *Die Entstehung der bürgerlichen Welt- und Lebensanschauung im Frankreich des 17. Jahrhunderts*, 2 vols., (Halle: M. Niemeyer, 1927–30), 1:64.

forms of idleness as well were condemned, prohibited, and prosecuted. Such efforts even aimed at the upper, wealthy groups of society, attempting to force everyone to be usefully active. The decrees of Frederick William I of Prussia and of Peter the Great of Russia were ample evidence of legislative and police measures designed to instill the new attitudes while punishing those who resisted them.

More important, however, were the positive steps taken to improve the conditions of life. These may be put in the category of philanthropy, and the expansion of humanitarian concern at the end of the seventeenth and the early decades of the eighteenth century was remarkable indeed. Under the watchful eyes of the administration a variety of philanthropic institutions and organizations were established to take care of the poor, the sick, and the orphaned. The need for such establishments was especially great in the Protestant lands that in the sixteenth century had lost the welfare institutions of the Church. But secular philanthropies were also spreading to the Catholic world as a consequence of the secularization of life in general and the authorities' desire to control all institutions, including the charitable ones. Although private initiative was readily countenanced, supervision and control were effectively kept in the hands of the authorities.[199]

The upshot of these endeavors was to instill a new attitude toward human life, an attitude that is frequently credited only to the propaganda of the "Party of Humanity": the conviction that life is not only sacred but also a valuable asset not to be wasted. Human life had to be respected, not just for God's sake but for society's, and positive action to save the life or health of an individual was a duty no subject should shirk whatever the consequences.[200] Ordinances set forth arguments and provided prescriptions for helping those in danger of drowning or those

---

199. Wolfenbüttel 31.I.1701, 5.X.1716 (special treatment to *pia corpora*); 21.XI.1742 (calendar sales to support widows); Bergius, *Sammlung,* 2:195–98 (16.XII.1774); 5:1–23 (Freiberg i. Breisgau, 1781, poor ordinance with philanthropic orientation); ibid. (Hebammen Ordnung Holstein, 18.II.1765, connects hospital for poor with training of midwives); ibid. (Waldeck Verordnung 3.I.1780: special institution of lying-in hospital for illegitimate births).

200. Mylius, *Continuatio,* 1:147.

who had attempted to commit suicide. Significantly, these ordinances stressed the moral obligation to overcome the squeamish disgust and fear of the drowned or hanged that religion had instilled and tradition hallowed. Only active intervention to save the victim's life, in disregard of one's own feelings and superstitious prejudices, would restore a useful member to society and fulfill one's primary obligations toward a fellow man.[201] A sense of social and human solidarity, respect for the individual life—these were the crowning achievements of the ordinances' drive for cultural progress. Obviously this achievement provided the necessary precondition for society's ongoing material progress and economic development, as well.

7. Administration

Administrative ordinances, then as now, depended for their success on the political and institutional framework within which they operated, and the latter in turn acquired some of their basic traits from the operation of the ordinances. In the process of promulgating and implementing police ordinances, territorial authorities had to establish or reform a number of institutional mechanisms and to create manpower pools to operate them effectively. For the purposes of the present essay, we need not go into the specific organization of the major institutions set up or used by the ordinances. It will suffice to assess their nature and their relationship to policy and to significant political developments. In a sense, it is the well-known chicken and egg problem. Did new tasks create a new administrative framework, or did a

201. Bergius, *Sammlung*, 5:125–36 (Braunschweig Verordnung 24.X.1780); ibid., 9:140–51 (Neipperg Verordnung 24.II.1785:

Eine traurige Erfahrung befürchten lässt, dass einerseits noch so viele Vorurteile, anderseits noch so viel Hartherzigkeit unter den meisten Menschen herrscht, dass sie Verunglückte Nebenmenschen hilfreiche Hände leisten entweder sich schämen oder kaltblütig zur Ersparung einiger Mühe oder Zeit vernachlässigen. . . . [Man folge Engländer, Holländer, Franzosen] welche ohnstreitig das Gesetz des Nächstenliebe nicht nur in Worten bestehen machen, sondern durch ihre Vorkehrung werktätiger, als andere Nationen und wir Deutschen bisher getan haben (pp. 141–42).

novel administrative organization extend and create its own realm of action? My preference, in line with the argument I have been developing, is to say that the political elite set directions and goals and then endeavored to devise the proper apparatus for their implementation. This is demonstrated in part by the administrators' resort to constituted bodies (*corps constitués,* in the sense of French ancien régime practice and legal theory) to assist them in administering the innovations. This also largely explains the ambivalent nature of the well-ordered police state, the gradual growth of conservative features that complemented its radical goals and intentions. It is, however, also fair to point out that administrative functions released immanent forces and trends that acquired a dynamic of their own. In this way administration, in the form of laws and regulations, became one of the vast impersonal forces moving within society that set limits to the freedom of action and choice of subsequent generations.

To begin with, we should take note of a few theoretical notions about government that usually found expression in the ordinances. Paradoxically, perhaps, we note a contradiction at first glance: on the one hand, as we have had occasion to observe, the ordinances promote a discrete approach, which stressed the desirability of specialization and the separation of functions. Yet on the other hand, in their preambles and theoretical justifications the ordinances put forth the notion of a body politic conceived of as a single organism and described in terms of organismic images. True, now and then there occur phrases conveying a mechanistic conception, but usually these were concerned with the performance of a specific operation, not with the relationship between the polity and a social or administrative function within it. The ordinances addressed specific problems in a *body* politic, but like doctors they tried to cure and repair individual functions in terms of the total health and well-being of the organism. Such an approach focused on the separate organic functions while stressing their strong organic ties. In this way, too, it provided a rational justification for preserving the traditional hierarchies of functional roles, that is, a stratification based on "orders" (or estates) with specifically assigned tasks in society. This may seem to be in contradiction to the individual productive thrust of the ordinances analyzed earlier. We shall return to this problem in section 8.

Naturally, the point of departure of all administrative action, even the most interventionist and rationally constructivist, was the existing structure of society. The starting point was the medieval type of society that still prevailed and that was not going to be fully eliminated until much later, thanks largely to the effects of the ordinances. In view of the lingering notion of a limited universe, the determinant conception of social structure was that of basic harmony or, if one prefers, of a balance between the various orders, strata, and groups of society and of maintaining that balance among the activities of the various productive groups of society. Innovations, it was realized both intellectually and out of practical necessity, had to be based on tradition ("Erneuerung ist selektive Tradition"). Existing social structures had to be used and the balance among them maintained lest the whole system break apart in chaos. The violence and anarchic troubles that ensued from the religious crisis in the sixteenth century had been enough of a warning to avoid its recurrence in other areas.[202] The medieval notion of a harmonious whole to which every class and estate made its contribution was preserved in principle, while its workings were adapted to new purposes.

The contradictory character of the ordinances arose from the fact that their stress on the productive individual and on new standards of efficiency and productivity went counter to the notion of a harmonious socioeconomic organism. But it was precisely this contradiction (which in all fairness, could not have been as apparent to contemporaries as it is to us who know the outcome) that justified the issuing of ordinances by authority of the sovereign power and validated legislating and intervening in the domains of social and economic life. Since the separate orders and estates had different functions, someone had to harmonize and coordinate them.[203] In the absence of the modern view of a mechancial harmony and automatic balance of the forces of

202. From Wolfenbüttel, *Des . . . Herrn Augusti . . . Canzlei Ordnung* (1651); Bergius, *Sammlung*, 4:183–86 (Braunschweig 22.XI.1768); *Des . . . Herrn Augusti . . . HofgerichtOrdnung—Tax Ordnung*, p. 351; *Fürstlich Anhaltische Process-Ordnung* (1666), p. 61; Mylius, 5(2):7.

203. This is different from the notion of the ruler's sovereignty and absolute

nature, a view which an age that viewed God as the creator and
harmonizer of the universe and that still accepted the possibility
of His direct intervention could not bring itself to embrace, a
sovereign artificer was needed. The sovereign used laws to
maintain balance and to protect individual group interests, so that
each institution and estate played its assigned role in the polity;
in short, the body politic had to be headed by an absolute sovereign (monarch or republican government), albeit an enlightened
one.[204]

There was another explicit justification for the ordinances that
was related to the notion of an organic body politic, namely the
idea that the ruler and legislator existed to promote the *gemeine
Beste,* the common good. Of course, we have here, on the whole, a
negative notion of government. It could be interpreted, as it had
been over the centuries, in the sense that the ruler's and legislator's function was merely to preserve law and to secure order and
justice. Yet the concept of the common good also contained a
dynamic, positive, action-laden element. Indeed the *Beste* is not a
given quality, as *Gute* (good) or *Wohl* (weal) would be, but rather a
hypothetical superlative state to be pursued; it implied a goal to
be worked for and eventually to be attained. To attain it clearly
required a striving and consequently a movement with the
implications of progress and possible realization of the desired
state of things in the future.[205] But for such a movement to be
"safe," it had to proceed under the supervision and control of the

power, as well as from the ruler's traditional role of protector and justicer of the
commonwealth. *Pfaltz Landesordnung* (1599), p. 22; *Hohenlohe gemeinsame Landrecht*
(1738), introduction and pp. 189ff.; Bergius, *Sammlung,* 4:211–14 (Hessen Darmstadt 1.XI.1750, establishing Öconomie Deputation) and ibid., 6:123 (Schleswig
Holstein Policey Ordnung 29.I.1768).

204. O. Brunner, "Das ganze Haus und die alteuropäische Ökonomik," *Neue
Wege der Verfassungs- und Sozial-geschichte* (Göttingen: Vandenhoeck & Ruprecht,
1968), points out the classical, Aristotelian origins of this political theory.

205. Admittedly, this is my own reading of the phrase "gemeine Beste," to
contrast it with "gemeiner Nutzen," "gemeines Gut" or "Wohl," and "gemein
Wesen." But *Grimms Deutsche Wörterbuch* (s.v.) justifies my interpretation as one of
the secondary meanings of *Beste.* Contrast to *Pfaltz Landesordnung* (Amberg: 1599),
p. 166, stressing the personal element, and *Mecklenburg Ordnung* (1562), under-
scoring material benefits. The 1590 *Ritter Raths . . . Fränckischen Craises . . .
Satzungen und Ordnungen* refer to *salus populi* (p. 11). See also *Des . . . Herrn Augusti
. . . Tax Ordnung* (1645), introduction.

authorities. This is where the role of administrator and administration came in: they represented the means of striving for the
gemeine Beste, and they made explicit the goal—the best and
most effective opening up of productive potentials that would
result in the whole community's enjoyment of the fruits of
creative labor. In the process, the authorities were to provide the
necessary external security and the social peace and order to
serve as the most suitable framework for these efforts.

For a similar reason, the ordinances of the period under study
may be viewed in the perspective of the development of modern
law. This was the case not only in the obvious sense that the
ordinances constituted law for many domains of the territories'
public and social life. The ordinances also promoted, disseminat-
ed, and consolidated the new fundamental notion that positive
prescriptive laws were required to regulate the activities of the
polity's members, a function of law that went beyond the traditional concept of equitable (*sui cuique tribuere*) settlement of
conflicts and grievances. Such a conception of law, which became
basic to the West, enabled legislation to play its eminently constructivist role as a connective link in men's relationships to things
and fellow men. It should be noted, however, that this new
orientation in law followed in the voluntaristic spirit and heritage
of scholastic nominalist positivism. In fact, positive law as embodied in ordinances tended to blur the distinction between law
and administrative regulation: the ordinances served to make
acceptable as well as familiar the notion that positive law was an
expression of human will to administer things and men, to shape
their relationships—in brief, to shape society's attitudes toward
economic and sociocultural activity. The blurring of the hierarchical relationship among law, custom, and regulations may have
proven to be unfortunate in the long run, but it was an almost
inescapable by-product of the positive, voluntaristic role of leadership assumed by the territorial authorities in seeking and
promoting the gemeine Beste.[206]

206. Cf. Michel Villey, *La Formation de la pensée juridique moderne* (Paris: Editions
Montchrestien, 1968); *Leçons d'histoire de la philosophie du droit* (Paris: Dalloz, 1962)
and H. Coing, ed., *Handbuch der Quellen und Literatur der neueren europäischen
Privatrechtsgeschichte* (Munich: C. H. Beck, 1973–). Also the stimulating Carl

Similar motivations and developments set the stage for the appearance, rapid expansion, and significance of codifications. The work of codification was not only the result of long-felt needs; it also was initiated by ordinance as a deliberate administrative practice. Indeed, if laws were to play the regulatory and shaping role we have just mentioned, they had to be clear, readily available, and well known by all concerned.[207] Such a role could not be played by customs transmitted orally or by mere compilation of such customs; only the systematization of their norms and the imposition of verbal and conceptual uniformity would endow laws with an immanent force for growth and for application to new situations. By giving a rigid form and a coherent organization to basic juridical norms and concepts, the codes provided the judges and administrators with tools for numerous practical variations to fit novel and unforeseen circumstances. In this way codification imparted an inherent dynamic to jurisprudence and turned law into a particularly convenient instrument for shaping and changing economies and cultures. The codification of laws and ordinances thus marked the culminating effort of the well-ordered police state, for it faithfully "codified" the immanent features released by the new production-oriented cultural attitudes and norms.

In the codification of positive law, Western societies found an instrument that enabled them to maintain an evolutionary impetus and a dynamic within a normative and formal framework that assured a degree of stability and order.[208] Whether such a result

---

Schmitt, *Der Nomos der Erde, im Völkerrecht des Jus Publicum Europaeum* (Berlin: Duncker & Humblot, 1950).

207. Mylius, *Corpus . . . Magdeburgicarum*, introduction, 1:a-a$_2$.

208. Calenberg 1739, introduction (no pagination). Cf. F. Wieacker, "Aufstieg, Blüte und Krise der Kodifikationsidee," in *Festschrift für G. Boehmer* (Bonn: Ludwig Röhrscheid Verlag, 1954), pp. 34–50. The promulgation of the Code Civil may be considered the highest achievement of Napoleon's rule, which was a delayed manifestation of the well-ordered police state in France. Naturally, the delay itself became a formative factor in subsequent developments. This was even more the case in Russia, where codification was delayed until the 1830s (and where the law never obtained the final form of a genuine code), although many of the practices of the well-ordered police state had been introduced in the eighteenth century (cf. pt. 3).

would be automatically achieved by mechanically applying the letter of the law or whether one had to bring to bear individual reason and will in interpreting the law were questions that gave rise to much disagreement and dispute among contemporaries. But the fact that the argument could arise at all indicated that the notion of the autonomous working of law as a factor of change and progress had become accepted and internalized by the mid-eighteenth century.[209] Indeed the very notion of progress as *natural*—that is, as the manifestation of Natural Law or of the laws of nature over which man had significant but limited control—was directly connected with this new conception of the role of law and codification.

The institutional framework that the ordinances assumed or established had a concrete and almost immediate impact. Quite naturally, as stated earlier, the ordinances relied on a central power as the source of their legislative authority, although it should be pointed out that centralization did not necessarily mean that a central institution had in fact an exclusive monopoly on the exercise of power. It meant rather that there was but a single source of sovereignty, dictated by the needs of guiding and harmonizing public life; this did not prevent multiple, at times overlapping, jurisdicitons and authorities, both local and functional. The crucial aspect of the institutional situation we are dealing with was singleness of sovereign authority that enabled it to initiate progressive legislation that endeavored to encompass and transmit similar *dirigiste* purposes to all local and functional institutions. One should, it seems to me, speak not of a concentration of the ruler's power but rather of a reaching out of the chanceries' authority to every administrative and local institution. In the long run authority and responsibility were to become monocratic on all levels rather than dispersed, but in our period this was only a trend that the ordinances had just inaugurated.

In any event, whatever the form and status of the political unit it was viewed as a single entity, an organic whole to be dealt with

209. *Fürstliche Privilegia . . . der Heinrich Stadt* (1602), §7, and John P. Dawson, *The Oracles of the Law* (Westport, Conn.: Greenwood Press, 1978; repr. from University of Michigan Press, 1968) for best discussion of history of question in comparative European perspective.

in toto for the sake of the gemeine Beste, with an emphasis on *gemeine*, meaning the whole community, the commonwealth. It enabled the central directing authority to select and emphasize particular areas for special attention, not so much in response to private needs, interests, and prejudices as in an effort to push forward the whole polity. Gone was the traditional view that a new territorial or social component remained an autonomous, separate entity within a more or less loose federation of distinct possessions assembled by the accidents of inheritance and dynastic policy. For example, Frederick II's policy with respect to Silesia pointed the way to be pursued by multiregional and multiethnic empires, such as the Russian, with the ideological assistance of the developmental philosophy of history and culture provided by the Enlightenment.[210]

Another facet of the new political culture was its repeatedly stressed belief that the central political authority, be it the ruler or an institution, had to assume the guiding role in loco parentis. In this instance the organic image of the body social was transformed into an idealization of the relationship between a father and his children, as graphically illustrated by the term *Landesvater* applied to the ruler.[211] It was suggested that the people (especially the productive and also the less sophisticated and less well-educated individuals) had to be guided and raised—schooled and disciplined—for their future role as builders of material and sociocultural progress. As parents saw to it that their children were trained to participate most fully and effectively in society, so the sovereign power guided and educated society as a whole, in particular its "younger" and less developed classes, for the sake of a dynamic modernizing polity. Local institutions, authorities,

210. See in particular the legislation of Frederick II with respect to Silesia after its conquest. Bergius, *Sammlung*, 3:21–25 (24.XI.1765); pp. 26–27 (Circular, n.d.); 50 (22.II.1765); 443–44 (Circular 16.X.1765, with admittedly wider implications); ibid., 7:309–30 (6.XII.1764, re Spinnschulen).

211. *Hohenlohe gemeinsames Landtrecht* (1738), introduction; *Des . . . Herrn Augusti . . . Schul Ordnung* (1651), p. 1; Bergius, *Sammlung*, 2:347–57 (Baden Durlach Müller Ordnung 5.I.1714, p. 357). Examples of use of the term *Landesvater* (and its derivatives) are too numerous to cite, although Mylius' compendium suggests that they become much rarer in Prussia under Frederick II (Mylius, V-3, p. 12).

solidarities, and cooperative bonds would be co-opted to the degree that the central power first succeeded in attaining its own purpose. Wherever local historical ties, *Bindungen*, were able to offer resistance in defense of traditionally conceived selfish interests, they had to be broken. This was the most important factor in the struggle between princes and estates (*Fürsten und Stände*) which has dominated the traditional political historiography of the period.

The concentration of legislative authority could not be effective without adequate instruments for its implementation. Given the technological limitations of the time, the central administration *sensu strictu* was unable to take effective care of everything and never really expected to; of necessity its instruments had to be local, regional, and estate institutions. It sufficed that the central power held the initiative and coordinated the performance, which enabled it to set the overall direction of the dynamic development. The central sovereign authority also endeavored to impose its own modus operandi locally, so as to make possible a uniform and efficient participation of local institutions without their becoming a threat. It is perfectly true that the main assault of the central institutions seemed directed at regional "formations," usually based on traditional estates and their privileged positions. As Dietrich Gerhard has well shown, the estates continued to play a significant role locally, even when it looked as if absolutism had triumphed.[212] One of the reasons for the continued influence of the estates—and it is a warning against overstating the role of the nobility—was the fact that already-constituted bodies could be co-opted easily for the new policies. Thus alongside the erosion of some regional estate structures we observe the preservation, although with a changed policy focus and source of authority, of many traditional bodies and institutions (such as guilds and corporations) that now undertook the task of implementing the ordinances and legislation issuing from the capital.

In the urban framework, the coopting of existing institutions proved relatively easy, since in the German territories the ruler's residence was normally in smaller towns, which facilitated interac-

212. Cf. D. Gerhard, *Alte und neue Welt* (Göttingen: Vandenhoeck & Ruprecht, 1962), and also his *Ständische Vertretung*, as well as G. Oestreich in Gebhardt's *Handbuch*.

tion between officials and the elites of constituted bodies.[213] Also, the task of supervising those who had been so recruited was, of course, much easier. Local administrative talent was co-opted to implement the ordinances dealing with guilds and crafts, as well as with most economic matters. The usual pattern was to entrust the enforcement and supervision of the ordinances to the bodies most immediately affected. There were also instances when the elites of such constituted bodies and interest groups were actually lured into becoming part of the official administrative machinery of the territory.[214] In Protestant states the church settlements provided perhaps an unconscious but most convenient model: under the supervision of an official or someone nominated by the sovereign, a body composed of pastors and their assistants was put in charge of church matters.[215] Thus affairs pertaining to schools and the administration of poor laws could easily be delegated to similar bodies, and medical boards set up in the second half of the seventeenth and in the eighteenth centuries followed the same pattern. Economic matters, such as supervision of markets, weights and measures, and the collection of duties and tolls, could similarly be delegated to members of the guilds and corporations concerned, under the supervision of the ruler's officials.[216] How much corruption could and did take place under the circumstances is a question that should be posed but need not be resolved here. We do know from some legislation of cases of illegal collusion; on the other hand, it is also evident that the partnership often worked for the general benefit of the polity.[217]

213. Note, however, the caveat of Mack Walker, *The German Home Towns: Community, State and General Estate, 1648–1871* (Ithaca, N.Y.: Cornell University Press, 1971). *Augusti Hofgerichts Ordnung* (1663), pp. 567, 781; Mylius, *Corpus . . . Magdeburgicarum,* 3:73ff.; *LandsOrdnung . . . Tirol* (1573), p. 2.

214. *Magdeburgische Ordnungen* (1673), Policey Ordnung, 1652, pp. 490, 493ff.; *Fürstliche Privilegia . . . der Heinrich Stadt* (1602), §7; Bergius, *Sammlung,* 5:223–30 (Policei Ordnung Giessen, 15.III.1776, with reference to that of Marburg); Patent . . . die Juridiction in Policey Sachen Berlin 16.VII.1735, especially §23; Mylius, 4(2):297.

215. Bergius, *Sammlung,* 6:132 (Schleswig Holstein Post Ordnung, 29.I.1768) and references in sections 2, 5–6 above.

216. Cf. section 5.

217. On government corruption in premodern societies, see van Klaveren, "Die historische Erscheinung der Korruption . . . ," *Vierteljahrschrift für Sozial- und*

Since each facet of town administration was better taken care of by specialized professionals, whether officials or members of a particular economic and social enterprise, greater compartmentalization of administrative life resulted. In the urban setting, therefore, professionalization of administration went hand in glove with growing stress on technical expertise, although the line separating the areas of communal and state concerns was not always sharply drawn; it tended to blur in favor of technical efficiency as regulated by the central state establishment.

The situation was somewhat different in the countryside and in the villages. There was a dearth of proficient officials who would reside or could be ordered to reside in the villages; at the same time, local society was less structured, with fewer constituted bodies and less specialized expertise available for co-optation. In some areas, however, the task was not impossible and, mutatis mutandis, an arrangement not much different from the urban solution could be made. For example, in the case of forestry the foresters and rangers were supplemented by local inhabitants to enforce the ordinances more effectively locally, exercising the sovereign's authority by delegation.[218] In simplified manner a situation like that in towns could be brought about for country churches and schools, since the local minister could play a role similar to that of his urban confrere. Finally, for the supervision of markets and taverns, the upkeep of roads, and the establishment and manning of barriers and enclosures, the population itself had to furnish the necessary manpower, usually under the supervision of the appointed or elected mayor or *Schultheiss* (or whatever the local title).[219]

There was still another manpower resource available in the rural setting, although its success and effectiveness depended

---

Wirtschaftsgeschichte 44 (1957):289–324; Freyberg, 2:368 (1616); Wolfenbüttel, 20.III.1742. Calenberg 1739, 2:670–72 (10.I.1636) and 676–78 (15.IV.1705) punish dishonesty of officials, but note the (traditional?) religious sanction of disinterment if the crime was found out after death of the culprit. Ibid., 4(5):47–49 (confirmation of Amts Ordnung 18.V.1683).

218. Bergius, *Sammlung*, 5:259ff. (8.IX.1777 Gebirgsforst Commission); 7:207ff. (Bauer. Hofcammerverordnung 1779).

219. Wolfenbüttel, 22.X.1688; *Des . . . Herrn Augusti . . . Landes Ordnung* (1647), p. 12; Bergius, *Sammlung*, 6:132ff. (Schleswig Holstein PO 29.I.1768).

very much on the degree of organization and structured control
that the central authorities could bring about. This resource was
the landowning nobility. In territories where the control of the
sovereign was firmest and those where the policies embodied in
the ordinances were pursued with the greatest consistency and
esprit de suite, this local elite was drawn upon on the basis of its
traditional role. Such a co-optation usually worked well from the
point of view of the well-ordered police state, for it secured the
services of a personnel that had a tradition of leadership and
command, that presumably was accepted by the local population,
and that could safeguard the interests of the region by adapting
policies ordered from above to the special circumstances of the
locality. It also guaranteed the preservation of the social balance
or of the hierarchical pyramid—a major requirement for effectively implementing the ordinances, as we have seen. The "ideal
type" (in the Weberian, value-free sense of the term) of this kind
of arrangement was Prussia, with its noble *Landrat.*

In order to bring village communities under the umbrella of a
well-ordered administration *(gute Polizey),* a structuring of rural
activities along functional lines had to take the place of traditional
regional structuring. The village had to be organized in such a
way as to enhance its productive potential and to encourage its
population to strive for progress. In the pursuit of this aim a
number of general police ordinances for the village were drafted
in the late seventeenth and early eighteenth centuries. Most of
them remained in the stage of plans and projects; only a few were
implemented. Their very existence is evidence of the similarity of
goals set for both villages and towns, but in the country the
difficulties facing their implementation proved to be nearly
insuperable. It is not surprising that these ordinances were a mix
of didactic economic precepts and institutional arrangements, the
latter serving to promote the former. They serve to illustrate
graphically the notion held by the well-ordered police state that
an enlightened evolution could be sponsored and guided, as
reflected in their highly paternalistic tone when they addressed
the peasantry, and their circumscribed pragmatism.[220]

---

220. Cf. sec. 4, above. See also model Dorfordnung in B. von Rohr, *Compendieuse Havshaltungsbibliothek* (1716).

In spite of the varied, complex, but on the whole pragmatic arrangements on the institutional level, the imposition of new administrative techniques on all facets of life resulted in basically uniform patterns. First came the realization that an administration aiming at guiding and leading in the transformation of society could not do so without comprehensive and accurate information. Such awareness brought about consistent efforts to secure complete and coherent data on all the activities of concern to the legislator. It was discovered that the desired statistical data were best gathered by imposing uniform rules and standards for their collection and organization.[221] In our period, therefore, the gathering of data was much expanded, and greater reliance was placed on it when drafting ordinances and general legislation. To ensure the usefulness of the data collected, standard questionnaires, forms, and units of measurements were devised and introduced. Uniform formularies and forms came into widespread use, and as a result administrative operations became more bureaucratized and routinized.[222] Such statistical inquiries, however clumsy and primitive their techniques in comparison to later developments, enhanced the effectiveness of legislation and permitted the taking of long-range views in developing plans for the future. Standardization and increasing routinization of administrative action, however, could not but affect the character of the personnel of government and their recruitment and training.

It should cause no surprise to learn that this personnel was being transformed into an incipient bureaucracy. Yet in our period it would be more accurate to speak not of a bureaucracy but of an officialdom, since *bureaucracy* carries connotations that

221. "Hessische Verordnung die Städtischen Cämmereyen betreffend" (1.III.1695, Cassel Verordnung re accounting instructions) confirmed 2.X.1745 (role of elites in audit procedure). Wolfenbüttel, 8.VIII.1700, Sept. 1705 (sample of forms); Calenberg 1739, 1:449, 451ff. (Monita generalia 26.VIII.1727) and 4:26–30 (Erneuerte Amts Ordnung 1674, §§14–18).

222. This was also a source of revenue, because of the required use of stamped paper. For example, *Varia Ordnungen* (Prussian Renoviertes Edict . . . 22.IV.1722); Wolfenbüttel Nov. 1692, standard, regular forms for tax payments; ibid., n.d. (ca. 1705), formularies for accounting of grain and payments through local authorities; ibid., 20.VI.1726, standard forms for periodic reports; Mylius, *Corpus . . . Magdeburgicarum* (Process Ordnung 1686).

did not appear before Napoleonic institutions and "mass society." In the late seventeenth and early eighteenth centuries, professionalization only made its beginnings; the *cursus honorum* and operating procedures were not yet rigid and fully rationalized. Essentially we are dealing with the creation of a group of officials who could administer in a more or less structured, uniform, and hierarchical manner. To this end, ordinances aimed at developing the very practices we have come to associate with rational management and efficient administration. It was a matter of breaking down customary forms and traditions that had not recognized a separation between the public and the private domains; that had not kept administration apart from justice; that because of a reliance on personal and family ties, had not seen administrators as being sharply distinct from those they administered; and that had not organized the tasks and timing of public affairs in a methodical, rational fashion.

An evolution toward the development of these practices can be followed in collections of ordinances like that of Mylius for Brandenburg. The increasing functional differentiation of the administration led first to a clearer discrimination between judiciary and administrative (executive) matters. The earlier *Hofgerichts-ordnungen* had included administrative matters as well as judiciary ones.[223] Later the Hofgerichtsordnungen were concerned exclusively with judicial procedure, while *Kammer-* and *Process-ordnungen* dealt with chancery and office routines. The establishment of various functional councils and bodies within or under supervision of the ruler's own chancery were further instances of this evolution.[224] Furthermore, from the middle seventeenth century on ordinances aimed at reorganizing the ruler's chancery

---

223. Magdeburg Process Ordnung 1686. Mylius, *Corpus . . . Magdeburgicarum,* 2:1–96; *Des . . . Herrn Augusti . . . Canzlei Ordnung* (1651) and *. . . Hofgericht Ordnung* (1663).

224. Cf. O. Hintze, studies in his *Gesammelte Abhandlungen,* edited by G. Oestreich, vol. 1 (Göttingen: Vandenhoeck & Ruprecht, 1962); vol. 2 (Göttingen: Vandenhoeck & Ruprecht, 1967). The separation of the administration from the judiciary was explicitly stated for France in the "Édit portant sur la création d'un Lieutenant de Police de Paris" (Oct. 1699) in Isambert, *Recueil général* (Paris: 1829), edict 501, 18:100–02.

by isolating its activities from the public and the daily life of the subjects and by endowing its officials with some of the arcane prestige of the sovereign. In more concrete terms, the new chancery procedures prevented direct contact between adminis-'trative personnel and the public, whether in judicial or purely administrative matters. In the course of our period procedures became exclusively written, oral and verbal communications playing a dramatically decreasing role. By excluding direct contact between subjects and officials, these procedures enhanced the role of lawyers and solicitors who could handle the required written communications. The physical separation between governed and governors was underscored by regulations that set aside separate rooms for the transaction of business, rooms that were accessible only to staff. The latter were forbidden to take papers home or to collect opinions of council members at their homes, and the like.[225] Other ordinances provided the conditions and facilities to enable officials to work in peace and keep records and papers in good and secure order. Administrative work was moved to special rooms with appropriate furniture, and secret and privileged matters were separated from public business; an efficient, routine work pattern was set up, and regular hours, compulsory attendance, and standard operating procedures for every transaction were imposed on all.[226] We may smile at the

225. The traditional conception of the monarch is then desacrilized by providing that all matters be forwarded through bureaucratic channels and by prohibiting direct petitioning of the monarch on an individual basis. Pfaltz 1599, p. 171; *Magdeburgische Ordnungen* (1673), Process Ordnung 1652, p. 873; "[Hessische] Ordnung die Rechtssachen bei den Ämtern . . ." 29.III/9.IV.1732; *Sammlung Anhalt-Dessau*, no. 103, 24.X.1780 and *Fürstlich Anhaltische Landes- und Process-Ordnung* (1777), p. 106; Bergius, *Sammlung*, 3 (15.XI.1765, only sworn personnel allowed to process administrative and judicial matters); 4:91–96 (10.II.1775 Hessen Cassel); ibid., p. 186 (Braunschweig Verordnung 22.XI.1768); Mylius, 2(1):45, 63, 103, 219, 357, 563; Mylius, *Corpus . . . Magdeburgicarum* (Process Ordnung 1686).

226. Also the requirement of written procedure and going through channels, which yielded additional income in fees paid to central authorities. *Magdeburgische Ordnungen* (1673), ordinance of 1570; *Halberstadtische Canzley Ordnung* (1652), p. 22; *Sammlung Anhalt-Dessau*, no. 6 (6.VIII.1710, fees for civil and criminal procedures) and no. 42 (26.IV.1765, increasing weekly sessions); "Hessische Gerichts Ordnungen," 1497–1735, especially that of 1733 re increase in litigations;

pettiness and triviality of these ordinances which included such minutiae as prescribing the number of inkwells and the proper way of taking care of them. But in fact they offer graphic illustration of the sustained efforts at creating a bureaucratic ambience and style of work.[227] In central Europe such pedantic prescriptions disappeared with the eighteenth century; we may assume that a bureaucratic apparatus was in place by then.

The physical separation between administrators and administered reinforced the feeling of separation between the sovereign authority and the population. The rulers isolated themselves more and more from the nation by retiring to suburban residences and also through an elaborate court ceremonial and etiquette, of which the court at Versailles was the ultimate expression as well as a model for many Germany sovereigns. While such isolation might enhance the aura and prestige of the ruler as an individual, who might be graphically represented in the guise of a "god in uniform" in statues and portraits, it also served to give concrete form to the concept of the state. The state, of course, was (and remains) an abstraction, but this abstraction received body and meaning from the fact that administrators spoke in the name of rulers who were remote from their subjects, practically invisible, except when they appeared in the awe-inspiring surroundings of court ceremonials. Along with the positively active administration and directive officials there also developed the notion of the state as a guiding power and disciplining force, personified by rulers remote in the majesty of their rare and well-staged public appearances.[228]

It was difficult to transfer the personal charisma attaching to the ruler or hereditary elite to an official who did not come from an exalted family and who in the past may even have been a lowly

---

Policey Ordnung Nürnberg (1672), p. 22; Wolfenbüttel, 18.V.1714, 20.V.1718, 2.III.1737; Calenberg 1739, 2:607 (10.I.1734); 4:17ff. (Amts Ordnung 1674), 2 (19.X.1719).

227. *Sammelband . . . Wolfenbüttel* (Canzlei Ordnung 1651 gives detailed schedule). Calenberg 1739 (Oberappell Gerichts Ordnung 1712) and p. 202 (17. VII.1716, re access to chambers; similarly 10.I.1734, p. 607).

228. Ernst H. Kantorowicz, "Gods in Uniform," in *Selected Studies* (Locust Valley, N.Y.: J. J. Augustine, 1965), pp. 7–25.

flunkey. The detailed prescriptions for the administrative setting and procedures aimed at generating deference toward officials and their tasks and at securing prestige and respect even for subordinate officials on the grounds of their offices and public functions, rather than their personal status or qualities.

The new bureaucratic procedures had to be consistent and permanent, for they implemented policies designed to bring about long-range transformations. It was essential, therefore, to preserve good records of what was being done and keep in readiness the information on which the policies were based. Good archival organization for the safekeeping of official documents was required, which led to the setting aside of a place where the physical preservation of the records could be assured and access to them limited. It further necessitated rational classification and organization of the documents, so that they could be easily retrieved when needed. A well-functioning archive assured permanent availability of basic regulations and laws and in so doing provided security and protection to both officials and subjects. Most important of all, the existence of accessibility of the body of legislative sources created a sense of ongoing purposefulness and stability that were more or less impervious to the caprices and vagaries of individual officials.[229] An almost autonomous, inherent control mechanism had thus been introduced into the administration, a mechanism that was reinforced by the compilation and drafting of codes based on the legislative and legal documents preserved in chancery archives.

The need for regularity, routinization, and uniformity affected the very form of the documents. Papers, questionnaires, and records were standardized and simplified, especially with respect to titles and preambles. While the didactic intent continued to find expression in form and style, the references to old times and

229. *Würtemberg allerhand Ordnungen* (1670) (Hofgerichts Ordnung 1654, §14); *Quedlingburgische Constitution* (Quedlingburg: 1634); Bergius, *Sammlung,* 7:109–26 (Bayerische Oberlandesregierung Instruction 1779, p. 123, re archives—most comprehensive, though of late date); Calenberg 1739, 3 (Amts Ordnung 1674); Braunschweig Canzlei Ordnung 1651, introduction, pp. 2, 16, 78; *Holstein Hofgerichts—Ordnung* (1640), pp. 8–9, 47.

traditions became briefer and on occasion disappeared altogether.[230] The officials had to become familiar with the established formulations, and proper mastery of language and of
its use was an essential prerequisite. German now claimed its right
as the language of direct and didactic communication with those
to be administered, thus superseding Latin, which had been used
for the preservation of traditional formulae and symbols. The
teaching and learning of good and comprehensible German was
stressed in all school and chancery directives, and the new
requirement found its clearest expression in the publication of
numerous manuals for secretaries and for letter writing. Finally,
in the eighteenth century, special chancery schools were established and textbooks on chancery procedure published—
compelling evidence that the routinization of the administrative
and political life of the German territories had been completed.[231]

These changes also were reflected in a changed order of
priorities: in the eighteenth-century ordinances secular, material
concerns were taking precedence over religious and moral ones,
as is easily noted by looking at the table of contents of compendia,
codes, and general Landesordnungen. Finally, regular and uniform methods of publication and dissemination of legislative acts
were adopted: separate ordinances were printed in greater quantity and given wider distribution than in earlier times, and a
standard, handy format made collecting and storing them for
later reference much easier.[232] It may be noted in passing,
however, that the wide distribution of ordinances resulted in their
being treated as ephemera, so that complete collections are quite
scarce, to be found only in a few depositories and libraries. The

---

230. *Halberstadtische Cantzley Ordnung* (1617), preamble; Wolfenbüttel, *Augusti
Canzlei Ordnung* (1651), p. 23; *Allgemeine Verordnung des Lüneburgischen Zucht- und
Werck-hauses* (1702), didactic argument; also *Hohenlohe gemein sames Landrecht*
(1738), introduction.

231. Cf. manuals on *Secretarial Kunst* by Spaeth, Moser.

232. *Magdeburgische Ordnungen* (1673), Policey Ordnung 1652; *Rhein Policey
Ordnung* (1579) (under Pfalz); *Policey Ordnung Nürnberg* (1672). For stark contrast,
see Mecklenburg Landes Ordnung 1572 and Bavarian instruction for Oberlandes
Regierung 1779 (Bergius, *Sammlung*, 8:110ff.).

ordinances were written in uniform language that transcended the boundaries of territorial jurisdictions, thereby initiating a process that strengthened the sense of national belonging, which in turn lent support to the future drive for national unity.

To be effective on any level, an official had to be well prepared and trained for the routines of administrative procedures. Future officials and bureaucrats were subjected to a period of training that definitely had a professional, specialized, and technical content. Naturally the legal profession took the lead in the process, since its subject matter and procedural forms fostered most effectively the required bent of mind and behavior.[233] At first training was essentially an apprenticeship, especially in the case of those who were not rich or lucky enough to obtain the university preparation that was offered in some centers. True, highest status was reserved for those with university experience, mainly because it gave a general cosmopolitan education. But since such an education did not train students in the routine skills of administration, it did not displace the apprenticeship system but rather complemented it; the university graduate, too, was expected to acquire administrative skills in a subaltern position, under the direction of a member of his own family or a patron.

Whether in school or through practice, the future official was expected to develop certain traits deemed as particularly desirable. Most highly valued were those facilities of mind that made for a logical and rational approach to administrative tasks and problems. Much stress, therefore, was laid on training in rhetoric and logic; not only the form but also the concepts of administrative policy were strongly suffused with Ramist and Cartesian norms and logic. Of even greater significance was the neo-Stoic moral thrust that gave pride of place to human will and to voluntaristic active intervention by the ruler and administrator for the sake of a dynamic transformation of society. Neo-Stoic reliance on the active role of human will, guided by a proper understanding of the laws of nature, gave the administration self-

233. *Anhalt Policey und Landes Ordenung* (1572) already complains of the excessive increase in the number of lawyers, etc., taking population away from productive process. Calenberg, 2:214–16, 247ff. (Canzlei Ordnung 1663); *Augusti Hofgerichts Ordnung* (1663), p. 14; *Holstein Hofgerichts-Ordnung* (1640), p. 8; Mylius, *Corpus . . . Magdeburgicarum*, 2:216.

assurance and conviction in selecting and pursuing the right course for the polity.

Another aspect of greater bureaucratization was the expansion of the staff of various institutions and the recruiting of new people to implement the policies on the local level. Much has been made of the alleged penetration of the bourgeoisie into the expanded officialdom. There is no denying such a trend, but it is far from being the whole story; more interesting and significant was the co-optation of the old elites, who had easier access to education. This was accomplished primarily by insisting on relatively high levels of education and training. The members of the privileged elites were expected to pursue careers in administration (whether military or civilian); in preparation they had to attend schools and universities, undertake foreign travel, and enter what we would call internships. Because of the emphasis on education, the administration found candidates not only among members of the upper nobility but also among members of the academic estate, which by the twelfth century had become an autonomous group with its own characteristics, interests, and loyalties.[234] The most successful officials from the academic establishment easily moved over into the nobility, as titles, estates, and ranks were conferred upon them and as they acquired the property requisite for their new style of life. In other instances, the success of individuals from local elites who joined the administration would enable their descendants, within a couple of generations, to acquire wealth and landed property, to become part of the academic estate and regular officialdom, and most frequently also to be ennobled.[235] In the process, estate and class origins tended to lose their significance; what mattered was technical preparation, loyalty to the sovereign, and commitment to the new policies of development. Eventually there developed a new public style of life and an official outlook that were the most important

234. Cf. Erich Trunz, "Der deutsche Späthumanismus um 1600 als Standeskultur," *Zeitschrift fur Geschischte der Erziehung und des Unterrichts* 21 (1931):17–53.

235. Wolfenbüttel, Bergfreiheit 1716, 20/30.III.1733 (re appellate court), in Bergius, *Sammlung,* 2:440–42 (Baden Durlach 8.X.1768, office of "Hatschier"); Calenberg 1739 (Oberappellgerichts Ordn. 1712); Mylius, *Corpus . . . Magdeburgicarum* 3:501–2 (re foreign travel) and p. 20 (nobles in "civil service").

prerequisites for membership in the country's administrative, social, and cultural elite. This was perhaps the true meaning of the process that we usually label the "growth and triumph of the centralized modern state."

We may say that this co-optation took place in two forms and on two levels. In a narrow and specific sense, the sovereign admitted or attracted members of the so-called feudal elites, as well as children of other classes and groupings, into the administrative establishment. For members of the former feudal elite, it meant merely adjusting the traditional service role by accepting the new educational requirements. In the case of the members from other groups or classes, it meant transferring their specialized training and know-how to the service of the state. Participation in the life-style and patterns of thought of the administrative elites enabled the former commoner to play an active role in the higher culture of the state establishment, whose basic norms of behavior had an aristocratic origin. This resulted in a basic uniformity of outlook and life-style among administrators that, in the long run, led to the emergence of a distinct class of officials whose coherence as a group stemmed not as much from common social origins as from shared common service values.[236]

It was not a process of democratization, for it did not eliminate from society traditional class distinctions and hierarchies or cultural cleavages, but it did entail a transformation of the basic pattern of institutional and social structures. The traditional nomenclature of feudal estates loses all meaning when applied to a description and interpretation of the transformations ushered in by the territorial Polizeiordnungen. This transformation resulted in increasing the number of class groupings, foreshadowing the emergence of new ones. It is this pattern of social fragmentation that constitutes a major hallmark of modernity. The administrative system of the well-ordered police state was a prime mover in initiating and furthering this development in continental Europe.

---

236. Prussian Patent re Berlin administration, 16.VIII.1735 (Instruction to Policeymeister, §2); *Halberstadtische Canzlei Ordnung* (1652).

8. Conclusion

The nature of the material, and even more the necessity of an analytically clear presentation, may have resulted in the downplaying of chronology and the blurring of the evolution that the police ordinances underwent over a period of more than a century. It is appropriate now to see what trend emerges from the steady stream of ordinances and to try to assess its significance for the development of modern Europe. In fact, we detect a double trend: first an extension in geographic area and in the scope of the ordinances' objectives and second a transformation in approach and attitudes.

In the late sixteenth century the ordinances started out by being mainly concerned with the urban situation, even when their jurisdiction embraced an entire territory or the Empire as a whole (for example, the Imperial Police Ordinance of 1530). They were primarily concerned with problems peculiar to the towns and to their relationship with the surrounding countryside. A graphic though perhaps extreme illustration of this approach may be found in France in the Ordonnance du Roy: it was specifically addressed to Paris but with the proviso that it should be extended to all other towns (*villes*) of the kingdom, the countryside being involved only peripherally and by implication.[237] But as the authority of the political establishment reached out more effectively to the whole country, the ordinances encompassed wider and wider geographic areas. In the seventeenth century most ordinances involved the entire jurisdiction of the ruler, while in the eighteenth century they at times had an almost national character (as in Prussia) or even an imperial one (as in Austria).

In the second place, late sixteenth-century legislation was essentially negative; it prohibited actions and practices deemed harmful, and it did so for a negative reason: its major concern was defensive, to protect the inhabitants and the territory from

237. *Ordonnance du Roy* (1578). Also the classic article of G. von Below, "Die städtische Verwaltung des Mittelalters . . . ," *Historische Zeitschrift* (1895), 75:396–463, and the subsequent discussion culminating, for the time being, in Friedrich Lütge, *Studien zur Sozial- und Wirtschafts-geschichte (Gesammelte Abhandlungen)* (Stuttgart: G. Fischer, 1963).

dangerous elements and threats believed to come always from outside.[238] "Outside," however, referred either literally to "beyond the boundaries of the territory" (for example, foreign countries) or to individuals who were outsiders by definition, such as beggars, vagrants, Jews, Gypsies, and dissidents who had become outsiders by virtue of their beliefs or attitudes—people such as heretics, criminals, and those believed to be sorcerers, witches, and Anabaptists. The ordinances of that period took it for granted that a prince's true subject, a subject who followed the "right" ways and "correct" beliefs, could not be an outsider; thus such a subject could not be an offender against the polity as a whole except accidentally, owing to external pressures that it was the ruler's duty to deal with and for which purpose the country had to furnish the means.

What was perceived most acutely as a threat was an internal problem stemming from subjects who had become alienated from the traditional ways and beliefs, largely because certain traditional institutions (such as the Roman Church) were no longer effectively operating. Under the circumstances, it should cause no surprise that the early ordinances—and in many cases down to the second half of the seventeenth century—made religion their point of departure.[239] They were issued, it was said, to prevent the population from following the ways that had angered the deity, bringing disasters onto society, and they were enforced to compel the population to abide by the tenets of their faith and the behavior it prescribed. Religion, both as a body of beliefs and as a pattern of behavior within an institutional framework, was the primary concern of the early ordinances. It always headed the list of topics covered by the Landesordnungen, and it provided the main justification for the specific rules prescribed by the ordinances. It followed quite naturally and logically from this that the tone of the early ordinances was hortatory and moralizing. They preached, while ordering or threatening punishment in case of disobedience. The note of futility and desperation that strikes the

---

238. For example, *Minden Policey Ordnung* (1613); *LandsOrdnung Tirol* (1573).

239. *Sachsen Policey* (1583), Ordnung 1543 of Moritz von Sachsen; *Des . . . Herrn Augusti . . . Landesordnung* (1647).

twentieth-century ear derived from contemporaries' failure to see in what ways universal ethical norms and the specific religious beliefs that had ceased to be shared by all could be brought together to secure proper modes of social behavior. The moralizing tone suggests an insecurity about the connection between belief and behavior. Subsequent ordinances, especially in the seventeenth century, strove to overcome this sense of insecurity by providing a new intellectual and ideological foundation.

Over the roughly one century and a half we are dealing with, the exclusively urban interests were gradually displaced by new areas of concern. In the first place, ordinances now were more specifically designed for particular functions. They came to deal with major aspects of social, economic, and cultural life that were not geographically circumscribed. Ordinances dealing with trade, education, agriculture, manufacturing, and those regulating institutions and patterns of behavior were no longer necessarily limited to a specific locale. This made for a more comprehensive as well as sophisticated approach to the problems tackled by the ordinances and for a general disregard of the original subjective and religious–moral motivations. In the second place, the ordinances began to be extended to the rural situation, dealing with the problems of the agrarian population and its modes of life. The political concerns and intellectual attitudes of the governing elites were spread to the villages in an effort to bring about uniformity of culture and behavior in the entire country or nation. The end result was to erode the boundaries between town and country with respect to "high culture" and institutional organization.[240]

The originally passive and negative features of the ordinances gave way to positive and constructivist ones. The most striking feature of the ordinance legislation at its peak—that is, in the second half of the seventeenth century and the early decades of the eighteenth—was that it was not content to issue moral injunctions and religious prohibitions, threatening punishment for trespass. Rather, the ordinances proposed concrete and

240. Calenberg 1739, vol. 3 (various ordinances of 1730s, pp. 960ff). Cf. Bauernordnungen, cited above in n. 138.

positive steps to bring about new conditions.[241] They taught, and to that extent they still relied on moral and religious suasion, but they taught not in order to maintain and preserve the old ways; on the contrary, they taught to bring about a new social and institutional framework, to make it possible for new patterns of behavior and new values to be accepted.

Naturally such a new constructivist approach assumed positive action based on will, and it implied goals; it had to be anchored in definite ideas capable of structuring the proposed pattern of behavior coherently and rationally. Significantly, the ordinances of the seventeenth century relied on rationalist principles and arguments, since setting social goals and issuing constructivist legislation involved intrinsically rationalist procedures based on the uniformity and regularities discovered and made explicit by human reason and will.[242] That these tasks were not always accomplished and the goals attained should be no cause for wonder. Quite clearly, goals or tasks set by rationality and imposed by will (whether that of a ruler or a social group) were bound to meet with resistance from traditions, customs, talents, and regional and social differences. For this reason, in the course of the seventeenth century and progressively more so in the eighteenth, in addition to the rationalism and voluntarism that never disappeared, a strong note of pragmatism, or of reliance on the lessons of experience, emerges. This did not imply automatic reliance on what had gone on before, which would have meant merely a return to traditional and customary behavior. It signified, rather, a readjustment of the tactics used to attain goals set for society by reason and will grounded in a coherent view of the universe.[243] It required greater self-confidence, greater flexibility,

241. Contrast for example, "Privilegia, Statuta . . . Heinrich Stadt, 1602" and in Bergius, *Sammlung*, 7:336–38, Heilbronn Verordnung re burials, 10.IV.1783.

242. *Magdeburgische Ordnungen* (1673), Bauer Gesinde . . . Ordnung 6.VII. 1652, p. 647: "Dass alles unter guter Regul hinwieder gebracht und darin beständig erhalten werden möge."

243. Bergius, *Sammlung*, 2 (28.IV.1774, Hessen Cassel ordinance against gambling no longer contains any reference to moral and religious considerations). Ibid., 7:109ff. (Instruction for Oberlandesregierung Bayern, 1779). See Heilbronn burial ordinance cited in n. 241. Calenberg 1739, vol. 1, introduction (no pagination). Also Amthor, *Project der Oeconomia* and May, *Weisheit der Menschen nach der Vernunft*.

and awareness of differences to bring about gradual change and progress. As legislation became more pragmatic, the means began to assume the status of an end in itself. No longer did ordinances aim at expansion only in order to provide the means for a happier existence (though this concern was still present); they aimed rather at modernization for modernity's sake, production for productivity's sake, and "progress," rather than the old transcendent and ethical goals.

In short, the conservative and passive ordinances of the sixteenth century, designed for a world that had witnessed the collapse of its traditional and spiritual framework, helped to turn legislation into a tool for bringing about dynamic modernization as an end in itself.[244] Today the innovative and dynamic features of late seventeenth-century ordinances are obvious, and they were obvious to their authors as well; in the long run the ordinances came to legislate for individual freedom of action and enterprise and in so doing paved the way for the withdrawal of the political establishment from many areas of social and economic life.[245] In a sense the ordinances served to break down the barriers of tradition and custom that had stood in the way of the creativity of individuals and maximum utilization of their productive potential. Paradoxically, though not illogically, the legislation by ordinance of the late eighteenth century turned into self-denying ordinances by the administrative and political establishments of the ancien régime, pointing the road to the "night watchman" state of the nineteenth century. From now on, for most of the nineteenth century in central Europe as well, the political task will again be conceived in a passive and negative manner, but this time not to protect and secure traditions and established values but rather to secure the freedom of action of individual subjects for unending material progress.

244. Compendia that are arranged chronologically, such as Mylius and Freyberg, illustrate the evolution very graphically. One should note that the ordinances with this intellectual thrust antedate the full acceptance and impact of the Enlightenment, though they are based on seventeenth-century rationalism and science.

245. Freyberg, 2:356 (re trade ordinance, 1616); Bergius, *Sammlung*, 4:183ff. (Braunschweig Verordnung 22.XI.1768); Calenberg 1739, 4 (28.III.1716), liberalizing *Abzugsrecht* on the specified model of England).

We may approach the same problem from a different perspective. In the sixteenth century ordinances were predicated on the notion that the ruler was responsible for the people, the subjects, in moral and religious terms. Any failure on the part of the ruler, as well as on that of the subjects, would incur the wrath of God and bring about all kinds of material disasters. The rulers' function was to see to it that the people did not incur God's wrath, which meant that sovereigns had to prevent subjects from violating religious rules and ethical norms; this the rulers could best do by providing for the subjects' security and peace.[246] It was but a short step from this to the notion that the ordinances served primarily the rulers' interest, although still in the sense of expressing a moral responsibility for society. To enable sovereigns to carry out their duties and to enforce God's commands, rulers had to be provided with the necessary material means, and ordinances were issued to secure them. In the seventeenth century, as a result of the disarray brought about by religious strife and the destruction resulting from the Thirty Years War, the idea of the ruler's responsibility before God weakened. With the restoration of peace, the interest of rulers was narrowly interpreted to mean the state's international standing and the sovereigns' own prestige. By extension, this allowed rulers to argue the identity of their own interests with those of the country and society. To repair effectively the damages wrought by war and to lay the ground for further progress, the interests of the country as a whole had to be put uppermost and made the object of legislative action. In this way, by the end of the seventeenth century (whatever the legislator's sincerity and ulterior motives), the interests and welfare of the country, *gemeine Nutz* and *gemeine Beste*, came to motivate the issuing of specific ordinances. The welfare of society rebounded to the glory and might of the rulers, so that both interests were served. Unquestionably, however, the concept of the commonweal reinforced the rational constructivist outlook, since it required taking a global view of society and setting a goal for dynamic furtherance of its progress.[247]

246. Imperial Police ordinances (in Koch, *Sammlung*) of 1530, 1548, for example. Sachsen Ordnung 1583.

247. The various treatises of the seventeenth century cited in the bibliography yield a plethora of illustrations.

Concern for the common good most obviously and most frequently meant concern for increased production of wealth, since wealth, in all forms, provided the best means of securing all other benefits for society.[248] Thereupon the focus of the ordinances automatically shifted to the production of wealth, to productivity *tout court*. Enterprise for productive purposes became an end in itself, but by succeeding in creating conditions and mental attitudes favorable to this end the police legislation abolished its own raison d'être.[249]

This brings us quite naturally to the serious paradoxes that beset the enterprise of the well-ordered police state, paradoxes at which we had occasion to hint in the course of the earlier discussion. In the first place, the most obvious contradiction or ambivalence consisted in the desire, rooted in the experience and awareness of scarcity, to check expenditures, consumption, or display while at the same time encouraging ever-expanding material productivity. In partial recognition of this dilemma, at the end of the seventeenth century the ordinances came to emphasize not so much limiting expenditures and display as husbanding resources for future investment in productive activities. As might be expected, in the long run the ordinances restricting expenditures and display became rarer and rarer, and they disappeared altogether toward the third quarter of the eighteenth century. They were replaced by legislation that assured security for long-range planning and made possible a high time horizon. Conceivably the regulations imposing limits on consumption and display did hamper productivity and development; on the other hand, in an economy of scarcity they brought about enforced savings that were not all fruitless.[250] Only specialized and detailed analysis of economic behavior and development in key areas might yield a balance sheet permitting us to see

248. Instruction for Oberlandesregierung in Bavaria in Bergius, *Sammlung*, 7:109–26.

249. Calenberg 1739, 4 (28.III.1716); Freyberg, 2:163 (14.V.1700) and 166 (1.I.1737), setting forth intention of government to withdraw from certain areas of life. Of course, the treatises and publicistic writings of the eighteenth century (cf. bibliography) also offer many cogent and graphic statements.

250. "Hessische Policey Verordnung Sittlichkeit, Luxus, Spielen und Lotterie betreffend" (1526–1774), e.g., folio 46ff., n.d.

whether, as Adam Smith and the liberal economists of the nineteenth century believed, the restrictive economic legislation of cameralism and mercantilism was indeed a handicap or whether as subsequent economists and planners would argue it helped society to save for investment in future heightened productivity, a saving that would never have come about without the compulsory restraint on spending.

The second area of ambivalence, or even paradox and contradiction, has already been referred to: on the one hand, the police ordinances insisted on social harmony and the stability of prevailing distinctions between classes and orders of society; on the other, they advocated dynamic drive and display of productive entrepreneurial energy on the part of all individuals capable of so doing.[251] The latter aim could be implemented fully only by eliminating traditional notions of permanent and God-ordained social relationships and harmony. The political leadership endeavored to avoid the dilemma by co-opting the members of traditional orders and estates and forcing them to become agents of new purposes and new methods. In this way the traditional elites were to be integrated into the process of modernization of which they eventually, and at any rate in the short run, became the loyal promoters. In the long run, however, the process served to undermine their claims to cultural and political leadership and special privilege. This did not become apparent until the process had gone too far to be reversed, and thus the traditional elites, too, became the victims of the very modernization many of them had eagerly advanced.

In the course of this development, as we have seen, new elites were promoted and secured positions of influence and power. Membership in the new elites was not defined primarily by social origin but rather by professional competence, so that members of both old and new strata could join them. The old elites, as defined by birth and outdated functions, were displaced by professional technicians. The latter reinforced the basic trend toward reliance

251. Hessian ordinance cited in n. 250. "Hessische Verordnungen in Consistorial und Kirchen Sachen" (9.VIII.1651 and May 1660, the latter emphasizing again division of society into estates). Marriage ordinance, *Ernsten Herzogen zu Sachsen Ordnungen . . . Hochzeiten* (Gotha: 1646), stressing class differentiation.

on reason, knowledge of the regularity of the universe, and familiarity with the laws of nature, and they strove for uniformity and consistency in society as well—the very features that had characterized the classical police ordinances from the beginning.

A third ambiguity stemmed from the fact that the ordinances were designed for a self-contained, relatively isolated and limited territorial unit and for a society that it was presumed would be stable. Yet the world they helped into being was an ever-expanding one, full of diverse states in conflict and competition. Surrounded as it was by equally dynamic and enterprising political entities, the single territory could not survive in isolation. The strain between isolationist, protectionist concerns and the urge to take advantage of membership in a broader concert of active players grew increasingly stronger. The stimulation of production often seemed to require protective barriers; on the other hand, ongoing productivity might best be promoted by some sort of division of labor on an international scale. The ordinances, of course, did not resolve the conflict. The policies they inaugurated, especially in their cameralist and later physiocratic forms, tended to stress isolation and self-sufficiency at the risk of forsaking the opportunities offered by international competition. It was a timidity that may have been well advised in some cases; at any rate it clearly reflected earlier views and traditional ways. Only the great technological breakthroughs of the late eighteenth and nineteenth centuries helped to change the isolationist outlook somewhat (and not always successfully at that), and to fault the authors of the ordinances for not seeing the problem and not dealing with it in the liberal nineteenth-century manner is anachronistic.

Finally, in the light of the experience of the last centuries, we are in a position to pinpoint a fundamental contradiction between the means used and the goals aimed at: were not strict direction and control, activization of enterprise by legislative command, and the setting of limits to this activity in order to preserve social harmony and stability in conflict with and in opposition to dynamic expansion? This was the case indeed, but it was not as yet perceived. Only at the end of the eighteenth century did it become clear to many that left to themselves, on their own initiative, members of society would be more productive and that the administrative institutions created by the ordinances of the absolutist state were sufficient to maintain the required social peace and harmony. However, this very awareness was a product of the education that the police ordinances had given the societies of central Europe. The upsetting experience of the French Revolution jolted administrators and elites into a realization of the inherent conflict. Recent historiography on the preconditions of the French Revolution has shown that it was not so much a revolt against paternalism or the desire to strike a balance between social harmony and dynamic production that were at the bottom of the revolutionary ferment; it was rather the unequal distribution of benefits, a sense of diminishing scope for active entrepreneurial engagement, as well as the establishment's inelasticity in accommodating itself to the results it had promoted. The resulting sense of frustration and discontent eventually led to a reaction against the entire social and political system.[252] But this was true only of France, where the well-ordered police state had never taken firm hold; in Prussia and other German states the compromise solution of the well-ordered police state worked tolerably well, preventing a violent, revolutionary upheaval and paving the way for the founding and triumph of a modern capitalist and industrial polity, however one may assess such an outcome in the light of the latter's fate in the twentieth century.

In some measure these ambivalences and paradoxes stemmed from the need to justify the ordinances and policies in terms that had themselves undergone a change over the period of a century and a half. Obviously the justification had to be in terms of what was known and more or less universally accepted by society. That is why the rationale or justifications lagged behind the intellectual and cultural reality that the ordinances aimed at bringing about. Inasmuch as the ordinances turned into positive, constructivist, future-oriented legislation, they could not avoid the discrepancy between traditional justifications and their innovative purposes and goals. The earlier justifications, as we have seen, were

252. Robert Furet, *Penser la révolution française* (Paris: Gallimard, 1978); E. Hinrichs and R. Vierhaus, eds., *Vom Ancien Regime zur französischen Revolution: Forschungen und Perspektiven* (Göttingen: Vandenhoeck & Ruprecht, 1978).

conservative, negative, and primarily moral or religious. The
tension between the traditional rationale and the new mental
outlook later became glaringly apparent and had to be covered
up. This explains the very strong sense of discontinuity and
primitiveness that we experience when we read the early ordinances, with their jumbled organization, contradictory thrusts,
and ad hoc quality.[253] But once it became possible to have
recourse to rational justifications and explanations, the ordinances ceased to display an *écart* between what they wanted to
achieve and the justifications they offered. The rational approach
also made it possible to leave the final result open, allowing for
adjustments and flexibility in implementation, and it became
easier to harness the energy of members of society.[254] Finally,
rational justification admits of only one criterion: absolute rationality or coherence, or something close to it. This allows for
perfectibility, improvement, and development, as well as assessment in terms of a universal and absolute standard.

Implicit though almost never stated in so many words was also
the assumption of human nature's malleability. Change was
justified by the needs and ends of human nature, which entailed
the full development of man's potential (not defined more
specifically) beyond the limits set by scriptural tradition, which
had ceased to be a binding norm. Once this admission was made,
it was easy to claim that human nature was essentially malleable,
that it could be fashioned by will and external circumstances.
Growing awareness of diversity and relativity in human conduct
confirmed the legislators' belief that man could be shaped into a
desirable state, and successes attained in one place or one area
gave encouragement to more sweeping and global efforts at
transforming attitudes and behavior by legislative fiat.[255]

The observations we have made on the trends released and
supported by the police ordinances lead us to quite simple and on
the whole not unexpected conclusions. The evolution of the

253. *Magdeburgische Ordnungen* (1673), Policey Ordnung 1652.
254. Bergius, *Sammlung*, 3:43–44 (21.X.1765); Prussian Postordnung 1712
(Mylius, 4:963–1022).
255. Calenberg 1739, introduction; *Fürstliche . . . Privilegia . . . der Stadt Heinrich*
(1602), §7, where the extension to *Staat* is made explicitly.

ordinances showed clearly that the political and administrative authorities paved the way for what we call the secularization of European society. They put priority on the productive, material aspects of human life and activity and discarded appeal to and sanction by religious, ethical, or metaphysical values. In so doing they promoted judgment and evaluation on the basis of "interest" in the broadest sense—"benefits" ("happiness," in Enlightenment rhetoric) to the ruler, to groups and individuals, to the country as a whole, and even—in its most extreme and utopian expression at the end of the eighteenth century—to mankind in general.[256] The ordinances set themselves the task of educating and developing a new breed of men, of shaping their actions, thoughts, and behavior in such a way as to clear the way for the energetic, productive, "beneficial" individual. They led the effort long before Rousseau and others gave it ideological sanctification. But in so doing, of course, the ordinances also prepared the ground for the great paradox of modern Western society, the paradox that Rousseau so fiercely struggled to resolve, namely that of the relative significance and role of individual freedom and will, on the one hand, and man's obligation to the group or to society, on the other.[257] The ordinances tried to establish an institutional framework that would balance the claims of both men and subjects (or citizens). In their emphasis on the productive, creative side of man's life, however, they paved the way for upsetting the tenuous balance they had hoped to strike by preserving the traditional organic conception of society.

The well-ordered police state helped bring into being for the modern world the antinomy between the claims of individual and group that classical political thought had resolved within the framework of the city state and its civic religion (and which medieval Christendom had downplayed or ignored in favor of a transcendent notion of spiritual harmony). In addition, the conception and practices of the well-ordered police state gave

256. In the eighteenth century, "interest" *(intérêt)* and welfare were given identical status with "happiness" *(bonheur)*. Cf. A. Mauzi, *L'Idée du bonheur dans la littérature et la pensée française au XVIIIe siècle* (Paris: Armand Colin, 1960).

257. The best brief statement of problem is in J. Shklar, *Man and Citizen: A Study of Rousseau's Theory* (Cambridge, England: Cambridge University Press, 1969).

pragmatic illustration of the paradoxical role of the legislator: might not the role assigned to the legislator, the administrator, the ruler, or the elite in shaping the future be in opposition to the full development of the creative personality? And could the full development of the individual occur outside the group and outside a system of traditional and ethical values?[258] One could not have it both ways, yet the well-ordered police state tried to have it so: to preserve the interests of the group, the cohesion of society and the hierarchical structure of the world and at the same time encourage the active, enterprising, unfettered, and creative individual citizen or subject and promote material wealth and progress as well. Perhaps it might have been possible to achieve both goals had the power of the ruler and of the elites remained sanctified by transcendent authority. But this was precisely the Achilles' heel of the system, the point at which the system broke down and ended in failure in its own terms, for it failed to preserve the social, cultural, and political status quo of the ancien régime. For us, *sub specie historiae*, it was not a failure, for it released the energies and the dynamic potential of those individuals who shaped the world we call modern today. This was achieved, we realize today, only at the expense of the destruction of ancient social ties, communal groupings, and loyalties.

258. Cf. L. Krieger, *An Essay on the Theory of Enlightened Despotism* (Chicago: University of Chicago Press, 1975).

PART THREE
The Russian Experience

Eighteenth-century Russia did not know legislative acts compara-
ble in scope, frequency, and comprehensiveness to the Polizei-
and Landes-ordnungen we have considered in the case of the
German states. Yet some of the major notions and practices aimed
at by the police ordinances in Germany found an echo in the
Russian empire. Moreover, following the example set by Peter the
Great, the imperial governments endeavored to import and
acclimatize some of the goals of the *état bien policé* of Western and
central Europe. Due to differences of environment and circumstances, however, these efforts changed the nature and import of
the cameralist theories and practices. It is instructive, both for a
better understanding of the Russian development and for a
firmer grasp of the dynamics implicit in the practice and theory
of the well-ordered police state, to examine the administrative
and legislative activities of the Russians in the eighteenth century.
For reasons that I trust will become clear in the course of our
exposition, our focus will be on the reigns of Peter I (1689–1725)
and Catherine II (1762–1796). There will be no need to duplicate
the approach we have taken in analyzing the German materials.
In the absence of similarly comprehensive acts and coherent
practices in Russia, we shall focus our attention on the broader
issues involved in the attempt to implement cameralism in Russia
and on the relationship of the Russian ordinances to social
structure, issues that, in my view, are the significant aspects of the
Russian experience.

By the second half of the sixteenth century, the Muscovite
culture, society, and political system, in the process of development since the late fifteenth century, had achieved a degree of

coherence and stability. They had been subjected to a most serious crisis that almost destroyed them during the so-called Times of Troubles (from 1598 or 1605 to 1613). But with the accession of Michael Romanov, a reconstruction of the Muscovite polity was undertaken and carried through in the spirit of the late sixteenth century, with some readjustments of course. In 1649 the code of Tsar Alexis *(Ulozhenie)* gave final juridical form to the institutional and idelogical system of Muscovy.

At this point, too, Muscovy entered a period that revealed— increasingly so as the century wore on—the inner disarray and institutional weakening of the patterns defined in the Ulozhenie. The process was quite rapid and reached a critical state after the death of Tsar Fedor in 1682; ultimately the crisis ended in 1696 with the assumption of full personal power by Peter I, who, as is all too well known, proceeded to transform the institutional and cultural face of Muscovite Russia and to fashion the St. Petersburg empire that was to last until 1917. His reign was marked by the introduction of contemporary Western European norms in the political, cultural, and institutional spheres—in short, a conscious taking over of the basic ideas of the well-ordered police state and of mercantilism and an effort to implement them in practice. My purpose is to trace the change of pattern resulting from the attempt to transfer the ideas and practices of central Europe's well-ordered police state to another cultural and socioinstitutional milieu. But first a brief analytical description of the Muscovite polity is in order.

The first thing that strikes the observer of traditional Muscovite political culture is the fusion, almost an identification, of church and state, a fusion that did not, however, prevent the tsar from having the decisive role in all matters public and institutional. The Byzantine formula of a "symphony" between church and state, the fundamentally religious basis of Muscovite civilization, clearly emerges from a perusal of the decrees and acts collected in volume 1 of the *Complete Collection of Laws of the Russian Empire (Polnoe sobranie zakonov rossiiskoi imperii* [hereafter *PSZ*]). The church was present at every function of the state; the state often took the lead in prescribing religious and hieratic actions, while the church (headed by the patriarch), for its part, took the legislative initiative in areas both ecclesiastical and public. Even in as critical and paramount an event as the condemnation of the Patriarch Nikon and of the traditional rites, which led to the emergence of the Old Belief, it is difficult to distinguish between the parts played by the state and by the church. While the state's role was enhanced by the institutional and political repercussions of the religious conflict, this occurred solely on condition that the state enforce the reformed ritual adopted by the church. As a result, many put the cultural and spiritual leadership of both state and church in question, undermining the traditional Muscovite cultural and political consensus based on the harmony between the two. The ideal of a symphony between state and church remained, however, and it would seem that the Muscovite tsar acted the part of the concertmaster.

The hieratic character of Moscow's rulers endowed their authority with an aura of absoluteness that made them autocrats in every sense of the word. Their power was enhanced by the fact that in Byzantine and Eastern tradition it was cloistered from the outside world, manifesting itself publicly only on rare and specified occasions, within the framework of a strictly regulated ceremonial. It thus partook of the magically divine and exacted absolute obedience of all subjects who, in principle, all had the same servile status. More important still, the fusion between the religious and secular spheres meant that Muscovy's sense of identity and its political culture and self-definition rested on an absolute consensus of religious tenets. Outside this consensus there existed only an alien and inimical world: either one was fully integrated into Muscovite political culture and accepted unquestionably all its values and norms, or one was read out of the community and branded an impious traitor (this explains the virulence of the persecution of Old Believers and all dissenters). The wholeness of Muscovite culture and the demand of total acquiescence in its norms resulted in a rigidity and inflexibility that made it difficult for this society to adopt new ways without feeling that it was threatened in its very existence. Arrogant self-righteousness and self-satisfaction combined with a basic insecurity to produce mortal fear of any innovation, especially when coming from outside, as a betrayal and existential threat. For these reasons the new elements that did penetrate into Muscovy were not incorporated in such a way as to play a dynamic and organic role; the innovations remained largely external and ornamental, yet their increase could not but weaken the structure to which they were attached.

It might be noted at this point that the Kremlin court was more open to outside influences (in taste, costume, speech, appearance, and behavior) than is at times realized. Under Tsar Alexis, for example, one can speak of far-reaching Polonization (that is, westernization) of the court—witness the careful and European education he gave his children. But like the ruler, the Kremlin court was isolated from the rest of the country, even from Moscow. It did not dare to display its innovative spirit too openly for fear that it would be misunderstood by the people, branded as unorthodox and treacherous, as it always was during the uprisings that punctuated the political life of the country in the second half of the seventeenth century. The innovations of the courtiers did not strike roots in the society at large and did not play a constructive role in initiating or leading a gradual organic transformation of Muscovite polity and culture.

From an institutional perspective, the political system of Moscow consisted of an autocratic tsar who reigned with the help of his immediate advisors—the members of the *boiar duma* (council)—and a rather limited body of high-ranking servitors and clerks in a number of chanceries (*prikazy*). The basic principle that needs stressing was that the tsar's assistants occupied their positions and played their roles strictly as the ruler's servitors, at his pleasure, not by virtue of any claim to office by birthright or family possession. While it is true that in fact only a small number of families or clans provided most of the members of the Kremlin establishment, this was an outcome of the circumscribed circle of potential candidates and of ad hoc individual appointments. Furthermore, rank, prestige, and rewards were ultimately dependent on service and the tsar's recognition of it (though extraordinary service by one servitor could give an edge, but no guaranty, for his descendants' prominence). In principle, and this is undeniable, everyone was a "slave" or *kholop* of the tsar, appointed and maintained in office at the discretion of the monarch. Service was

THE RUSSIAN EXPERIENCE 185

the basic principle of Moscow's political structure: in fact, society consisted of two classes of servitors, those who served by paying taxes—the common people—and those who served in person by performing military and administrative tasks—the nobles. The latter's service function determined their status in the hierarchy: members of the boiar duma, courtiers, Moscow service nobles, provincial noblemen, and rank-and-file servitors of various categories. Service was of rather limited definition or nature, consisting primarily in participation in military campaigns or in central and local administration. Military service was essentially in the form of membership in a noble militia that was called up in time of need as well as for training and maneuvers. The servitors in Moscow were full-time officials taking care of routine administrative and judiciary functions; they were sent out to the main provincial centers to take command of garrisons, to recruit and supervise the training of local service nobility, and to act as tax collectors and judges. They were frequently moved about from one place and function to another, so that there was no pattern of functional specialization or geographic ties.

Since the personnel pool was extremely small (at the end of its existence, when its membership had been overinflated, the boiar duma had fewer than one hundred members; during the first half of the seventeenth century, however, its membership had hovered at about only twenty-five), the tsar's servitors in the provinces only performed "errands" for the ruler or merely forwarded to Moscow monies collected, criminals caught, and new servitors recruited locally.[1] They interfered very little at the lowest local levels; most of the peasantry lived in village communes and enjoyed a great deal of latitude of action as long as law and order reigned and taxes were paid regularly. Similarly, the governor of provincial centers, the *voievoda*, rarely interfered in

1. Robert O. Crummey, "Crown and Boiars under Fedor Ivanovich and Michael Romanov," *Canadian American Slavic Studies* 6 (1972):549–74 and "Court Groupings and Politics in Russia 1645–1649," *Forschungen zur osteuropäischen Geschichte*, no. 24 (Berlin: Osteuropa Institut der Freien Universitä ([Berlin, 1978]):179–202; H. J. Torke, "Oligarchie in der Autokratie: Der Machtverfall der Bojarenduma im 17. Jahrhundert," ibid., pp. 179–201; and of course the classical works by V. O. Kliuchevsky, *Boiarskaia duma* and *Istoriia soslovii*.

the daily routine. The loose network of authority explains why revolts, when they did occur, spread rapidly and had to be put down by calling in military forces from outside.

Compared to Western and central European societies, Muscovy's was loosely structured. To be sure, there were social classes and institutions, groupings for a variety of purposes, the parish first of all. One of the basic elements of structure, as we have pointed out, was the universal service obligation toward the tsar (or state). But the principle of this structure was a one-way or one-dimensional affair: obligations, without definitely stated and guaranteed rights and privileges for subjects. Under the circumstances, it is not surprising that in Muscovy we do not meet with the solid, permanent, often very strong and powerful corporations and constituted bodies that provided the framework of premodern European society and that were used by the well-ordered police states, as we have seen, in disciplining and modernizing society. Nor was Muscovy, for the same reason, acquainted with the stress on individual and group initiatives, the solidarities and autonomies, that were made possible by the rights and privileges of such constituted bodies. To be sure, there developed in the course of the seventeenth century some embryonic manifestations of such corporate ties, especially on the local level of peasant life, in some provinces and towns and on the periphery of the tsardom; to a limited extent, such bodies also participated in the country's public life. But as H. J. Torke has so well shown, these were mere beginnings that were cut short by the crisis preceding the Petrine reforms and dealt a death blow by the Petrine state.[2] A basic reason for the weakness of these bodies was the fact that they had been promoted and developed only to perform tasks for the state, so that Torke could felicitously characterize Muscovite society as *staatsbedingte* (state-determined). Their activities were not carried on on their own initiative or on their own behalf, and in addition they had to follow the directives and commands of state officials even in performing their assigned

2. Hans-Joachim Torke, *Die Staatsbedingte Gesellschaft im Moskauer Reich: Zar und Zemlja in der altrussischen Herrschaftsverfassung 1613–1789* (Leiden: E. J. Brill, 1974).

tasks for society. Weakened or destroyed by the disarray of
Muscovite culture and the reforms of Peter the Great, these
corporate solidarities maintained themselves only in the peripheral territories, among those sectors of the population that for
religious or occupational reasons had not yet been fully integrated into the regular Muscovite pattern—the Cossacks, *streltsy*, non-
Russian natives, and Old Believers. These groups fiercely opposed all efforts at integration or modernization; consequently
they could not be co-opted to promote the purposes of the well-
ordered police state.

Under the circumstances, it is not surprising that the political
and administrative activities of the tsar's government were primarily negative—that is, they were concerned with maintaining
Orthodoxy and domestic peace and with protecting the country's
borders (which did not exclude taking offensive steps whenever
circumstances permitted, as was the case with respect to Poland or
the Crimea). Of course, the tsar was also chief justicer and
maintained law by enforcing the resolution of conflicts among his
subjects. To perform these tasks, the tsar's government needed
resources in men and money, and to this end it had to take
positive steps. But even here the approach was traditional and
negative: taxes remained stable over long periods, and their
collection was delegated to the communities themselves. As for his
manpower needs, the tsar relied on the universal service system
that included all members of society. Even some peasants and
urban laborers had to render service as well as pay taxes—
obligations that prevented them from playing an entrepreneurial
and economically dynamic role. It meant that most of the legislative activity of the government was repressive: the laws forbade
those actions that might bring the social system into disorder, and
it punished (or threatened to punish) failures to pay taxes and
furnish manpower. The majority of the acts in the *PSZ* spell out
state obligations and threaten punishment for nonperformance.
A principal function of the Muscovite administration was to keep
track of and mobilize service personnel. Since the service obligations were usually resented, attempts at avoidance were normal,
and legislative measures dealt with the calling up of servitors and
the punishment of the recalcitrant.

Lastly, the government's activities were Moscow-centered. Taxes and service were levied to satisfy the needs of Moscow, not those of other localities. All administrative measures of a welfare, police, or social nature taken by the government were restricted to Moscow. We have no counterpart to the Western police ordinances that dealt with a problem or an activity regardless of location. Only the population of Moscow was in the government's purview, except for the unusual cases of rebellions or large-scale violence in provincial towns or areas. Clearly the government did not even try to reach out to the local level; in fact the tsar in the Kremlin was little concerned with the world beyond Moscow, satisfied that its communal ways would suffice to bring in the taxes and furnish the manpower he required for his God-ordained tasks of preserving Orthodoxy from domestic and foreign threats.

No polity remains static or unchanged over several generations, and so it was with Muscovy, where, in spite of apparent immobility, beneath the surface changes did take place and bring about a crisis. Indeed, the polity's very rigidity precluded a gradual modification or reforms that would have preserved its basic identity while admitting of far-reaching changes. In seventeenth-century Muscovy the transformation took on an accelerated and aggravated character as a result of the religious schism and the establishment's turning to the West.

The schism of the Old Belief, the *Raskol,* had essentially two consequences for the polity. In the first place, it separated and then alienated from the Muscovite consensus a goodly portion of the people, especially among the lower clergy, the small towns-people, the peasantry, the cossacks, and the streltsy, about 30 percent of the total population. Because of the practically Manichean outlook that dominated muscovite norms, the Old Believers found themselves outside the bounds of normally recognized society, and they, in turn, firm in their conviction of being the guardians of true orthodoxy in the face of impiety and the coming of Antichrist, firmly rejected the state as an instrument of the devil. Whether, as a result, the more energetic and dynamic elements of the population found themselves outside the pale or their being outside the pale turned the Old Believers into the nation's more dynamic and energetic elements may be a moot question.[3] In any event, in the long run the Old Believers turned out to have withheld a significant potential of enterpreneurial and productive energies—witness the exceptional history of the Vyg community tolerated by Peter the Great for its economic value.[4]

In the second place, the Raskol initiated the process that led to the cultural separation between church and state and that dissolved the very essence of a polity that had rested on the fusion of secular and religious norms, the one supporting and promoting the other. This development might best be described as a waning of the church's moral authority and its replacement by the disciplining power of the state. Far from separating state and church institutionally, with each going its independent way, the process of dissolution created a spiritual and moral vacuum that resulted in the government's taking over the cultural leadership and many public functions that had previously been the church's—not unlike the effects of the Protestant revolution in Europe. To be sure, in seventeenth-century Moscow the process did not reach the extremes and display the same form as it did in the West in the sixteenth century. Religious life remained within the institutional framework of the official church; what was at issue was a more subtle disappearance of the church's moral authority. In any event, the Raskol pushed the church as an institution into the background and left the state with an absolute monopoly of authority, both spiritual and secular. The state persecuted Old Believers with vicious ferocity as enemies and "gravediggers" of the nation, while the Old Believers, in turn, became involved in all the rebellions against a tsar who in their eyes was the embodiment of Antichrist. In this conflict the Old Believers also clung rigidly and firmly to the traditional culture of the people, and in so doing they helped preserve that culture throughout the eighteenth and early nineteenth centuries, isolat-

3. Alexander Gerschenkron, "Lecture 2," *Europe in the Russian Mirror: Four Lectures in Economic History* (Cambridge, England: Cambridge University Press, 1970) pp. 23–61.

4. Robert O. Crummey, *The Old Believers and the World of Antichrist: The Vyg Community and the Russian State, 1694–1855* (Madison: University of Wisconsin Press, 1970).

ing it from the transformations experienced by the culture of the elite.

By pushing the active role of the church into the background, the Raskol also helped the expansion of government activities and furthered the development of bureaucratization. As in the case of Western Europe in the sixteenth century, the Muscovite state had to assume guardianship of behavioral norms that heretofore had been the preserve of church discipline. Thus in the second half of the seventeenth century the government issued laws, restricted in their application to the capital, that were reminiscent of the blue laws in the West, to enforce the decorum and sanctity of holidays and Sundays.[5] Efforts were also made to separate feast days from religious events and to bring about greater order and discipline. Once that path was taken, other areas fell into the purview of state legislation as well, since the moral suasion and disciplinary control of the church were no longer adequate. Yet compared to what had taken place in central Europe in the sixteenth century and was going to occur in Russia in the eighteenth, the area of Muscovite governmental regulation remained narrowly restricted; the state interfered only on an ad hoc basis; we detect no trace of a comprehensive or systematic approach such as would be present in a normal Policeyordnung in the West.

Such as they were, these innovations and Moscow's greater involvement with the outside world required that more attention be given to an efficient bureaucratic organization of administration. Compared to that of Western European states, by the eighth decade of the seventeenth century it was still quite primitive, but it was a beginning. The number of executive offices or chanceries, the prikazy, increased, and their personnel and organization assumed more regular and institutionalized forms.[6] The professional staff of these institutions, the *diaki* or clerks, were assuming a greater role in policymaking, albeit under the guidance of the

5. *Polnoe sobranie zakonov rossiiskoi imperii* 1st series, 48 vols. (St. Petersburg: 1830–39), hereafter *PSZ. PSZ*, no. 976 (18.XII.1682).

6. See descriptive summary in Borivoj Plavsic, "Seventeenth Century Chanceries and their Staffs," *Russian Officialdom: The Bureaucratization of Russian Society from the Seventeenth to the Twentieth Century,* edited by W. McK. Pintner and D. K. Rowney (Chapel Hill: University of North Carolina Press, 1980), pp. 19–45.

head of the *prikaz*, usually a boiar or high courtier. The boiar
duma itself was broken up into sections that dealt with specific
problems and left basic policy decisions to a select committee; as
to the permanent clerks of the duma, they became members of
the highest elite, being granted the right to be listed with their
patronymics.[7]

The second major aspect of the transformation to be felt in
Muscovy by the middle of the seventeenth century was the
establishment's deliberate and definitive turn to the West. It is
often forgotten that up to that time, certainly until the end of the
sixteenth century when the Livonian War and consequent Times
of Troubles interrupted a century-old pattern, Muscovy had
faced east (and southeast). Its major enemies had been on the
border of the steppe, its major trade contacts were with the
Ottoman empire and the Caucasus, and its elites in the Kremlin
copied Eastern fashions in dress, arms, decorations, and even life-
style. Professor Keenan has correctly observed that Muscovy was
one of the heirs of the Mongol steppe *oikoemene*, and thus it is not
surprising to find so many Eastern and steppe elements in its
political orientation and cultural preferences.[8] Partly as a consequence of the Times of Troubles, partly as a result of Western
Europe's economic expansionism, the Eastern orientation weakened and was displaced by a Western one involving active trade
contacts with England and Holland and political and cultural
contact with Poland. The immediately noticeable consequence
was the greater number of Westerners coming to Moscow and
sometimes even striking roots there. The so-called foreign suburb
(*nemetskaia sloboda*) of Moscow revived in the middle of the
seventeenth century, harboring many Western traders, artisans,
military experts, and adventurers, and it provided an example of
another way of life and civilization. The tsar's government, too,

7. *PSZ*, no. 851 (21.XII.1680), no. 1243 (8.V.1687), no. 1436 (1.III.1692).
8. Personal communication. Muscovy's conflicts with Lithuania and Poland
in the late fifteenth and sixteenth centuries may be viewed as part of the struggle
for the heritage of the Golden Horde's steppe empire. The focusing on the East is
not disproven by Ivan IV's Livonian War, which marked a sudden (and arbitrary?)
turn to the West that created the difficulties leading to the Times of Troubles and
almost destroyed the Muscovite state.

employed a growing number of foreigners, quite a few in important positions, especially in the army. By the last quarter of the seventeenth century Moscow was becoming a part of the European world and was well acquainted with its representatives. The latter not only introduced technical innovations, they also exemplified another mentality and a modern vision of society's purpose and norms.[9]

Significant as these Western Europeans were for some areas of life—military techniques, foreign trade, and the life-style of the court—even more important was the role of the Ukraine. This is not the place for detailed discussion of the complexities of Muscovite-Ukrainian relations—political, military, social, and cultural. The annexation of the Ukraine (treaty of Pereiaslavl', 1654) had most far-reaching consequences. It consolidated the cultural ties (partly ecclesiastical) that bound Moscow to Kiev and enabled the graduates of Ukrainian schools to play a major role in the modification of Moscow's intellectual life and to facilitate Peter's revolutionary transformation. Put very simply, the Ukrainian schools, in particular the Theological Academy at Kiev, served as a conduit for Western European intellectual norms. Thanks to the churchmen and scholars trained in Kiev who were attracted or sent to Moscow, the ruling elites of the Kremlin gained access to neoscholastic philosophy and the concept of Natural Law, acquired a staff trained in the logic, rhetoric, and language of the West, and also became somewhat acquainted with the best-known political literature of contemporary Europe. Thus in the guise of Orthodox ecclesiastic concerns the main features of Western European political culture became accessible to Moscow, as shown by the books that were read and translated and the curiosity about European administrative, legal, and political practices that permeated the correspondence and intellectual life of the Muscovite elites.[10] In short, through its learned

9. S. I. Kotkov, ed., *Vesti-Kuranty, 1600–1639* (Moscow: 1972) and *Vesti-Kuranty, 1642–1644* (Moscow: 1976); Martin Welke, "Russland in der deutschen Publizistik des 17. Jahrhunderts (1613–1689), *Forschungen zur osteuropäischen Geschichte*, no. 23 (Berlin, 1976), pp. 105–276.

10. S. P. Luppov, *Kniga v. Rossii v. XVII veke* (Leningrad: 1970) and M. I. Slukhovskii, *Russkaia biblioteka XVI–XVII vv.* (Moscow: 1973) give introductory

ecclesiastics (such as M. Smotritskii, S. Iavorskii, S. Polotskii, and F. Prokopovich) the Ukraine paved the way by which the dominant intellectual and political trends of the West reached the Muscovite elites.

This preparation was the *conditio sine qua non* of Peter the Great's reforms, and it also suggested the direction in which he would turn for inspiration. Naturally all of this did not go forward without provoking resistance, so that in fact Ukrainian influences contributed their share to the destruction of the cultural consensus to which the Raskol had delivered the first and most damaging blow. The Ukrainian influence was to be felt most strongly in one specific area, as a result of the church's displacement from the center of the society. The Muscovite clergy was replaced by the more aggressive, better-educated, and sophisticated clergymen from the Ukraine. These Ukrainians came to staff the upper rungs of the hierarchy (and in so doing helped to widen the gulf between the official church and the religious life of the people), and they proved to be the most capable and energetic collaborators in the government's reform efforts. In the intellectual reorientation of Moscow, the Ukrainians may be said to have played a role similar to that of the pastors and lawyers in sixteenth-century Western and central Europe.

These trends introduced slow and insidious changes into the body of the Muscovite polity; the old consensus was disintegrating, and crisis was ripening. Moscow was losing its self-confidence and sense of cultural identity. But the establishment, too, was in disarray; the old ways no longer functioned adequately, while nothing seemed readily available to overcome the deepening crisis. This impression is confirmed not only by the many revolts and rebellions among some classes of society, the streltsy and cossacks in particular (in the second half of the seventeenth century), but also by the conflicts over the succession to the throne that arose after the death of Tsar Fedor (1682). The disarray manifested itself even in the realm of normal civil relationships:

survey and bibliographical guidance to knowledge of Western literature in the seventeenth century. Also, *Puteshestviia russkikh poslov XVI–XVII vv.—Stateinye spiski* (Moscow–Leningrad: 1954); *Biblioteka Petra I—ukazatel' spravochnik* (Leningrad: 1954).

the mainstay of the old service system, the *mestnichestvo* (service hierarchy based on a combination of family and personal service ranks) no longer functioned adequately, and it was formally abolished in 1682, creating a fluid situation that increased the sense of disorientation;[11] there was a sharp increase in judicial and administrative cases involving disputes over land and property rights, and it was becoming more difficult to control the peasantry and resolve intraurban conflicts by legislative means alone.[12] At the same time, traditional modes of cultural life were breaking down too, with the noble elites as well as church hierarchs adopting Western literary and artistic styles (for example, the "Moscow baroque," new fashions in portraiture and icon painting, and the introduction of new literary genres such as drama, secular tales, and history).

Additional strains were caused by greater military involvement (for example, wars against Poland, Sweden, and the Crimea), more active commercial contacts with the West, and also by the problems arising out of the multiethnic and multireligious character of the empire. Nor did there seem to be alternative forces readily available for regenerating the policy, at least as far as we can gauge from the perspective of hindsight and from what we may infer from contemporary statements. To be sure, no one knows how things might have worked out had the situation lasted nor what a reconstituted and transformed Muscovy might have been. But, as we do know, the crisis was resolved by bringing to Russia the ideas of change and some of the practices of organization that were to be found in Western and central Europe. This solution was facilitated by the relatively coherent and exportable nature of the concepts and practices of the well-ordered police state, and this is precisely what Muscovy attempted to take over, at first hesitatingly, under the regent Sophie and her favorite, V. V. Golitsyn, then energetically and systematically under Peter the Great.

With the help of resident foreigners and Ukrainian intellectuals

---

11. "Sobornoe deianie o mestnichestve," *PSZ*, no. 905 (12.I.1682).

12. *Pamiatniki russkogo prava*, vols. 7–8 (to date) (*Vtoraia polovina XVII v.*) (Moscow: 1952–63); K. Pobedonostsev, *Istoricheskiia issledovaniia i stat'i* (St. Petersburg: 1876).

(soon to be joined by military and administrative personnel drawn from the upper echelons of the cossack *starshyna* and Ukrainian *szlachta*), young Tsar Peter and his collaborators became well acquainted with European political practices and theories. Books and information had also reached Russia through diplomatic agents and travelers whom the tsars had sent out to the West.[13] Tsar Fedor's and Tsarevna Sophie's efforts to modernize the military, better husband the resources of the government, and increase and broaden commercial and diplomatic relations with Western powers had prepared the ground for the sharp turn taken by Peter in imitating the West. It is therefore quite arguable that even before Peter's accession Moscow embarked on the path that the future emperor was to pursue much more aggressively and systematically. It should be pointed out, however, that Fedor's, Sophie's, and Golitsyn's timidity, as well as the difficulties they encountered in coping with the opposition and inertia of Muscovite society, make the likelihood that they would have succeeded rather small.

In the transformation wrought by Peter the Great, his personality was certainly a major factor.[14] We need only list its dominant traits: energy, impetuousness, moodiness, wide-ranging curiosity, eagerness to learn, manual dexterity, ruthlessness, as well as cautious shrewdness when needed—all make of Peter a Renaissance personality who would have been at home in the West in the century of the condottiere, state builders, and conquistadores. He was, literally as well as figuratively, larger than lifesize, and there was something Rabelaisian, in both the positive and pejorative

13. See the curious description of a Russian traveler-diplomat in the fictitious dialogue by E. Francisci, *Ost und West Indischer und Chinesischer Lust- und Staatsgarten* (Nürnberg: 1668), vol. 1, cols. 1433–34. Also *Puteshestviia russkikh poslov,* and for a somewhat later example A. D. Lublinskaia, ed., *Russkii diplomat vo Frantsii (Zapiski Andreia Matveieva)* (Leningrad: 1972).

14. On Peter I's personality, see the classical portrait by V. O. Kliuchevsky, the collection of materials of M. M. Bogslovskii, *Petr I. (Materialy k biografii),* 5 vols. (Moscow: 1940–48), vol. 1; the psychoanalytical approach in A. Besançon, *Le Tsarévitch immolé* (Paris: Plon, 1967); and V. O. Klyuchevsky, *Peter the Great,* translated by L. Archibald (New York: Random House, 1958), as well as the fictionalized but perceptive representations of A. Pushkin ("Poltava," "The Negro of Peter the Great") and D. Merezhkovskii *(Peter and Alexis).*

senses, about the tsar. Peter's personality was a crucial factor in making the well-ordered police state the basic framework of the Russian imperial regime, for as we have seen, the *état bien policé* required the guiding spirit, driving force, and unified authority of an absolute sovereign. It is important to add, however, that the condition of Muscovy no longer satisfied the more energetic, aggressive, and ambitious members of the elites. There were many Muscovites, as well as foreign and Ukrainian newcomers, who welcomed a radical transformation to satisfy their own hunger for action, recognition, and influence. The presence of such people and Peter's ability to detect and attract them gave greater effect to the tsar's personality and encouraged him to undertake tasks of a magnitude that would have daunted anyone else. Of course Peter was forced into tackling some problems almost accidentally, at times even against his will or better judgment, by the necessities of the moment. Yet even in such instances the basic reason for the problems' having arisen in the first place had been Peter's fundamental decision to consciously and actively pursue the Europeanization (or modernization, if one will) of the country.

We are now ready to turn to an analysis of the Petrine "system," a system that had set itself the task of rooting Western culture in Muscovy and of making Russia (as Muscovy will be called from now on) into a well-ordered police state, *reguliarnoe politseiskoe gosudarstvo,* on a par with Europe's major powers.[15]

In sharp contrast with the Muscovite polity, the state and government that Peter the Great bequeathed to his successors ended the organic symbiosis between church and state that had been the characteristic pillar of the tsar's realm. The patriarchate disappeared when the office became vacant in 1700 and no successor was appointed; eventually, in 1721, Peter installed an ecclesiastical college, the Holy Synod, to take care of religious affairs on the model of the German Lutheran state churches. Peter not only severed the links that had bound state and church;

15. The most comprehensive recent summary of Peter's reign is R. Wittram, *Peter I, Czar und Kaiser,* 2 vols. (Göttingen: Vandenhoeck & Ruprecht, 1964); cf. also N. Pavlenko, *Petr Pervyi* (Moscow: 1975); B. Syromiatnikov, *"Reguliarnoe" gosudarstvo Petra Pervogo i ego ideologiia,* pt. 1 (Moscow-Leningrad: 1943).

he also initiated a truly secularized policy. Not that he destroyed religion or even tried to do so; in his idiosyncratic way he was even personally devout. But from now on religious matters were to play a subordinate role, since the state viewed them in strictly instrumental terms, and as one of the disciplining agents of society the ecclesiastical establishment was saddled with new tasks of public welfare and public education. To be sure, the empire remained an Orthodox one; only the Orthodox had full status as subjects of the empire (exceptions were made for western European foreigners and the Protestant Baltic elites whose services the establishment needed so much). In any event, the secular needs of the state were to have absolute priority in determining policies; spiritual and religious affairs were taken into account only if and when they had a direct bearing on state interests.

The military and fiscal needs of the government, always in the forefront of the state's concerns, grew and expanded enormously in consequence of Peter's policies. The military needs quite naturally grew out of the long-protracted and difficult war Peter waged against Sweden and the several subsequent campaigns in the East. The wars necessitated the modernization and expansion of the military establishment, both land and sea forces, on a scale hitherto unknown. The cost was so huge that fiscal concerns could never be far from the tsar's mind: the country was poor, and more important still the government did not possess the means to collect effectively what was its due. Muscovy's fiscal apparatus had been wide-meshed, and as its needs were much more modest than Peter's it had failed to work out an efficient and comprehensive system of collection. Peter's needs were so pressing that he constantly had to devise ways to obtain money immediately. In the West, tax returns were greater, and the taxes were more easily collected, not only because the countries there were more developed economically and richer (Russia was bigger and had more people) but because the administrative apparatus effectively tapped the sources of revenue with the assistance of local institutions and social groups. In Peter's Russia, however, the government tried to raise more money by shifting the basis of taxation from the homestead (*dvor*) to the individual male peasant, "soul" (*dusha*). This only increased the administrative problem, even though more money was collected at first. Later censuses and checks revealed that a very large number of souls had escaped, by one means or another, the fiscal dragnet of the government. In the end, the responsibility for delivering the soul tax was placed on the individual landlord. In this manner the peasants became tied to the individual landowner, and their bonds to the land and to the community were loosened. It further resulted in the atomization and total enserfment of the peasantry. The individual peasant serfs turned into virtual chattel, to be moved and disposed of at will by their masters, for their traditional relationships to land, community, and family no longer counted in the eyes of the state. Under the circumstances, Peter's government had to seek other means of raising revenue, and quite a few of his social and economic policies were simply dictated by the need to obtain money immediately, regardless of long-range effects; that is why so many of the measures proved short-lived and uneconomical.

It has been frequently asserted that all of Peter's policies in the important domains of public life were also dictated exclusively by the needs of war. On the surface this seems to have been true, and there is no gainsaying that bringing to successful conclusion the protracted and difficult struggle against Sweden was uppermost in Peter's mind. But it is hard to believe that this was the only or even main motive for all his measures. Had this been the case, the transformation he wrought would have been less dramatic, less impetuous, and less complete. Indeed, even before the victory at Poltava (1709), Russia's military position in the war had turned favorable. After Poltava, eventual success could be taken for granted, and the efforts required to continue the war against Sweden were no longer superhuman (the disastrous campaign on the Pruth in 1711 proved to be only a temporary setback); Sweden was brought to terms by its own exhaustion. In any case, the fairly coherent program of internal administrative changes and the emperor's energetic and goal-directed policies with respect to education, trade, social organization, and cultural life cannot be accounted for as a mere sequence of ad hoc measures taken to meet military contingencies and day-to-day fiscal needs.

Peter the Great did have an overall goal and a general conception of what he wanted to accomplish, or he had one at any rate after about 1701, following his return from his first trip to Western Europe and after overcoming the critical situation created by his defeat at Narva. He himself stated his goal on a number of occasions, and there is no reason not to take him seriously, the more so that the sum total of his measures did amount to a coherent and sustained effort to achieve a specific purpose. Peter wanted to modernize, to Europeanize Russia's establishment. He obviously did not care to Europeanize the peasantry and common people, for he believed that they would eventually follow, provided the upper classes of society performed their leadership functions well. This also implied the westernization, or making over on a European model, of the administration, the military, the court, and the elite's culture or *sociabilité*, to use a more specific and more accurate term borrowed from contemporary French historiography. Dress, social life, entertainment, scientific and intellectual activities, as well as changes in the government apparatus, contacts with the outside world, introduction of Western ways, manners, and styles—all were part of a broad plan to transform the members of Moscow's service and boiar elites, who had been isolated from Europe and rooted in traditions that owed much to the East, into contemporary Western Europeans. Peter wanted for Russia an elite composed of individuals capable of playing an active role in transforming society—not slaves *(kholopy)* but loyal servants of the emperor and of the fatherland whose central concerns were to be the nation's welfare, prosperity, and progress.

Finally, the reign reflected Peter's own personality—his impatience, driving energy, and ruthlessness. Indeed, the transformations introduced by the tsar-reformer were rushed through, brooking no opposition; any attempt at resistance was pitilessly crushed. Peter rode roughshod over his people, the country, even his family, disregarding difficulties and resistances and quite unmindful of the high price paid by the population. The furious tempo of his reign created the impression of relentless hurry and impatience, as if centuries of Western European experience had to be crammed into the twenty-five years of the reign. Gone were the passivity and deliberateness of Muscovy as Peter intervened positively and aggressively in every domain of national life. Peter's impetuosity passed like a whirlwind over the empire. The changes seemed dramatic, almost total, and breathtaking. This alone has given Peter's reign its historiographic and mythical stamp; it raised the crucial question of historical continuity to be debated by generations of Russian thinkers and writers. As for the common people, they experienced Peter as a ruthless and harsh tyrant whom they could not understand and whose actions seemed unnecessary, bringing new burdens of foreign origin.

Because of its impetuousness and seemingly disconnected pattern, Peter's reign appeared at first to have had only a superficial effect. Many innovations were abandoned, many a member of the elite was happy to slide back into the old grooves.[16] Some institutional and administrative changes that had not produced the expected results were quietly set aside. For a brief moment, at least, it seemed as if Russia was to return from St. Petersburg to Moscow (symbolically, the government of Peter II [1727–30] had made that move on the eve of his early death). But if we look more carefully we realize that this was not quite the case. To be sure, some innovations were not maintained, at any rate not at the Petrine level of effectiveness (the navy is the best example). But the changes introduced by Peter with respect to the elites, especially at the new capital (and St. Petersburg did remain the empire's capital) and with respect to the formal structure of the imperial administration did in fact survive. There was no going back to Muscovy. The essential innovations in the institutional organization and life-style of the elites were not allowed to die out. Although the Russian elites were not as yet fully Europeanized, they had broken with the Muscovite past and had taken the road that would bring their descendants to full-fledged membership in Europe's cultural elites. But it is time to turn to those specific transformations wrought by Peter the Great that are relevant to the issues dealt with in this essay.

The governmental structure of the Petrine empire took shape gradually and with uneven progress over a period of twenty

16. There is no evidence of systematic follow-up as in the case of the German police ordinances.

years, but eventually the government did attain a coherence of form that provided a framework for all of Peter's other innovative enterprises as well as the institutional basis of the imperial regime throughout the remainder of its existence. It is therefore appropriate to give a summary overview of the governmental structure as it emerged in the 1720s. Following the tradition of Muscovy, but increasing the tendency, the Petrine structure of government was centralistic. All efforts made to deconcentrate administrative functions—for example, by delegating fiscal and administrative duties to regimental commanders in the provincial garrisons—failed, and by the time of Peter's death (January 1725), the government of the empire was highly centralized. What proved even more significant was the effort at functional organization. The large number of Muscovite prikazy, which had frequently been established on the basis of geographic criteria or more often were the result of historical accident, had overlapping jurisdictions and competences. These prikazy were replaced by eleven government colleges, each having a distinct administrative and political function.[17] The collegial setup, although partly a carryover of Muscovite patterns, was of course more importantly a copy of Western, especially Swedish, models popular at the time: rooted in a traditional medieval conception, the collegial pattern served to distribute the burden of responsibility and accountability among several individuals, although at the expense of singleness of purpose and executive efficiency.

The Senate (created in 1711) was meant to give cohesiveness and direction to long-range policy, and as such it was empowered to act in the emperor's name in his absence. It coordinated and centralized imperial decisions and also exercised general control over the colleges and other central institutions (for example, the Holy Synod). In fact, however, reflecting a fundamental evolutionary predisposition, the Senate, too, soon assumed the character of a super-college, supervising and deciding matters beyond the competence of a single college or serving as a body of

17. The rationale is given in the preamble to the *General'nyi reglament, PSZ*, no. 3534 (28.II.1720). For the history of its drafting, cf. N. A. Voskresenskii, *Zakonodatel'nye akty Petra I*, (Moscow and Leningrad: 1945), vol. 1, sec. 7.

administrative appeal.[18] After the death of Peter the Great, the primacy of the Senate passed to a new institution, the Supreme Privy Council, set up to assist and act on behalf of the weak and incompetent empress Catherine I and her successor Peter II. The evolution of the Senate into primarily an administrative institution demonstrated the centralistic tendency that aimed at excluding all subordinate and local institutions. The rapid development of senatorial procedures in the first years of its existence not only showed the centralized and functional character of the Petrine system but also its well-nigh exclusive reliance on paperwork. The protocols and minutes of the Senate offer clear evidence that all problems were dealt with in writing (decisions were based on papers submitted and resolutions were registered in writing), in contrast to Muscovite reliance on oral transactions.

The Muscovite administration had developed regular chancery procedures quite early, but they were cumbersome and largely oral, adapted to the semipatriarchal and personal regimen of the Kremlin. Nor was the administrative apparatus very extensive; since the clerical personnel was quite small, the main clerks, or diaki, participated in deciding policies as well as in administering them. This situation changed drastically in Peter's times. He introduced and firmly rooted Western chancery techniques, with their emphasis on the written document. As a matter of fact, this approach was initiated quite early in his reign when he decreed that henceforth all documents were to be kept in book fashion rather than in scrolls (where each paper was stitched to the top of the next following).[19] The preamble of the decree justified the change on the ground of efficiency, asserting that the new form of documents would be easier to find, consult, and use. This showed clearly the direction of the innovations in administrative practices. The many detailed and specific ordinances for modernizing chancery techniques found their ultimate and comprehensive expression in the *General'nyi reglament* (General Regulation),

18. For legislative history, cf. N. A. Voskresenskii, *Zakonodatel'nye akty Petra I*, and for evolution of the Senate's functions see *Doklady i progovory Senata v tsarstvovanie Petra Velikogo*, 6 vols. (St. Petersburg: 1880–1901).

19. *PSZ*, no. 1797 (12.VI.1700), and the earlier decree prescribing that land-grant charters be printed, *PSZ*, no. 988 (15.I.1683).

dated 28 February 1720, its first draft dating from 1718, which
was to be the foundation of all administrative and chancery
procedures for the remainder of the life of the empire.[20] Besides
establishing the eleven colleges mentioned earlier, the General
Regulation also set forth the standards and rules that were to
govern the behavior of the clerical staff of the colleges and the
administration at large. Read naively, these rules strike us as a bit
childish in the attention they pay to minutiae and minor technical
details such as inkwells, furniture, office hours, arrangement of
office space, and the restricting of all business to the premises of
college chanceries. But we have already seen that in the early
seventeenth century similar rules had been established by the
police ordinances of German territories. The significant traits of
the new chancery procedures represented two aspects of a single
feature: in the first place, business had to be transacted only in
places specifically designated and set aside for the purpose (we
recall similar prescriptions in the police ordinances), so as to do
away with the earlier personal and informal administrative practices that left no traces in the written record and easily turned into
arbitrary capriciousness. In the second place, and also reminiscent of the police ordinance pattern, a strict separation between
the administered and the administrators was introduced and
secured thanks to the physical arrangement of the offices, since
petitioners were kept standing in anterooms or behind wooden
barriers.

In short, government was to be completely separated from the
population's life pattern; administration had to partake of the
aura of the arcane possessed by the sovereign ruler. Naturally this
meant a great increase in the technical tasks of writing and
keeping the papers needed for administration, so that more
personnel were needed. At the same time the role of the copyist
or clerk diminished as his task became more mechanical and
routinized, and the gap separating the staff of responsible officials
from the scriveners who performed mechanical tasks grew wider.
This is not to deny—quite the contrary—that the copyist's and
clerk's power might not have increased with respect to the little

20. Cited in n. 17 above.

people who, more than ever, depended on him as the effective intermediary between themselves and those in authority. While the sovereign power was attempting to remove itself from the population and depersonalize the administration by relying on written procedure, the traditional personal element of authority did not disappear, either in decision making (done by the monarch and his personal agents) or in the technical carrying out of policy (done by the clerks).

These procedural innovations were not merely due to Peter's copying of Western models and to his desire to have a more efficient administrative apparatus to perform the traditional governmental functions of the Muscovite state. Had this been the case, fewer and less costly changes would have sufficed. The more important reason is that in Europe, and now in Russia, the very conception of the function of government and administration had undergone a basic change. In Muscovy, as we have seen, the main functions of government had been passive or negative in nature. These functions were not eliminated, of course, since the state had to maintain law and order, preserve external security, and find the financial resources for these purposes. To the extent that Peter pursued very active military and diplomatic policies, these traditional concerns of government were merely magnified during his reign. Peter's innovation, however, consisted in his turning to active, directly constructive—even rationally construc-tivistic—domestic policies. Put very simply—and the General Regulation reflected this overall intention while other decrees provided more specific instances—Peter attempted to turn the imperial government into an agency for the direction and organization of a dynamic, production-oriented society. No longer was the task of government to be the passive care of internal and external safety; it was to be that of aggressive promotion of all the country's potential, social as well as material. The civilian colleges had been set up and provided with the General Regulation in order to perform some of these functions. The military and naval establishments, too, were directed to work for the same purpose, in addition to fulfilling their specific task of defense and mainte-nance of the empire's military power.

The Petrine government extended its concern and active

participation to a variety of domains—economic, commercial, educational, and scientific—in order to increase the empire's productive potential as much as possible. Closely modeled, consciously or not, on the Prussian ordinances concerning manufacturing techniques, Peter the Great's decrees instructed the population on how to innovate in various technical and economic domains.[21] He established manufacturing concerns, trading companies, and factories, introduced new industries and crops, and gave specific instructions on how traditional methods should be replaced by more efficient and productive modern ones (for example, using saws instead of axes to cut lumber). We need not enter into the details of these decrees and regulations, many of which could not be implemented in full or were effectively resisted by the population. In Prussia such specific regulations proved more effective because they helped to promote industries and techniques by relying on gradually acquired patterns and notions, but in Russia the innovations were too drastic and their purpose rarely understood. Nor did Peter's personality make for consistent follow-up; he was prone to enthusiasms that cooled easily when success fell below his sanguine expectations. The important thing, however, and a lasting consequence of his measures, was the fact that from then on the government conceived its policy task as positive, rational constructivist action with a high time horizon. Henceforth it was prepared to direct and sponsor policies that would yield results in the long run and to organize and discipline the nation for that purpose.

To be sure, this implied regulation and prescription; Peter's legislation was highly prescriptive, at times brutally and ruthlessly so. In that, it differed from the German police ordinances we have studied, for the latter counted on the collaboration and participation of some sectors of the population. Peter, however,

21. See a summary of Peter's economic policies in Simone Blanc, "A propos de la politique économique de Pierre le Grand," *Cahiers du monde russe et soviétique* 3 (1962): 122–39. Also E. B. Spiridonova, *Ekonomicheskaia politika i ekonomicheskie vzgliady Petra I* (Moscow: 1952); Dm. Baburin, *Ocherki po istorii manufaktur kollegii* (Moscow: 1939); A. Gerschenkron, *Europe in the Russian Mirror*. And of course, the classical study of P. Miliukov, *Gosudarstvennoe khoziaistvo Rossii v pervoi chetverti XVIII veka i reformy Petra Velikogo*, 2d. ed. (St. Petersburg: 1905).

made no such assumption, and rightly so; he acted on the
assumption that all of his innovations would be resented and
resisted.[22] This was one of the main reasons why we do not find in
Peter's acts anything that might be considered the equivalent of
a police ordinance, in the sense of a set of laws or decrees
.endeavoring to produce a new pattern of behavior in the operation of existing aspects of public, economic, and social life. In
Russia we have the direct command that introduces and orders
something altogether new under threat of dire punishment. Old
patterns of behavior were forbidden outright, without any suggestion of alternative paths, while new ways were commanded
without regard to whether the presuppositions existed for them
or not. Little wonder that so much of this kind of legislation of
Peter's proved stillborn. The didacticism of the tsar's decrees,
mirroring that of Prussian ordinances, was more than a trifle
artificial in the Russian context and all too verbose and hortatory.
Peter lectured his audience at length on the grounds for this or
that practice; he appealed to his subjects' reason and self-interest,
but he did so in terms of very long-range plans for the future that
were neither easily understood by nor convincing to most. In the
final analysis, only the central institutions of government could
promote and supervise these innovations; the emperor's dumb
and mute subjects would be at best the unwilling instruments
under threat of punishment.

We see therefore that Peter not only set the state new tasks
but introduced a new style of government as well: a dynamic,
interventionist, and coercive state assumed the task of initiating
and directing the productive concerns of society. Its new operating style was also in contrast to the Muscovite tradition of securing
religious sanction for all its important actions. Peter, on the
contrary, not only claimed for the sovereign the absolute right to
exercise his power and will as he deemed fit but also justified his
legislative acts by appealing to rational and pragmatic arguments.[23] He discarded the claims of tradition and scorned reli-

22. Peter's contemporary and collaborator I.T. Pososhkov put it graphically
when he spoke of the emperor hauling the country uphill while millions of his
subjects were pulling him downhill.

23. For didactic justification of decrees (for example, the act of succession),
PSZ, no. 3893 (5.II.1722) and on single inheritance PSZ, no. 2789 (23.III.1714),

ance on religious norms. Whenever reference was made to tradition, precedent, and religion, the argument rested not so much on the Russian experience as on the lessons of universal history and the philosophic concepts of Natural Law (as shown most graphically in *Pravda voli monarshei*, 1718).

This change in political style, while quite drastic in its formal expressions, was not without its contradictions and ambiguities. On the one hand, an abstract conception of the state (or even of the fatherland) now became the prime object of the government's concern, and all subjects' behavior was to be subordinated to this state. True, the notion of state, *gosudarstvo*, had on occasion crept into Muscovite laws, though rather as an exception,[24] but with Peter the interests of the institutional abstraction became the all-important end.[25] On the other hand, the personal authority of the sovereign, far from being narrowed, experienced an increase and extension; it was the sovereign, who, like the engineer of the universe, put the new machine in motion and gave it direction and purpose. It was his will—and his was the final decision in all cases brought to his attention—that provided the sole ground for legislation. The personal aspect of state authority in Russia needs to be stressed, for it provides added evidence for the absence of social structures capable of serving as conduits for policy, of advocating change, or of actively participating in matters of the public interest.

The new style of government had more far-reaching consequences than might appear at first glance. Indeed, it meant that all state personnel had to acquire and accept a similar rationalistic, constructivist, didactic approach to government. Paradoxical as it may sound, it was in transforming the life-style and behavior of the elite that Peter's policies may be deemed most successful.[26]

---

and most extensively and dramatically in the so-called Spiritual Regulations, *PSZ*, no. 3718 (25.I.1721) now in English, translated by Alexander V. Muller (Seattle: University of Washington Press, 1972).

24. *PSZ*, no. 864 (3.V.1681), in which the tsar thanks merchants for their contribution in the war against Turkey after conclusion of an armistice.

25. Peter's proclamation to his troops on the eve of the battle of Poltava expresses the conception best.

26. This was in contrast to the West, where the upper nobility was among the most recalcitrant to modernization. Cf. the illuminating remarks in Simon Blanc,

Harnessed to minister to the needs of the dynamic emperor and the new activist state, members of the service elite adapted their ways to the role. Of prime importance to this end was the acquisition of rational modes of behavior and thought. Not only did this entail obtaining a modernized education or practical preparation; it also meant internalizing the prevailing Western patterns of thought and behavior on which the new political culture was based. Clearly such a transformation could not take place without conflicts and inner strains; in many instances the process of adaptation took more than a generation to complete. Yet in the overwhelming majority of instances it proceeded quickly and was completed by the middle of the eighteenth century. One reason for this success was the attraction the new ways and opportunities had for the type of personality that had chafed under Muscovite inertia. There was also the obvious attraction of participating in an expanding establishment and sharing all the advantages that this entailed. But of equal importance, in my opinion, was the regime's preservation of the personal character of authority: it was the sovereign emperor, the ruler in person, who provided impetus and direction and also distributed the rewards. The notion of individual service and recompense was essential to the system; let us examine it briefly.

Obviously the success of a policy of such generalized character as Peter the Great's depended on the manner of implementation. In the case of the well-ordered police state in the West, as we have seen, the governments relied on the collaboration of already constituted bodies *(corps intermédiaires)* and on the training of a professionalized bureaucracy in modern educational institutions. The latter were to assume the primary directing role, while the former served as the instruments for specific and local implementation. As we had occasion to remark, Muscovy lacked any well-developed, autonomous, and strong corps intermédiaires, so that the Petrine government could not co-opt them. It had to make use of whatever personnel there was and, of necessity, to expand and develop its own local cadres, a major task beyond the capacities of

Un disciple de Pierre le Grand dans la Russie du XVIIIᵉ siècle: V. N. Tatiščev, 1686–1750 (thèse présentée devant l'Université de Paris IV, 20 Feb. 1971), 2 vols. (Lille: Université de Lille, Service de Publication de Thèses, 1972), pt. 3.

Peter's state. The first emperor was acutely conscious of the fact that his central institutions hardly penetrated to the provincial and local levels; they could not even serve as a "grid system" for reaching the peasantry.

As had been true of Muscovy and all so-called medieval societies, the nobility constituted the main pool of state servitors. In Russia the nobles were traditionally at the beck and call of the government; they constituted the only class that by virtue of upbringing and experience was more or less prepared for a leadership role in the modernized establishment of the first emperor. Thus the traditional military and court servitor had to be reeducated for the new, westernized army and administration. The Muscovite noble resented and resisted the new army rules that forced him to acquire modern ways and rational thought patterns that could also be applied to the realm of administration, just as nobles in German had also resented it. The new military could and did serve as the disciplining and westernizing agent for the civilian sector as well. But the traditional noble militia could not suffice for the task; it was necessary to find other sources of administrative manpower.

The system devised by Peter recognized that the state had to reach out beyond the traditional categories of servitors and provide the mechanism by which the pool might be further broadened in the future. Usefulness, in the Petrine administration, meant a ready acceptance and internalization of the new goals and forms of government and the ability to display initiative and energy in guiding society along the path indicated by the state; it demanded a capacity to function in an efficient and comprehensive institutional framework that relied on rationality, written records, and generalized rules. In short, a genuinely bureaucratic, routinizing mentality was required, as well as a display of individual drive and responsibility. Peter had few men of such type; he had to fashion them. Some were drawn from the old prikazy and their staffs; a few more, but very few, were found among the merchant and urban classes. Foreigners, of course, furnished a significant contingent; some were especially recruited abroad, others were found among older residents of Russia or the newly conquered territories. But as had been true in the West at

earlier times the main effort was directed at reeducating the
traditional service groups, at helping them adapt to the new ways.
Since Muscovy possessed no lawyers and academics who could
readily provide technical competence and leadership, the Petrine
government had to create cadres of its own entirely out of the
traditional service class. To this end Peter imposed an educational
requirement on all young servitors, a requirement that eventually
became the main criterion for membership in the establishment.
All male members of the younger generation of the service class
were forced to go to school (or study on their own and pass an
examination) before being granted full legal rights (for example,
the right to marry) and admitted to regular service. This requirement was new and burdensome, for there were few schools or
other educational institutions; moreover, the knowledge that had
to be acquired was outside the traditional religious instruction
that had been provided in Muscovy. Modern, service-oriented
knowledge had to be imparted by force; all efforts at evading it
were severely punished. Yet in spite of the fierce resistance it
encountered and the obvious difficulty in acquiring education,
within a generation or so the Petrine policy had taken hold; the
young noble henceforth acquired the minimum of instruction
that prepared him for effective service in either the military or
civilian branches. Even more remarkable, the notion that education was desirable and the criterion for belonging to the elite had
taken hold among the nobility; education became the single most
significant factor affecting admission to and recognition of membership in the elite class of the empire.

Another feature of the pattern of state service Peter devised
was its compulsory and lifelong character. Compulsion was meant
to enlist all potential servitors, while lifelong service aimed at
effectively retaining all useful members. In spite of the resistance
that led to some alleviation later, state service retained these two
major features throughout the first two-thirds of the eighteenth
century, instilling in the nobility an almost exclusive preoccupation with state service careers. The availability of servitors on a
compulsory and lifelong basis obviated the necessity of looking
elsewhere for administrators and officers. In fact, after they had
internalized the idea that service careers were compulsory for

them, the noblemen tried to shut their ranks against newcomers from other classes, although they did not succeed in turning their own estate into a closed caste.[27] In particular, the state was able to recruit more personnel, especially for its civilian needs, from among sons of the clergy, who received a better education than laymen. Finally, the personnel requirements of the state were also met through the atomization of the service class: in contrast to the traditional Muscovite pattern, where each served in prefixed categories and functions, the Petrine government separated the individual servitor from his peers and his family and cut his local ties by assigning him at will to whatever task, in whatever locality, was considered best for the interest of the state. On the other hand, and it is an important contrast to the situation prevailing in the West, the system delayed the professionalization and functional specialization of the state apparatus. The main reason for this state of affairs, however, was the absence in Russia of a nucleus of professionals—the lawyers, university professors, and ministers (in Protestant lands) who were available to the Western European polities.

The Petrine service system, though, put Russia in a better position than the central European states to organize the administrative and military services along hierarchical lines and to insist that rank and promotion be based on performance and length of service. The Table of Ranks of Peter the Great provided a rigid framework for the service pattern; at the same time it opened state service careers to non-nobles and rewarded them for successful participation in the government.[28] This is not the place to consider the rather complicated and central aspect of the Table of Ranks—its contribution to social mobility, to use our contempo-

27. Brenda Meehan-Waters, "Social and Career Characteristics of the Administrative Elite, 1689–1761," in Pintner and Rowney eds., *Russian Officialdom*, pp. 76–105, and more generally A. Romanovich-Slavatinskii, *Dvorianstvo v Rossii ot nachala XVIII veka do otmeny krepostnogo prava*, 2d ed. (Kiev: 1912); S. A. Korf, *Dvorianstvo i ego soslovnoe upravlenie za stoletie 1762–1855 godov* (St. Petersburg: 1906); S. M. Troitskii, *Russkii absoliutizm i dvorianstvo v XVIII v.—Formirovanie biurokratii* (Moscow: 1974); M. Raeff, *Origins of the Russian Intelligentsia: The Eighteenth Century Nobility* (New York: Harcourt Brace Jovanovich, 1966).

28. Table of Ranks, *PSZ*, no. 3890 (24.I.1722). The history of the drafting of the table (and its sources) is in Troitskii, *Russkii absoliutizm.*

rary jargon. It will suffice to say that it routinized enrollment, promotion, and appointment patterns, and in so doing it became the principal avenue for the recognition of social status and prestige. By the same token, members of the government apparatus were completely enmeshed in the system and hierarchy of the Table of Ranks, which put them at the discretion and mercy of their superiors; in this way the Table of Ranks proved also a most effective instrument for controlling and disciplining the personnel of the establishment. There were almost no ways of securing status and prestige outside the Table of Ranks hierarchy. And while the first step on the Table's ladder was made very difficult for the outsider, especially in the earlier decades of the eighteenth century, the Table also offered the means by which the non-noble could achieve positions of responsibility and influence. In every case, however, the prerequisite was education, and in the final analysis it was access to the channels of education that determined social stratification and social mobility in Russia in the eighteenth century.

The patterns of compulsion imposed on the nobility was extended to others as Peter I tried to enroll various groups of the population in the productive and modernizing endeavors of the state. Not surprisingly, the nobleman in the military or the bureaucracy did not prove very effective in the economic domain. Quite clearly the assets and services of traders and artisans had to be drawn upon to provide the income needed to support the administration, the army, and the court. In good cameralist fashion, Peter was convinced of the necessity of developing manufactures and trade to the maximum possible extent. He believed that the towns were the main source of strength and support of the Western European states' power and material wealth. In this he shared the preconceptions of his seventeenth-century Western contemporaries (from whom he had learned them) in underestimating the role of agriculture as a valuable contributor to a productive and progress-oriented society. Conscious of the backwardness and inadequacy of the Russian merchants and entrepreneurs, Peter tried to organize them along European lines, so as to increase their material contribution and make it more effective. But again he resorted to the only methods he knew: state service and compulsion.

The merchants and townsmen (*posadskie liudi*) were forced to join a government guild organization, not for their own benefit but to provide for the interests and needs of the government. They were not only forced to accept a centralized organization but were also compelled to orient their activities (not merely their fiscal and administrative obligations) toward the needs of the state.[29] Far from encouraging the liberating creative initiative and fostering the development of voluntary, production-determined associations, Peter's policy had the reverse effect of impoverishing the urban strata and undermining their capacity for self-regulation, autonomy, and enterprise. In a sense, although he was aiming at imitating the West, Peter in fact reversed the model: he made private activities dependent on state needs and service, thereby weakening and even destroying long-range productive capacities. By contrast, the Western well-ordered police states, as we have seen, aimed first at expanding private production and wealth so that the state could share in their benefits. Cameralism did not undertake a basic restructuring of social hierarchies, nor did Peter think of reshaping the basic relationships of Russian society. The emperor was therefore loath to undertake a fundamental reordering and disciplining of society for the sake of ongoing productive progress. No doubt he envisaged such a reordering as a distant goal, but it can be safely said that he took no concrete measures to that end. In Petrine legislation we do not find an equivalent of the police ordinances that aimed at eliminating traditional customs, introducing and rooting modern, rational modes of behavior; in particular, such efforts directed at the common people, the rural population, found no counterpart in Russia. On the other hand, however, and paradoxically, at first glance, but quite rationally in view of what we have said so far, Peter, as we have seen, made strenuous efforts to change the customs, norms, and behavior of the upper class, the nobility (the class that in the West had normally performed the role of guide and leader because it had been the first to be transformed along modern lines). With respect to this noble service class Peter succeeded beyond all expectations, for within a generation or two

---

29. *Reglament Glavnogo magistrata*, PSZ, no. 3708 (16.I.1721) and *Doklady i prigovory Senata*, passim.

it had been turned into an elite with a Western cultural orientation, sharing fully the values of the Petrine state and developing a life-style that corresponded to that of the leadership strata in Western and central Europe.

At this point, however, one may ask whether in fact the people, or at least some of its elements, did not participate more actively in the construction of the new system than might appear at first glance. Was it conceivable for a considerable modernization of the state and its elite to have taken place so rapidly and on the whole effectively without anyone but the nobility and a few individuals from the clergy, some clerks, and some foreigners taking part in it? The question needs to be asked but cannot be fully answered in the present state of knowledge. We can surmise such participation; otherwise the huge army could not have been provisioned or transported, the new capital not built, and so forth. In the sources we occasionally come across references to individual peasants who were huge contractors; we also have the case of Pososhkov, a peasant turned merchant who for a while was Master of the Mint. All this is important, for it implies that the delegation of governmental tasks was limited to select individuals for specific purposes.[30] But we do not find the delegation of broad tasks to social groupings, with the granting of a degree of jurisdictional autonomy, that had been the pattern in the West with regard to questions of economy and police.

Were there, in fact, any alternatives other than compulsion and the absorption into state service of dynamic members of society? The answer is clearly no, since Peter would personally have preferred not to depend on the traditional class of military servitors and to broaden the base of his personnel. In his time, the clergy was not readily available for government service, since except for the few eminent hierarchs (who did well the job entrusted to them) the bulk of the parish clergy and their children were quite unsuited for the tasks that Peter would have liked to confer on them. It needed the transformation wrought by his new ecclesiastical establishment and the influence of the Ukrainian

30. I. T. Pososhkov, *Kniga o skudosti i bogatstve, i drugie sochineniia* (Moscow: 1951); N. Pavlov-Sil'vanskii, *Proekty reform v zapiskakh sovremennikov Petra Velikogo* (St. Petersburg: 1897).

hierarchy through the modernization of the ecclesiastical school curriculum and the demographic pressures within the clerical estate to make children of the clergy available for state service by the middle of the eighteenth century.[31] The peasantry was out of the question, since it was ignorant, illiterate, tradition- and poverty-bound, and in most cases also enserfed. Besides, in the early eighteenth century the notion of the peasantry as a reservoir for administrative or leadership roles would have been as unthinkable in the West as it was in Russia. There remained the so-called urban classes, but, as we have noted, they were poor and weak in Muscovy, and the situation did not change under Peter. Many were Old Believers, which excluded them (or made them exclude themselves) from participation in the establishment. The merchants, with rare exceptions, were unenterprising, and the fiscal and service burdens to which they were subjected killed whatever interest they might have had in participating actively in the Petrine revolution. To Peter's mind there was no alternative to compulsory service, primarily by the nobility. Servants of emperor and state, few in number, the leading noble servitors had a centralistic perspective; their eyes were focused on the capital, not on the country at the local level.

Peter consciously turned to the models of Western and central Europe; he aimed at imitating and reproducing in Russia the conditions created by the well-ordered police state he had observed during his travels in the West. The more serious question is whether he fully grasped the nature of what he was imitating. As is frequently the case with such cultural borrowing, even with Third World leaders today, Peter noted the results and he knew of some of the practices. But he did not fully grasp (and even if he had, the question of its transfer and applicability would have remained) the basic mechanism by which these results had been achieved. Was he aware of the important role in implementing policies played by co-optation and delegation of authority to intermediary bodies whose members had in the course of the

31. Most conveniently now in Gregory L. Freeze, *The Russian Levites—Parish Clergy in the Eighteenth Century*, (Cambridge, Mass: Harvard University Press, 1977); also G. Florovskii, *Puti russkogo bogosloviia* (Paris: 1939; reprint ed., YMCA Press, 1982).

seventeenth century acquired the political and philosophic outlook of the governing elites and were ready to participate for the
sake of their own interests as well? The amorphousness and
relative primitiveness of the social structure of Muscovite Russia
was the main impediment to a genuine imitation of the well-
ordered police state model. But by trying to reproduce it by other
means—compulsion and state service—Peter not only precluded
the realization of his aims but also initiated trends that were
counterproductive to his goals. In short, needing to promote
initiative and independence of action in the economic, social, and
cultural spheres on the part of all groups of society, Peter in fact
stifled these qualities by resorting to force and by focusing
exclusively on the needs of the central establishment. The service
elite he had fashioned was so much the slave and instrument of
the state that it proved incapable of initiative, enterprise, and
independence even in the pursuit of its own private, selfish ends,
which, in turn, could have rebounded to the interest of the
empire as well.

What were then the results of Peter's turbulent reign?

The consciousness of rapid change on the part of the emperor
and his aides as well as on the part of the population was very
intense. The reign had an almost revolutionary character, largely
because of the drive, forcefulness, speed, and ruthlessness with
which the changes were pursued. Naturally the resistance was
almost equally great and violent. The transformations wrought by
the well-ordered police state in the West had been extensive and
had required determined efforts over a long period. Peter's
changes had been even greater, and they appeared to have rained
down like some tropical downpour. Moreover, in the West the
changes had been gradual and had been adjusted to special
conditions or to incorporate newly acquired insights. Peter's
actions were not only more impetuous but seemed capricious as
well, since he easily gave up measures that did not bring the
expected results as rapidly as he had hoped. He produced a sharp
break, sharper than anywhere in the West, in the psychological
outlook and makeup of Russian society. On the one hand, the
government—that is, the ruling elites—assimilated the goals,
purposes, and also the new practices and values of the rationally

constructivist state. The members of the elite had to assimilate the norms of a high time horizon, unlimited productive progress, and a bureaucratized administration. The people, on the other hand, all those who were not part of the elites—not only the peasantry but also urban classes, the clergy, and the non-Russians—were baffled and dispirited, and they reacted by sulkily withdrawing. The purpose of the changes were incomprehensible to them, and the new practices were unfamiliar and seemed to result only in harsher treatment and heavier burdens. It was therefore preferable to escape direct contact with all novelties. This psychological rift and consequent withdrawal made it even more difficult for the government to identify individuals and groups whom it could co-opt and to whom authority could be delegated to promote the aims of the tsar.

This situation reinforced the government's propensity toward limiting its purview to the central establishment—quite the opposite of the European well-ordered police state, which aimed at extending to the local level the policies and purposes of the central institutions. Instead of diffusing the new social and political conceptions and practices, the Russian government concentrated them at the center among a tiny minority of the population, the elites in the capitals. As a result, the government's impact was limited to a very narrow circle, and the huge state establishment seemed to float in midair, unconnected to the population and country at large. Furthermore, the small bureaucracy at the disposal of the state found itself overtaxed and overburdened. Its activities were many and the amount of paperwork huge, but its effectiveness and radius of action was quite narrow, confined mainly to the capitals, a few cities, and the military establishment. Even more important, because of overwork the government leadership had no time and energy left to think, plan, and conceive policies *de longue haleine*. Repression and compulsion were the only means available to the bureaucracy, and to a much greater degree than was the case in the West it had no overall control and direction, for there were no constituted bodies to limit its capricious tryanny or to make abuses known to higher institutions. The vastness of the territory, poor communications, and the technical backwardness and illiteracy of the empire's subjects only served to compound the difficulties. There was also a lack of overall direction; the Senate, as we have seen, had lost its directing role almost the moment it was put in operation, and no other institution succeeded in taking over the task. The job was left to the ruler, and after the death of Peter in 1725 until the accession of Catherine II in 1762 no one sovereign was truly up to the task. Even if there had been better rulers, no single person could have repeated the performance, such as it was, of Peter the Great. Consequently, for over a quarter of a century there seemed to be no coherence and consistency of policy in Russia, no capacity to follow through. Ad hoc measures predominated over planned actions; the high time horizon, the necessary presupposition of an état bien policé was lost sight of almost entirely. The post-Petrine state was quite weak, probably weaker than the Muscovite polity had been. Yet after Peter, willy nilly, the imperial government had to be more active, more involved in shaping reality, and as it tried to do more without being able to do so adequately it grew weaker.

A major reason for this weakness of the state and government was the very amorphousness of Russian society. It allowed the government neither to act effectively on society nor to draw on society to delegate responsibility for implementing its policies. A genuine division of social labor was precluded as well, since peasants and nobles engaged in activities that in the West were traditionally the function of urban classes and merchants. In their turn, merchants and townspeople engaged in the same enterprises as nobles and peasants. Such overlapping would have been of little consequence in a more open, dynamic, and productive society, but in Russia the absence of functional division of labor was a reflection of poverty, inadequacy of human resources, and of the weak condition of estates and corporate bodies.

The situation was complex, full of paradoxes that acted as a brake on the development of the country's productivity. The economic and social development of the empire proceeded on two distinct levels: in the capital and among the elites the state had a direct impact. There the government endeavored to implement Peter's policies and did so with some success in the cultural as well as military and diplomatic realms. In the provinces, however, among the peasantry, the government avoided active involvement in creating new resources and wealth. The gap between the two could not be bridged, for the empire lacked the resources and social structure needed to provide effective disciplining and control of the productive population.

At the same time, as a result of the Petrine reforms there was a great deal of social mobility in Russian society. The requirements of state service forced many members of the nobility to leave their families, estates, and home regions and to be constantly on the move. The large number of soldiers recruited from among the peasantry were moved about the land (and abroad) as military and other requirements necessitated. To maintain the military establishment and the service personnel, including those in the government offices and the court in the capital, peasants and townspeople were drafted to provide and transport food and material. The elites of peripheral, non-Russian regions flocked to the capitals to take up service—Ukrainians, Baltic Germans, and, as in earlier times, representatives of Eastern elites. Increased commercial contacts as well as the requirements of luxurious lifestyles made for travel and active contacts with the outside world. Finally, the westernized style of life adopted by the post-Petrine elites compelled many peasants to come to the capitals and garrison towns to provide produce, servants, and artisanal labor to build, decorate, and maintain townhouses and suburban estates and provide recreational activities. Yet Russian society was based on immobility: the nobles in compulsory service, the peasants attached to the land and to their masters, the urban classes restricted to their posady ("settlements"). Mobility, therefore, had to take place outside the officially recognized institutional framework; it was tolerated, and its rules were informal. That is the reason why the informal mobility could not be steered or guided and given the necessary security and regularity to maximize its benefits for the country as a whole. The government wavered between a permissiveness that favored private interests and the enforcement of compulsory service rules that benefited the state at the expense of the private sector, as we would term it. In the final event, the benefits of individual mobility and enterprise were lost both to the state (or society) and to the individual (or his class).

One gains the impression that whatever the accomplishments—
and at times they were quite remarkable, such as the founding of
the iron industries of the Urals, the building and provisioning of
the new capital, the spread of Western ways and articles to the
provinces—they did not benefit the country. Russia remained
poor and underdeveloped; it did not manifest those production-
oriented, conscious efforts that were at the root of the progress
achieved in Western and central Europe.

The inadequacies and problems inherited from the Petrine
system became quite apparent in the course of the several decades
that followed the death of the first emperor. The efforts made to
correct and reform the system had not reached very deep or very
far; in any case, they did not seem to have been effective. True,
there are important lacunae in our knowledge of the period,
especially with respect to the efforts of A. Volynski in the reign of
Anne and the policies of the brothers Shuvalov in the reign of
Elizabeth. In the latter case, we know that significant steps were
taken to promote manufacturing and to liberate trade. But the
Shuvalovs relied on the entrepreneurial and investment potential
of the nobility, especially the rich groups connected with the
court; it proved to be a costly and short-lived approach. The fate
of the Ural mining and metallurgical enterprises showed that
their policy had only prevented merchants and successful traders
from the ranks of free peasants and other groups from full
involvement at the time. The policy of liberalizing trade, however,
was more successful: in 1753 most internal tariffs and tolls were
abolished, opening the way for the expansion of commerce
throughout the empire.[32] The exchange circuit was appreciably
intensified, and this, in turn, served to underline the deficiencies
and paradoxes of the system on the administrative level.[33]

---

32. S. M. Troitskii, *Finansovaia politika russkogo absoliutizma v XVIII veke*
(Moscow: 1966); Roger Portal, *L'Oural au XVIIIe siècle—Etude d'histoire economique et
sociale* (Paris: Institut d'études Slaves, 1950); N. N. Firsov, *Russkiia torgovo-
promyshlennyia kompanii v 1-iu polovinu XVIII stoletiia* (Kazan': 1896; reprint ed.,
1974).

33. The "class character" of these measures upon which Soviet historians dwell
ad nauseum is immaterial in our context; what matters here was the impossibility
for the system to reform itself on the basis of Petrine presuppositions.

The ambiguous development led to the realization, at first slow and reluctant, that the Petrine transformation had not succeeded as it should have. It dawned upon contemporaries that the root of the trouble lay in the fact that Peter had been content to reshape the central government along modern lines and to win over the elite to a westernized style of life. The governing elite was also beginning to realize fully that the small central administrative apparatus was inadequate to the task of transforming Russia and Russian society, because it did not reach to the local levels where it counted most. In short, a structured society was needed first to discipline the population so that it could fulfill long-range productive tasks. Only members of society constituted in corporate bodies and endowed with rights and privileges would feel secure enough to display initiative and energy and reap the benefits of their activities without fearing capricious interference and confiscation by the authorities.

Two events occurred to make possible a more comprehensive and thorough approach to reform. Both were quite accidental: the first provided dramatic and graphic illustration of the system's political problems and weaknesses; the second was the emergence of a personality capable of pursuing more or less consistently an innovative policy based on experience and intellectual awareness. The two events were the short rule of Peter III and the accession and reign of Catherine II.

The reign of Peter III (December 1761–June 1762) showed how weak was the institutionalization of the Petrine system. A relatively well-working central administration that had waged a successful war in central Europe (the Seven Years War) and that had achieved some stability on the basis of the controlling role of the Senate and the imperial council was overthrown overnight by the new ruler. In its stead he (or his advisors) began to set up a very personal regime of favorites (many of whom were foreigners) supported by a nationwide police network in complete disregard of the Senate. The unpredictability and capriciousness of personalized sovereign power were thus again graphically demonstrated. Two measures taken by Peter III greatly troubled the politically conscious sectors of Russian society and the establishment, because they, too, seemed to seriously threaten the entire system. First, a radical and poorly conceived secularization of church property opened the door to peasant unrest, as the peasantry (about 800,000 souls) was removed from control of the church without being given adequate supervision by any other institution. The second measure, welcome in many respects but perplexing for the elite was the "freeing" of the nobility from compulsory state service. The measure removed a major pillar of the Petrine system and left the status of the nobility in great confusion, creating practical and psychological difficulties for its members. In any event, in addition to the ruler's personality and his foreign policy, the reign of Peter III threatened the Petrine system and demonstrated its instability. It brought the principal administrators to the realization or suspicion that the basic cause of the instability was a weakness in the structure of Russian society, since a capricious and poorly prepared monarch could so easily upset the balance of the polity.[34]

As in the case of Peter the Great, the personality and antecedent of Catherine II (whose coup d'état had overthrown Peter III) were of significance for the policies and direction she pursued during her reign. In her case, too, there had been a long period of preparation and gestation for the role she was to assume on the throne. Like Peter I, Catherine II had experienced the impact of Western ideas and practices which she learned of through her initial upbringing in Germany, her extensive reading, and active contacts with foreign personalities. We must also remember that she matured in the middle of the eighteenth century, when the ideas of cameralism and the practices of the état bien policé had been largely implemented in the West. As we have seen in the second part of this essay, they had been systematically expounded and given philosophic justification by jurists and political economists, and they were thus readily accessible to anyone interested in the administrative practices of the Prussia of Frederick II and the Austria of Maria Theresa. Catherine was also well aware of the implications that these notions and practices had for contemporary observers and the philosophes. But unlike Peter I, Catherine II had also absorbed the rhetoric of cameralist hopes

34. M. Raeff, "The Domestic Policies of Peter III and His Overthrow," *American Historical Review* 75 (1970): 1289–1310.

and intentions, a rhetoric that had found its expression in the literature of the Enlightenment. In her time, the rhetoric and philosophic implications of the "party of Progress" could no longer be separated from the pragmatism of administrative reform and legislation.

Indeed, by 1762 the language and the philosophy of the well-ordered police state had become fused with its practice to constitute the ideology of both enlightened absolutism and progressive intelligentsia on the eve of the French Revolution. Catherine's own "enlightened" rhetoric thus became very much part and parcel of her policies, but it also had the effect of giving false implications to her legislation. In my opinion, this rhetoric came to Catherine naturally, and she was not really aware of the contradiction that existed between the implications of her language and of her concrete political measures. In the minds of her readers, however, especially of those who shared the liberal presuppositions of the Enlightenment and had become aware of their historical consequences at the end of the eighteenth century, her rhetoric made for false expectations and erroneous interpretations. Indeed, it contributed to hide the limited, pragmatic character of Catherine's policies. The fact that the empress herself was a prisoner of her own rhetoric only compounded the difficulty in assessing her intentions and achievements correctly. Contemporaries and historians have been too much concerned with her words, her *scripta,* and not enough with her *acta,* and they have fallen victim to the *fata morgana* of the vocabulary that Western writers and philosophers forged to ideologize the état bien policé in the form of enlightened absolutism and revolutionary liberalism.

We should also mention another aspect of the chronological disjunction that has been a recurrent feature of Russian history. In Peter the Great's time, the *décalage* between Russia and the West had in fact been less than it became in Catherine's times, in spite of the strides in Europeanization made by Russia, more particularly by its cultural elites. At the dawn of the eighteenth century, Russia had to emulate practices that had just become established and were only beginning to bear fruit in the West. By the time of Catherine's accession, however, Western Europe had made enormous progress in the civilization for which the seventeenth century had laid the foundations. It was reaping its full economic and social benefits. Catherine came to the throne when the "take off" in agriculture had already occurred in Holland and England and was beginning to affect France and some parts of Germany, while the industrial revolution was taking hold and manufacturing and commerce were transformed at an increasing rate. The social and intellectual consequences of these developments had become the subject of critical analysis and discussion by the leading minds of the West. Russia, on the other hand, had barely managed to take hold of the political achievements of Peter the Great; it had not even kept pace with the modest social and economic progress of the German states and Austria. Catherine, therefore, was much more aware of Russia's lag than Peter had been, although she could think of her elite as being on the same level of culture and her empire in the same general historical-philosophic stage as the West, but it was precisely for that reason that she felt Russia's backwardness more acutely and had a greater urge to overcome it. Given the fact that the major instruments of state power had been available since Peter I, Russia's lag must be the fault of something else, of a more basic condition in her society that needed correction, and since the Russian elites had already acquired Western Europe's intellectual tools and culture, the task of overcoming the backwardness seemed both conceivable and feasible.

The ambivalences obtaining between Catherine's intellectual perception and rhetoric, on the one hand, and her concrete pragmatic measures on the other have often been explained by inconsistency or hypocrisy, categories of little use in historical analysis. Her words were compared to her acts, inconsistencies were found, and the coherence and purpose of her policies put in question. For my part, I believe that behind an apparently inconsistent pragmatism there was an overall goal, as there had been in the case of Peter the Great. For Catherine the ultimate goal was to bring about in Russia a social structure that would assist in implementing and realizing the principal notions and practices of the état bien policé.[35] In the pages to follow, which do

35. Dietrich Geyer, " 'Gesellschaft' als staatliche Veranstaltung: Bemerkung zur Sozialgeschichte der russischen Staatsverwaltung im 18. Jahrhundert," *Jahrbü-*

not attempt to be a comprehensive account of Catherine's reign,[36] I shall be concerned with this overall purpose to the extent that it serves to illustrate the dynamics of the well-ordered police state and to offer material for comparative observation.

Catherine did not change the administrative and political system introduced by Peter the Great; she improved and stream-lined it to make it more efficient. The Senate was consolidated in its position of chief supervisor and highest level of administrative control in the empire. This was largely achieved by subdividing it into several departments, to separate more clearly, though not completely, the judiciary from the administrative functions, on the model of the ordinance in seventeenth-century German states. The establishment in Moscow of Senate departments concerned with the adjudication of civil suits, mainly cases involv-ing estates and inheritances, brought the highest government institution closer to the subjects. The instructions given to A. A. Viazemskii upon his appointment as procurator general of the Senate made it quite clear that Catherine conceived of the body's role as primarily a supervisory, not a policymaking one.[37] Under the direction of Procurator General Viazemskii, a particularly efficient and experienced administrator, the Senate did indeed concentrate all information that flowed from the provinces and other subordinate agencies. At the time of his death in 1793 at the very end of Catherine's reign, Viazemskii had built up an efficient network of information gathering and controls on the provincial level that enabled his sovereign to make comprehensive and long-term plans.

There was no reorganization of the colleges, only some shifting about. But, more important, the colleges began to take on a pronouncedly monocratic character; as they abandoned their

cher für Gesch. Osteuropas, n.s., 14 (1966): 21–50 and idem., "Staatsausbau und Sozialverfassung: Probleme des russischen Absolutismus am Ende des 18. Jahr-hunderts," Cahiers du monde russe et soviétique 7 (1966): 366–77.

36. This has been splendidly done by Isabel de Madariaga, Russia in the Age of Catherine the Great (Yale University Press: New Haven, 1980).

37. "Ukaz o razdelenii Senata na departamenty" (17.IV.1763), Sbornik impera-torskogo russkogo istorichesko obshchestva (hereafter Sbornik IRIO), 7:279–80 and "Nastavlenie kn. Viazemskomu," ibid., pp. 345–48.

collegiate procedures their presidents acquired the position and authority of ministers.[38] This was especially true in the case of the colleges of commerce and war, and, naturally, the college of foreign affairs. Moreover, the private chancery of the ruler, staffed with efficient and knowledgeable secretaries, gained a dominant role in coordinating policies and preparing long-range initiatives.[39]

In spite of these changes, and they took hold gradually, striking root only after 1775, the network of subordinate institutions remained inadequate, so that effective implementation and long-term control of policies handed down from above were still sadly lagging. The government relied on ad hoc committees to deal with problems that suddenly and unexpectedly became pressing (for example, conduct of war or settlement of southern Russia). Catherine did, however, clearly innovate in one instance: to draft a code she convoked a special commission whose members were elected (on a relatively broad basis) and instructed to present statements *(nakazy)* from their constituents concerning the specific needs of their classes and regions. Although the Legislative Commission (or Great Commission) of 1767, as it is known, did not accomplish its assigned task of drafting a code, it did provide the government with an unsurpassed amount of information concerning the needs and desires of the most articulate elements of society.[40] We shall return to this event and its significance below. The government also heavily relied on ad hoc inspections and missions; the inspections by senators *(senatskaia reviziia)* became a routine and significant way of obtaining local information and of following up on the implementation of policies.[41] Naturally all of this did not really take the place of permanent

38. A. D. Gradovskii, "Vysshaia administratsiia Rossii XVIII st. i general prokurory," *Sochineniia* (St. Petersburg: 1899), 1:37–297.

39. N. Barsukov, ed., *Dnevnik A. V. Khrapovitskogo, 1782–1793* (St. Petersburg: 1874; a reprint is in preparation).

40. There is a vast literature on the commission, and a sizable number of the documents, including many *nakazy*, have been published. For the external history of the elections to and work of the commission, see A. V. Florovskii, *Sostav zakonodatel'noi kommissii 1767–1774 gg.* (Odessa: 1915).

41. The reports of the senatorial inspections are in TsGADA, collection XVI (Vysshii pravitel'stvuiushchii Senat), file nos. 643, 655, 726, 745, 828, to cite only a few.

and regular institutional networks of control such as existed in the West.[42] To make up for this deficiency, once the new provincial system (discussed below) had been set in place, the governors were required to furnish periodic reports on all aspects of their provinces' situation and activities. Compiled according to a set scheme and formulary, these reports were forwarded to the Senate, which could study and check them; in this way the Senate, or rather its procurator general, received an up-to-date picture of the changing conditions of a given locality or region.[43] Naturally the reports' accuracy and reliability as well as their comprehensiveness and intelligence varied widely with the governors and staff that put them together. But compared to the ignorance that had existed earlier, and in spite of their deficiencies and sometimes even outright distortions and lies, the governors' reports did over time provide the government with a body of concrete data on which to base its decisions and plans. And as we know, this was the sine qua non for a rational, constructivist policy.

The statute on the provinces of 1775 proved of the greatest importance in enabling the central authorities to penetrate to the local levels. As we have mentioned earlier, Peter the Great had largely ignored local administration, merely delegating fiscal responsibility to regiments garrisoned in the provinces. Such an improvised solution sufficed to maintain regiments in peacetime, although at high cost to the local population, but it did not offer the means of enforcing and implementing the policies of the well-ordered police state. The significant hiatus left by Peter was not bridged by his successors.[44] In part on the basis of the information provided by the nakazy to the Legislative Commission of

42. On the development of regular control institutions in Western states, cf. O. Hintze, "Der Commissarius und seine Bedeutung in der allgemeinen Verwaltungsgeschichte," in his *Staat und Verfassung* (Göttingen: Vandenhoeck & Ruprecht, 1962), pp. 242–74; R. Mousnier, "Etat et commissaire: Recherches sur la création des intendants des provinces 1634–1648" in his *La Plume, la faucille et le marteau* (Paris: Presses Universitaires de France, 1970), pp. 179–200 and *Les Institutions de la France sous la monarchie absolue* (Paris: Presses Universitaires de France, 1980), vol. 2.

43. E.g., TsGADA, collection XVI, file nos. 588, 594, 606, 636, 683, 696, 725, 729, 731, 785, 788, 1012, 1014.

44. Iu. V. Got'e, *Istoriia oblastnogo upravleniia v Rossii ot Petra I do Ekateriny II*, 2 vols. (Moscow: 1913; reprint ed., Moscow and Leningrad: 1941).

1767, in part in response to the challenge presented by the revolt of Pugachev, Catherine introduced a completely new system of local administration in 1775. We shall discuss it briefly, but it should be kept in mind that it was closely related to her basic effort at structuring Russian society (to be examined below). In summary, the statute on the provinces of 1775 divided the empire into more manageable and rational units of administration, the *guberniia* (provinces), subdivided into *uezdy* (districts).[45] Sometimes several gubernii were put under the overall supervision of a governor-general in a vice-gerency *(namestnichestvo)*; we may ignore this provision as not relevant in our context. The province was in the care of a governor responsible to the Senate, who had the right to communicate directly with the sovereign (although this right was not often used by the governors, it was regularly resorted to by the governors-general). We have mentioned the requirement for the governor to submit periodic reports to the procurator general of the Senate on all aspects of his territory. Assisting the governor was a collegial board that duplicated on the local level the major colleges involved in domestic policy; each functional department of the governor's board was responsible to its respective college in St. Petersburg. The main departments of the provincial boards were, of course, those concerned with finances (collection of taxes, administration of monopolies and franchises), trade, manufacturing, and general security and police. On the uezd levels there were embryonic counterparts of these institutions under the control of locally selected noble proprietors.

In essence, therefore, to the extent that it was successful the reform introduced a functional and rational routinization of administration on the provincial and to some extent on the district levels; it made for an easier flow of information to and from the center; it brought about clearer demarcation of jurisdiction and competences on functional principles. Lastly, the reform helped spread the network of state institutions, facilitating the penetration of administration and its policy aims to the provincial and district levels. A concomitant effect was to increase the

45. *PSZ*, nos. 14, 392 (7.XI.1775).

number of administrative and urban centers: many a village was promoted to town status for administrative purposes, and many a small town was enhanced by the implantation of an administrative staff.[46] In this manner the implementation of cameralist socioeconomic practices was facilitated on the local level. The new system required more numerous administrative staff, so that the scope of the service nobility's opportunities increased without removing its members from their estates and home regions. As a result we observe a return to the estate or a renewal of ties with the ancestral district on the part of many nobles; at the same time the didactic and cultural mission of the central administrator (governor and his chancery) was greatly enhanced as well. Whatever its deficiencies, the statute on the provinces of 1775 filled a gaping void, and it enabled the creation in Russia of an état bien policé, because for the first time in its history the state was in a position to affect and direct life-styles on the local level. One thing is sure—the act of 1775 brought the government nearer to the local population, precluding the repetition of large-scale peasant unrest and revolts such as Pugachev's. The Russian provinces and countryside had acquired the means of keeping peace and effectively maintaining law and order.

Catherine II shared the goals of the well-ordered police state—fullest development of the country's productive potential, a creatively active population, and investment in the future. Unlike Peter the Great, however, who had limited his efforts to prohibition and compulsion, Catherine believed Russia to be ready for a more positive approach and that government should sponsor and encourage society's (that is, its leading members') initiative and constructive activities. Her approach was feasible, for by the second half of the eighteenth century Russia possessed an elite that shared her notions, expectations, and goals. In one most important respect, however, the situation of Catherinian Russia was as far removed from central and Western Europe's as Petrine

46. TsGADA, collection 248, book 3823 (Reshennye dela po gorodam, 1769–1774). The classical study is by A. A. Kizevetter, *Posadskaia obshchina v Rossii XVIII stoletiia* (Moscow: 1903; reprint ed., Newtonville, Mass: Oriental Research Partners, 1978); cf. also G. Rozman, *Urban Networks in Russia, 1750–1800, and Premodern Periodization* (Princeton: Princeton University Press, 1976).

Russia had been: because of the nature of Russian serfdom, the state could not, except very marginally, have direct relations with and impact on the peasantry. This remained the exclusive domain of action of the individual landowner. This explains, to a large extent, the government's belief that it had first to transform the noble landowning elite in order to provide a viable basis for changing the life-style of the peasantry. We thus do not find Russian *Dorfordnungen* drafted by the state, although we have similar types of instructions issued by individual land- and serf-owners to improve the management of their estates. These instructions offer evidence of the elite's desire and endeavor to extend to the serf population the lessons and knowledge of cameralist principles and practices it had acquired in the service of the imperial government and imbibed in the intellectual atmosphere of court and capitals.[47]

For Catherine's government, as it had been for the German states in the seventeenth century and continued to be for enlightened absolutist rulers like Frederick II, population was the key element.[48] It was not a question of mere numbers, for Russia's population was considered to be large and it was rapidly expanding, although its distribution was very uneven. But there was a felt need to increase the skilled agricultural population; Catherine turned to the West to enlist and settle various Germans and others on the Volga, in the Ukraine, and in the east. Skilled groups among the empire's population were moved to more profitable areas, as illustrated by the successful settlement activity of G. A. Potemkin in South (New) Russia, who established, for example, specialized communities of Georgians, Armenians, Jews, and Greeks, many of whom eventually contributed to the growth of urban centers on the shores of the Black Sea (Odessa being the

47. "Instruktsii upraviteliam imenii XVIII v.," *Istoricheskii arkhiv* 4 (1949); 6 (1951); 8 (1953); M. Confino, "La Politique de tutelle des seigneurs russes envers leurs paysans vers la fin du XVIIIᵉ siècle," *Revue des études slaves* 37 (1960): 39–69; Raeff, *Origins of the Intelligentsia*, on militarism on the estates; and the well-known memoirs of A. T. Bolotov.

48. V. E. Den, *Naselenie Rossii po piatoi revizii*, 2 vols. (Moscow: 1902) and more recently V. M. Kabuzan, *Narodonaselenie Rossii v XVIII—pervoi polovine XIX v.* (Moscow: 1963) and *Izmeneniia v razmeshchenii naseleniia Rossii v XVIII—pervoi polovine XIX v.* (Moscow: 1971).

outstanding example). We need only to compare the administrative setup used for new settlers in the German states—for example, the resettlement of the Huguenots touched upon in part 2—with those of Catherine to see the world of difference that separated them. First of all, Catherine did not assume (and rightly so) that the settlers would come and stay in formed and closed communities, though she underestimated the strength of their cultural and linguistic conservatism.[49] Furthermore, she deemed it impossible to guarantee the rights and privileges they had enjoyed at home. True, the settlers were given some relief from taxation, and some of their values—especially with respect to religion—were to be taken into account in cases of conflict, but they had to submit to Russian law and practices. Unlike new settlers in central Europe, their integration into existing corporate and social structures could not be encouraged, for there were none that they could integrate into and in some cases they were settled in isolated and virtually desert areas. In the absence of such corporate structures, the Russian administration took complete charge of the new settlers; frequently the recruiters themselves doubled as the administrative and judicial authorities.[50] Lastly, the whole operation was controlled from the center through the "Board of Guardians of Foreign Settlers"—a significant title, it may be noted in passing. The implication was clearly that the settlers were to be treated like minors and kept under the supervision as well as protection of the central authorities; they were not granted local and social autonomy, let alone self-government. Needless to say, the experiment did not prove very successful. The most important function that the new settlers could have fulfilled, that of *Kulturträger*—pioneers in and teachers of better agricultural methods—they were unable to perform since they were kept administratively and socially separate from

49. A. Klaus, *Nashi kolonii: Opyty i materialy po istorii i statistike inostrannoi kolonizatsii v Rossii,* (St. Petersburg: 1869; reprint ed., Newtonville, Mass.: Oriental Research Partners, 1972), vol. 1. The important monograph by Roger Bartlett, *Human Capital* (Cambridge, England: Cambridge University Press, 1981) appeared too late for me to use.

50. *PSZ,* no. 11 879 (22.VII.1763) and 11 880 (same date, Manifesto, and previous version, no. 11 720, 4.XII.1762). The dossier of the chancery in TsGADA, collection 248, book 3398, 3762.

the rest of the population. Only the abandonment of bureaucratic paternalism enabled some German settlements to be integrated into the economy of the empire, though they still failed to have a significant impact on Russian peasant society.

With respect to trade, Catherine was in a position to pursue both the old police ordinance policies and those of the more recent Western experiences. She founded and supported a number of privileged trading companies, especially for foreign trade.[51] She also actively pursued the improvement of roads and canals and the elimination of tolls at the entrance of towns, and she eased the circulation of small traders from villages to towns by dropping the more restrictive passport requirements. She strongly encouraged freedom of enterprise in trade; witness the abolition of the state monopoly over the China trade at Kiakhta.[52] The nobility obtained the right to trade freely in their own produce, mainly distilled alcohol, which became their class monopoly. Free and state peasants as well as urban classes also obtained greater freedom to trade in the empire, and domestic commerce expanded significantly thanks to their entrepreneurial initiatives. Foreign trade remained largely in the hands of foreigners who had the necessary capital and tonnage, but they, too, were freed from many fiscal and administrative constraints. Compared to previous periods the commerce of Russia soared, and if it did not make up for the general economic backwardness of the country it was not for want of Catherine's trying but because of what economists would call structural constraints in the situation, in particular serfdom and the cost of transportation.

Similarly, Catherine encouraged manufacturing, giving greater scope to individual initiative and free entrepreneurial activity.

51. The classic study still remains N. N. Firsov, *Pravitel'stvo i obshchestvo v ikh otnosheniiakh k vneshnei torgovle Rossii v tsarstvovanie imperatritsy Ekateriny II* (Kazan: 1902; reprint ed., Newtonville, Mass.: Oriental Research Partners, 1972).

52. Clifford M. Foust, *Muscovite and Mandarin: Russia's Trade with China and its Setting, 1727–1805* (Chapel Hill: University of North Carolina Press, 1969) and James R. Gibson, *Feeding the Russian Fur Trade: Provisionment of the Okhotsk Seaboard and the Kamchatka Peninsula, 1639–1856* (Madison: University of Wisconsin Press, 1969) for two specialized but very suggestive studies of particular cases.

From indirect evidence it is possible to infer that the number of entrepreneurs from among the merchants, the small urban tradesmen, and even the peasants increased very significantly, as did the number of manufacturing centers and areas. Unlike Peter I, who had imposed specific types of manufactures and prescribed quality, quantity, and processing techniques, Catherine left such things to individual initiative and judgment. But in two areas her own legislative initiatives played a determining role: she gave owners of real estate full title to the resources of their subsoil, ending the restrictive state monopoly that Peter I had imposed.[53] She also initiated legislation (and its implementation) designed to ensure the security of titles to property, as well as extending the scope of personal security through more effective administration of justice. In the tradition of the seventeenth-century German ordinances, she showed concern for the ecological consequences of industrial development, indicating that she had a much higher time horizon and greater respect for personal welfare than previous Russian rulers.[54] For the first time in Russia we detect a systematic approach to the husbanding of natural resources, especially lumber, as well as direct interest in promoting the welfare of society for its own sake and not only because of state needs.[55] Steps were also taken to secure the circulation of instruments of credit with a law on bills of exchange.[56] The issuing of assignats was a measure dictated not only by the needs of war but also to facilitate trade exchange operations, since copper and silver coinage were proving in short supply and not liquid enough to satisfy expanding needs and to stimulate the economy.

True to the doctrine of the well-ordered police state, Catherine

53. *PSZ*, no. 15 447 (28.VI.1782); note the date, an anniversary of the accession gift!

54. John T. Alexander, "Catherine II, Bubonic Plague and the Problem of Industry in Moscow," *American Historical Review* 79 (1974):637–71.

55. D. Eeckaute, "La Législation des forêts au XVIIIᵉ siècle," *Cahiers du monde russe et soviétique* 9 (1968): 194–208.

56. Troitskii, *Finansovaia politika*, for background and the classical N. D. Chechulin, *Ocherki po istorii russkikh finansov v tsarstvovanie Ekateriny II* (St. Petersburg: 1906).

made serious efforts, not immediately successful, to encourage greater productivity in all areas—agriculture, manufacturing, and mining. As had the police ordinances in Germany in the seventeenth century, she endeavored to import and disseminate knowledge of new techniques and crops, and she energetically encouraged and supported the foundation and work of the Free Economic Society in this domain.[57] The history and record of these efforts show that the initiative and active participation was the government's; as a rule, society followed in the eighteenth century rather reluctantly the lead taken by the sovereign and high dignitaries at court and in government. Moreover, in Russia, contrary to central Europe, members of society who followed this lead expected rewards and recognition from the state; they were not satisfied with merely private accolades for their entrepreneurial initiatives, although they did not disdain their material benefits. One of the reasons for the situation was again the absence of social groupings and associations that might supplement and support state leadership and offer peer pressure and recognition.

Lastly, the state also took the lead in encouraging and providing the means for the cultural progress of society—or of the elites, at any rate. As we have seen in the case of the German-speaking territories, this was an important and necessary aspect of the program of a well-ordered police state, for only a knowledge of nature and the development of rational mental tools would ensure society's ongoing creative productivity as well as its material and spiritual progress. Following in the footsteps of Peter the Great, Catherine II encouraged education. But her purpose was broader, since she realized that technical know-how and mechanically acquired intellectual tools alone would not suffice. Unlike Peter, Catherine was not concerned to train a few specialists in some technical fields. Under the influence of the cultural and intellectual strides made in the West since the beginning of the century, she laid her primary emphasis on the formation of a

57. For an introduction to the role of the Free Economic Society, see John Brown, "The Publication and Distribution of the *Trudy* of the Free Economic Society, 1765–1796," *Russian Review* (1977): 341–50; Michael Confino, *Domaines et seigneurs en Russie vers la fin du XVIIIe siècle* (Paris: Institut d'etudes Slaves, 1963); and the ubiquitous memoirs of A. T. Bolotov.

society, or at any rate of an active elite, that would possess an education enabling it to display cultural and technical creativity on its own.[58] Her educational program, therefore, was designed to form a new type of men, men capable of making independent and creative intellectual, scientific, scholarly, and artistic contributions. Naturally this first concerned the noble ruling elites. The scope of their educational institutions was broadened and their number increased; the goal of such education was to fashion not merely obedient tools of the state, as had been the aim of Peter the Great, but men capable of showing the way and serving as models to the whole of society. Catherine went even further. Not content with forming a progress-minded elite, she envisioned the spread of education to the lower classes, at least to free or state peasants and to the urban population. Her plans proved too ambitious for her time and place, but it is notable that she made serious efforts to implement them; in so doing, she spread the benefits of a modern type of education to a significant number of individuals from all classes of society who could be expected to occupy key positions and serve as models to others.

More and better education was not sufficient to make Russia an état bien policé. Access to the products of the modern Western mind was still limited, and their dissemination was a sine qua non for the kind of dynamic and productive society that Catherine envisaged. To this end she took a most important step by ending the state monopoly of printing presses and opening up the printing trade to private initiative and enterprise. The number of titles and runs of publication soared immediately, so that both Western and Russian writings (technical, scholarly, and belles lettres) became readily accessible and penetrated even into the far provinces. From then on, printed reading matter could be depended upon as an instrument for the enlightenment and progress of all of Russian society. Catherine's policy with respect to censorship was on the whole liberal and encouraging by the

---

58. By now there is a vast literature on the history of Russian education, in Western languages as well as in Russian. For an introduction, see Alexander Vucinich, *Science in Russian Culture: A History to 1860* (Stanford: Stanford University Press, 1963); I. de Madariaga, "The Foundation of the Russian Educational System by Catherine II," *Slavonic and East European Review* 57 (1979): 369–95.

standards of her times. Only at the very end of her reign did she withdraw some of the freedoms and encouragements she had given earlier;[59] but the initial steps she had taken proved to be irreversible. The increase in publications, the relaxed censorship, and the educational policies had helped into being and consolidated an intellectual elite that was to play a leading role in the future progress of the empire.

Closely related was the encouragement Catherine gave to scholarship and science. Here, too, Peter had taken the first step and set an example by founding the Academy of Sciences, but his purpose had been narrowly practical, to help build an army and navy. Catherine saw farther and could benefit from the inspiration and experiences of the West. Her goal was to have a body of scientists capable of further exploring the empire and thereby contributing to the intellectual and scientific progress of Europe. She also needed scholars to develop a national culture by investigating the empire's history and traditions and to assist in drafting meliorative legislation rooted in an accurate knowledge of Russian reality. Last but not least, Catherine initiated the study of Russian law, both as an academic discipline and as a tool for future administrators. She sent students abroad to study law and invited foreign scholars to lecture on jurisprudence; she established the first chair of law at the University of Moscow and supported the compilation and publication of legal manuals and collections of laws for practical purposes.[60] These cultural initiatives of Catherine's encouraged the formation of an intellectual creative elite. Little did she realize at first that her maternalistic supervision and concern would backfire once this elite felt strong enough to break loose from the state's leading strings.

59. S. Frederick Starr and G. Marker have promised studies on book publishing in Russia in the eighteenth century that will complement those made recently for France. See J. L. Black, *Citizens for the Fatherland (Education, Educators, and Pedagogical Ideas in Eighteenth Century Russia)* (Boulder: East European Quarterly Publisher, 1979); K. A. Papmehl, *Freedom of Expression in Eighteenth Century Russia* (The Hague: Martinus Nijhoff, 1971).

60. A. N. Fateev, "K istorii iuridicheskoi obrazovannosti v Rossii," in *Uchenye zapiski osnovannye russkoi uchebnoi kollegiei v Prage* (Prague: 1934) 1(3): 129–256; A. G. Cross, *"By the Banks of the Thames": Russians in Eighteenth Century Britain* (Newtonville, Mass.: Oriental Research Partners, 1980) and the unmanageably extensive literature on A. Radishchev's years in Leipzig.

We come now to Catherine's most crucial and significant policy innovation, namely the effort at restructuring Russian society. As the preceding remarks have made clear, in resuming Peter the Great's drive for a well-ordered police state in Russia, Catherine reversed his approach. The first emperor had insisted on compulsion and state control, believing that westernization could take place only within the framework of the state and for its exclusive needs. Catherine, for her part, wanted to rely on the participation of society itself, for she also realized, as Peter had not, that in the West the success of the well-ordered police state had been due to its enlisting and co-opting society. This knowledge led the empress to the realization that Russia had no society in the sense of structured groups, corporations, and associations capable of acting together, independently, in a predictable and rational manner in pursuit of their own interests as well as of those of the community. Catherine's recognition of the beneficial role of a comprehensively structured society, rather than reliance on an atomized population ruled by state servants, constitutes her most important contribution to the political history of Russia. Her efforts to bring about a structured society are interesting not only for understanding the subsequent history of imperial Russia but also for an appreciation of the dynamics of the état bien policé as a form of modern political culture.

Catherine's plan to create by legislative fiat social classes or, more accurately perhaps, estates, in the vocabulary prevailing at the time, can be readily inferred from her attempts at setting up a third estate in Russia. "Attempts" may be saying a bit too much, perhaps; it was rather an intention, although in one specific instance the intention was translated into concrete measures. Catherine spoke repeatedly of the desirability of creating and firmly rooting a genuine third estate, meaning thereby a commercial, artisanal, and perhaps manufacturing class that might also include artists and professionals (such as musicians, painters, architects, and teachers).[61] Endowed with secure rights and privileges but astrained to the normal obligations of the empire's taxable *(podatnye)* subjects, members of this third estate would also

---

61. For example, see the letter of Catherine II to Comte de Münich, 9.II.1766, in *Sbornik IRIO* 10 (1872): 66–67.

serve to breach the solid front of serfdom, since freed serfs and peasants of undetermined categories would be automatically enrolled in this class. In actual fact, Catherine only provided that orphans and foundlings placed in the orphanages established by her advisor on educational affairs, I. I. Betskoi, were to be free persons and enrolled in this estate upon release from the institutions where they were to receive professional or artisanal training. Assisted by the government in starting a trade or business on their own, they would lay the foundation of an active and productive third estate and constitute a solid basis for Russia's material and cultural progress. Echoes of the Prussian orphanages and poorhouses (established by Hermann Francke in Halle and expanded by Frederick II) are unmistakable. Unfortunately we do not possess precise figures on the number of those who survived the orphanages to benefit from this legislation; the death rate in foundling homes and orphanages was notoriously high, and we know next to nothing about most "graduates," since their traces were easily lost.[62]

Naturally the legislated mutation of existing social groups into officially recognized estates proved more significant and durable. It found expression in two major legislative acts, the Charters (a significant term) to the Nobility and to the Towns, both issued on 21 April 1785, and in a projected parallel "charter" for state peasants (implemented in part only in some Ukrainian provinces). It may be argued that in fact the first step toward the structuring of the population into constituted bodies or estates had been taken in 1767 in connection with the elections to the Legislative Commission. Indeed, those entitled to elect deputies— provincial nobles, members of the urban population, some free and state peasants, non-Russian natives, as well as *odnodvortsy* (single householders), cossacks, and the relics of former service categories[63]—were to do so as members of that particular corpo-

62. "Plan général de la maison des enfans trouvés, fondée à Moscou," in Betzky [I. I. Betskoi], *Les plans et les status, des différents établissements ordonnés par Sa Majesté Impériale Catherine II pour l'éducation de la jeunesse et l'utilité génerale de son empire*, (Amsterdam: 1775), vol. 1.

63. Curiously enough, the clergy was not included, though it was the only group coming close to being a genuine estate. Individual clergymen sat in the commission as delegates of other groups, towns, or institutions.

rate body. For the nobility it meant recognition and reaffirmation (often also the discovery) of regional solidarities that had practically disappeared under Peter the Great's service rules. For the urban population the election implied recognizing legally and psychologically that the town constituted a unit with an identity of its own, regardless of the social and national makeup of its population.[64] A similar effect was produced in the other social units whose members became more conscious of their identity. Even though the deputy who was eventually sent to the commission might owe nomination to prominent personal status or to government connections, the very process of election and of drafting the deputy's instruction (*nakaz* or *cahier*) fostered a sense of group identity or coherence, an "estate consciousness" if one will, especially among the nobility and the elite sectors of the urban population.

The deputies' nakazy or cahiers were testimony of the groups' wish to have some rights and privileges recognized by the government and their public status given appropriate structure. It is noteworthy that the Russian provincial nobility scornfully rejected the suggestion of an estate structure on the model of the Baltic nobility's. The Russian nobles' sense of identity was still defined by their service status; they thought only of securing individual advantage and did not function as an autonomous corporate estate sharing administrative responsibility with the state. It was at the sovereign's initiative and at her prodding that some form of estate structure was eventually given to the leading social classes of the empire.[65]

A further step in this direction was taken by the statute on the provinces of 1775, which provided for the election by the local nobles of a constable to execute the governor's directives and to enforce law and order. As a last step, the charters of 1785 set up the necessary institutional framework for the estate organization of the provincial and urban elites. The Charter to the Nobility

64. François-Xavier Coquin, *La Grande Commission législative (1767–68): Les Cahiers de doléances urbains* (Paris and Louvain: 1972) and A. V. Florovskii, *Sostav zakonodatel'noi kommissii.*

65. Wilson R. Augustine, "Notes toward a Portrait of the Eighteenth Century Nobility," *Canadian American Slavic Studies* 4 (1970): 373–425; Raeff, *Origins of the Russian Intelligentsia.*

granted corporate status to the nobles of each province;[66] the provincial noble corporation was recognized as a constituted legal entity, and every three years it elected its leaders and spokesmen, the marshal of the nobility for the entire province, and a marshal for each district. The provincial marshal cared for the interests of the estates, appointed or acted himself as guardian of orphans, chaired the board administering charitable institutions for the nobility (including sometimes schools), and petitioned the sovereign in the name of his peers. The marshal on the uezd level had similar, albeit more restricted and subordinate functions. In addition, members of the nobility were freed from corporal punishment, they received the right to be judged by their peers (a right that was never clearly defined and in practice superogatory, since at that time all judges were members of the nobility anyway), and had the privilege of disposing freely of their property, including subsoil resources from their estates. The provincial assembly of the nobility kept a record of membership and decided on admission of newcomers (from other provinces, from abroad, or through ennoblement). These estate privileges received corporate life and existence at the members' periodic meetings to elect the marshals, constables, and their assistants. The meetings were a social occasion as well, helping to foster cultural life in the provinces and to bind together the members of the estate. Catherine and her government hoped that this structure and the security of person and property that it guaranteed would mold the nobility into a dynamic, enterprising, and productive class that would contribute to the empire's material and cultural progress. While these hopes proved too sanguine at the time, in the long run, in particular after 1812, Catherine's expectations did largely materialize.

In a practical administrative sense, the district nobility acted as an estate by electing a constable *(zemskii ispravnik)* who was the local police officer and "justice of the peace" (in fact a mediator rather than a judge). It was the constable who implemented the directives received from the center through the governor's office. As police officer, the constable punished serfs at their master's

66. *PSZ*, no. 16 187 (21.IV.1785).

request and in so doing helped weaken the paternalistic and domestic features of serfdom. However, neither the constable nor the marshal of the nobility acted in the name of the provincial corporation of the nobility; they did not personify it, nor were they empowered to take the initiative in institutional, economic, or cultural activities in the name of the estate or their fellow nobles. They could act in the domain of philanthropic or didactic institutions only with the permission of the central authorities or the governor, and on an individual basis. Nor did the "corporation" of a province's nobility have any resources of its own to be expended independently of state direction. It was out of the question for the local nobility to act ex officio as administrators and judges on the model of the *Landrat* in Prussia or the Baltic provinces. The Russian nobles could not constitute themselves into a corporate tribunal to adjudicate or settle disputes involving their members. The constable was merely a subordinate official, and as his job was neither well paid nor given adequate recognition in the Table of Ranks, it was not much sought after; frequently it devolved on the poorest and least energetic or on the protégé of an influential personage, who was likely to look after his patron's interests rather than those of his fellow nobles in the district. The survival of the service mentality and of the personal nature of authority resulted in the district or provincial marshal's being elected not so much for his qualities as spokesman of the estates as for his putative influence with a dignitary or a favorite; for this reason, too, he frequently resided in the capital, and his connections with the nobility that had elected him were rather tenuous. In short, the ambiguity of Catherine's enterprise stemmed from the fact that she had to create a convention that did not yet exist; to be successful, she would have had to give the nobility freer rein in managing their corporate affairs, something they were reluctant to do, as their reaction to the Baltic model showed. But greater autonomy, even if the nobles had taken advantage of it, would have led to Catherine's losing control over the situation in the provinces and relinquishing her role of sole initiator and director of the country's modernization. True, at one time Catherine seems to have seriously thought of giving the provincial nobles a political existence as well, like German territorial *Stände,* by having them participate with consultative voice in the formulation of important legislation. How serious she was about it we shall probably never know; we do know, however, that as she was pondering the matter she showed a preference for government-appointed representatives over those elected or nominated by the provincial corporations of nobility.[67]

The Charter to the Towns had a similar purpose and thrust but diverged in specifics, of course. In the towns, the registered urban population (which excluded many inhabitants, such as noblemen and their peasant domestics, and peasants in temporary, though at times virtually permanent, residence) also was to form a corporation composed of three guilds and the *meshchane* (urban commoners or "townspeople").[68] This urban structure helped to administer the town in a manner that paralleled the role of the nobility in the provinces (though with even less authority, for the appointed governor, police chief, or military commandant residing in the town exercised greater direct control). The urban commoners did not attain anything like corporate status; they remained a repressed social category that had to meet most of the tax and service obligations imposed on the town. Wealthier and professionally active urban dwellers were organized into three guilds, membership in which was based on capital declared and assessed. The guild members, however, especially those of the first two guilds, came to play an increasingly greater role in local administrative decisions and in implementing government policies. They acquired some sense of identity, yet their subordination to the purposes of the state precluded their attaining a firm foundation for autonomous action, although through their spokesmen before the administration their economic interests received better protection. Under the circumstances, Russia could not develop the equivalent of an urban third estate. Catherine was well aware of the fact, which explains her toying with the idea of using orphans to build up a third estate that eventually would include the productive sectors of the taxable population both in towns and in the country.

67. M. Raeff, "The Empress and the Vinerian Professor: Catherine II's Projects of Government Reforms and Blackstone's *Commentaries," Oxford Slavonic Papers,* n.s., 7 (1974): 18–41.

68. *PSZ,* no. 16 188 (21.IV.1785).

In imitation of the nobles' right to set up charitable institutions, Catherine allowed the urban leadership to establish and administer medical, philanthropic, and educational enterprises, as well as to supervise public health and security matters. To this end she created a special board, the *uprava blagochiniia* (Board of Public Decorum), by a legislative act that was the second attempt at implanting a comprehensive Polizei Ordnung on Russian soil, limited to the towns of course.[69] The *Ustav blagochiniia* (Statute of Decorum) has perhaps not been paid the attention it deserves. Its preamble, *"Zertsalo"* (mirror of decorum), appears to have been largely taken from de La Mare's *Traité de police*,[70] though it is really not necessary to look for specific textual borrowings, since the thrust and tone of the act were similar to those of many German police ordinances, in particular the most recent ones for Berlin. Be that as it may, the law endeavored to have the tasks of police and urban administration shared by representatives of the town population. Selected townsmen were put in charge of sections and subsections and made responsible for order, cleanliness, and morality, evidently on the pattern of the Berlin Polizey Ordnung of 1735. The urban administration was to introduce and supervise a number of practices to rationalize the routine measures concerning public hygiene, cleanliness, and law and order, and to provide a better environment for the economic activities of the population. Although it was dominated by state-appointed officials, the uprava blagochiniia did include select local representatives, and it may be said to have been a first step toward shared responsibility for the town's police and welfare needs. In striking contrast to the police ordinances for the German towns of the seventeenth century as well as to the later regulations for Berlin, the ustav emphasized the repressive and negative aspects of police law; half of the act dealt with punishments for violations rather than constructive measures.

Lastly, we should mention Catherine's intention to give an estatelike structure to the state peasantry. In the project she drafted, the state peasantry appeared as an estate in a rather

69. The first such effort had been the *Glavnyi magistrat* of Peter I.

70. *PSZ*, no. 15379 (8.IV.1782); Vl. Grigor'ev, "Zertsalo upravy blagochiniia (epizod iz istorii Ustava blagochiniia 1782 g.)," *Russkii istoricheskii zhurnal* 3–4 (1917): 73–103.

limited sense, for it remained under the paternalistic supervision of the officials.[71] In this respect the proposal was not so far removed from the Bauern or Dorf Ordnungen we had occasion to mention in part 2 of this essay. What is striking, however, is that Catherine's plan dealt exclusively with the administration of the peasants in their villages; they were not to be given any meaningful autonomy beyond the very narrow confines of regulating their daily routines. It also clearly emerges from the document that the Russian state did not have, or did not recognize, communal self-governing bodies and individuals to whom the main task of administrative supervision could be delegated as a matter of course. The project proposed to do so by providing for the election of ten and one hundred men (*desiatniki* and *sotskie*) to assist in the administration of the village community. Unlike Western police ordinances for the villages, Catherine's project gave no attention to material, cultural, or agricultural concerns. It was implied that once good administration was established productivity would follow, but the question was not given special consideration. In brief, Catherine's project was reminiscent of early seventeenth-century German approaches to village policing rather than of the comprehensive and progressive policies embodied in eighteenth-century Dorfordnungen.

Russian historiography has repeatedly stressed that Catherine did nothing about serfdom, yet was it not serfdom that precluded a society of estates or even a civil society from striking roots in Russia? The nobles, it is argued, depended on the state's protection against their peasant serfs, and no third estate could emerge as long as the overwhelming majority of the population was in virtual slavery. This is oversimplifying a bit. As I. de Madariaga has shown, Catherine was aware of the necessity of ending serfdom, at least in its existing form, so as to release the productive forces in society.[72] She wanted to do it gradually, starting with the serfs' right to acquire property and to enjoy this acquisition in security. Catherine never implemented this plan,

71. "Proekt imperatritsy Ekateriny II ob ustroistve svobodnykh sel'skikh obyvatelei," *Sbornik IRIO* 20 (1877):447–98.

72. I. de Madariaga, "Catherine II and the Serfs: A Reconsideration of Some Problems," *Slavonic and East European Review* (1974).

and we need not, in the present context, speculate about her motives. There is no question that the concern was present, and it is unlikely that it was motivated by political or humanitarian considerations, for in this domain Catherine always put the economic aspect first.

What did all these efforts and plans of Catherine's amount to? Clearly the empress wanted to restructure Russian society so as to introduce stable estates possessing the legal status of corporations as well as some degree of autonomy in the administration of their own affairs. Thereby she hoped to attain two goals: first, by giving greater security to individual members of the estates, stimulate them to greater creativity and entrepreneurial initiatives, and, by allowing them to become richer and more prosperous, increase the country's wealth, strengthen her own power, and further the empire's progress. Secondly, by granting the estates a modicum of administrative autonomy within the framework of their class interests, Catherine hoped to educate them to better citizenship and to relieve the burdens and pressures resting on a small, comparatively overworked, and all too thinly dispersed officialdom. The provincial institutions of self-administration would be helpful as pools for recruiting new and better officials, and she proved right in this respect, although it turned out to be counterproductive to her primary aim, that of fostering the estates.

We have mentioned that in one area Catherine's policies had been particularly successful, namely in opening up and improving the quality of cultural life. In so doing she laid the foundation for a civil society in the cultural domain. But she felt compelled to restrict the civil society's scope and freedom, especially at the end of her reign, when the winds from the West were blowing a little bit too radically for her taste. But the civil society of culture wanted to engage in public educational and philanthropic activities on its own independently of the state. This Catherine's government would not permit; it turned repressive and prosecuted those involved, thus effectively stymying their creative efforts. Not until the nineteenth century, more particularly as a result of the backlash to her son's brief reign, did some of the seeds that she had planted strike roots and sprout. For example, the nobility developed an autonomous cultural life in the provinces, which served to foster for the first time since Peter the Great its members' sense of identity. This sense of identity, however, was based on common cultural activities, not on economic interests or involvement in public life as had been the case in the West. It is not surprising, therefore, that the truly creative impulse occurred in the domains of literature, thought, and the arts, an impetus that propelled Russia to the avant garde of modern culture, while social and economic developments were to lag for much longer. Indeed, it proved easier to impose and initiate a cultural modernization and transformation of the elites under state guidance (although the contradiction between guidance and creative freedom eventually became apparent). It was more difficult, or rather impossible, to introduce the modernizing pattern of the well-ordered police state in the absence of social structures to co-opt for its implementation. The job had to be done by a centralized bureaucracy, and when in the second half of the nineteenth century the state tried to build up the social base it lacked, it had to face much more complex conditions and in a different climate.

We may stop at this point to consider very briefly one dimension of the Russian situation that has not been given its due so far. Unlike the German territories where the well-ordered police state was developed, the realm of the Russian emperors was a multinational empire. In Muscovite times this fact hardly preoccupied the rulers and their assistants, who were content to collect tribute and undertake lackadaisical and inconsistent efforts at converting the nonorthodox. Peter the Great, too, had other things on his mind, and while he was eager to accept those non-Russians (of Christian faith) who wanted to take up service in his government (such as the Ukrainians and the Baltic Germans), he hardly had a set policy toward all others. Some of his more intelligent collaborators, for example V. N. Tatishchev, realized the necessity of dealing with the nomadic natives on the frontiers of the empire on the basis of their peculiarities and differences. Tatishchev advocated diplomacy and sometimes devious but on the whole pacific and tolerant policies to tie these natives more closely to the Russian empire.[73] Things, however, took on a

73. S. Blanc, *Un disciple de Pierre le Grand.*

slightly different perspective once Catherine II decided to create a social structure to support the modernizing efforts of the state. Such a policy had to involve the non-Russian population as well, if only because the settlement of agriculturists in the south and on the eastern frontiers involved closer contacts with the non-Russians, but also because their participation in the Pugachev rebellion had given pause to the authorities in St. Petersburg.

Catherine's approach derived from the double source of the practice of the well-ordered police state and the intellectual framework provided by the philosophy of history of the seventeenth century and its "enlightened" projection onto the future. The police state aspect implied the inclusion of the empire's non-Russian areas and populations in promoting material and cultural progress, since the world was one, and nature, especially human nature, uniform in its laws. Furthermore, and this was the contribution of contemporary philosophic anthropology, it was believed that the state of nature was evil and that all mankind aimed at civilization and higher culture. The Enlightenment corollary was the belief in the existence of stages of cultural development and the desirability of raising a people to a higher stage by conscious and purposeful policies. As the Jesuits had done in the case of the Indians of the Plata, so the enlightened Westerners should do with the "inferior" and "savage" nations that were under their care. In other terms, the paternalism toward the peasants, considered to be still children, was to be extended to the non-Western nations within the empire; this gave the government a duty as well as necessity to protect and further the development of the wretched natives even against their will.[74] The Russians could, of course, then play the same role of Kulturträger with respect to the natives that the Western nations had played toward Russia in the late seventeenth and early eighteenth centuries.[75] To this were added the Enlightenment

74. Peter the Great had well expressed it when he compared the task of modernizing his people with the teaching of reading and writing to children—neither could be done without compulsion.

75. "Nastavlenie gr. Petru Rumiantsevu," *Sbornik IRIO* 7:376–91; letter of Catherine II to D. V. Volkov on his duties as administrator of Orenburg province, 13.VI.1763, in *Materialy po istorii Bashkirskoi ASSR* (Moscow: 1956), no. 491, vol. 4, pt. 2, pp. 452–53.

attitudes toward religion, reflected in Catherine's neutrality toward it.[76] Under the circumstances, it is not surprising to find
Catherine pursuing a policy of cultural Russification wherever
possible, but it was a policy aiming at Russifying the natives' way
of life, not their language, religion, traditions, or customs, unless
these were deemed outright harmful to society. In line with this
purpose Catherine inaugurated an active policy for the settling of
nomads and turning them to agricultural pursuits, increasing the
security of the borders and of the Russian settlers on the frontier
by extending Russian administrative practices. As for the still
more primitive hunters and fruit gatherers, it would be best if
they could be brought to the level of nomads and eventually
settled to agriculture as well.

This policy, too, proved illustrative of the paradox of the état
bien policé approach: it aimed at uniformity and recognized
primarily material factors as the standard of cultural levels and
progress. It was, moreover, believed that this goal could be
achieved by government initiative and compulsion, quite oblivious of the fact that the recipients of this "progress" might not wish
to accept its benefits, at least in the forms offered, since it might
interfere with traditions and customs and even destroy them.
Catherine, however, had also absorbed another lesson of the well-
ordered police state, namely a pragmatic and cautious approach
in achieving such remote goals. In the case of the non-Russians,
she endeavored to do what the état bien policé had done in the
seventeenth century with respect to its own social groups—
namely, co-opt them into helping in her efforts at modernization.
The effort at co-optation, in the absence of estate structures
similar to those of Western Europe, took the hallowed traditional
Russian form: co-optation and enlistment of the native elites into
the service of the Russian state. This resulted in their immediately

76. Alan W. Fisher, "Enlightened Despotism and Islam under Catherine II,"
Slavic Review, 27 (1968): 542–53; M. Raeff, "Patterns of Russian Imperial Policy
toward the Nationalities," in *Soviet Nationality Problems*, ed. Edward Allworth (New
York: Columbia University Press, 1971), pp. 22–41. For the nationalities of the
Volga see now: Andreas Kappeler, *Russlands erste Nationalitäten: Das Zarenreich und
die Völker der Mittleren Wolga vom 16. bis 19. Jahrhundert* (Cologne and Vienna:
Böhlau Verlag, 1982).

sharing the benefits of their contribution to the Russian state. Muscovy had proceeded in similar fashion when it expanded beyond the Russian ethnic boundaries (imitating, unconsciously perhaps, the patterns of its former Mongol and Tartar conquerors and masters). Catherine was not only willing to accept into service the native leadership—and entice the native elites into leading the way to the transformation of their nation's customary way of life; she also generously rewarded such efforts. She endeavored to persuade the chieftains of nomadic tribes to settle down and become agriculturists; she transformed existing agrarian elites (in the Crimea, for example) into Russian "nobles" by extending to them nearly all the benefits and privileges enjoyed by nobles without requiring them to convert to Christianity. Thus they gained control over peasant labor, access to ranks in service, and admission of their children to state educational institutions. In the long run the policy helped to bring the elites of the more advanced native populations into the orbit of Russian culture. The paradoxical remote consequence of promoting a nationalism that would threaten the survival of the empire could not have been foreseen by Catherine and her contemporaries.

The difficulties and dissonances of the Petrine heritage, the intellectual development of the elites, and the individual qualities of Catherine II enabled the latter to approach the implementation of the well-ordered police state in a new and more sophisticated manner. Her contribution was to realize that the état bien policé needed a structured, westernized type of society in order to operate. Catherine's government did not go all the way and grant the autonomy and self-government that the Western intermediate bodies had come to enjoy. It is also arguable that the social structure needed for the well-ordered police state never materialized in Russia; the concrete cameralist policies had to be imposed by a bureaucracy, which precluded their having the necessary impact on the modernization of the country. Yet with respect to the cultural life of the elites, Catherine did lay the foundation of a civil society that was to be the seedbed for Russia's cultural explosion in the nineteenth century, at the same time bringing into the open the tensions and conflicts that resulted from the limitations imposed by the autocracy on creative social initiative.

In central and Western Europe the well-ordered police state initiated a trend that not only brought about great material and cultural progress but also stimulated and strengthened individual initiative, enterprise, and rational or critical constructivist features of intellectual life. This dynamism could not be restrained, in the long run, by the leading strings of government authority and officialdom. A clash was hard to avoid. A civil society had come into existence, and because the état bien policé had made use of (even strengthened) basic social institutions, the clash was a purely political one. Once the barriers of bureaucracy and monarchy had been broken down (or a compromise had been reached), once the authoritarian political systems that had initiated the well-ordered police state and modernity had been removed, society was still there, and its members could go on being productively active on their own account. This was not to be the case in Russia. The state remained in command and retained the initiative until the end of the nineteenth century, for there was no comprehensively structured society either to defer to or to challenge it. When the imperial autocracy was eventually challenged, it was by the only kind of civil society that had been allowed to develop—namely, one based on cultural and ideological criteria incorporated by intelligentsia. When the challenge proved successful, the political system virtually collapsed, and the social void became visible to all. A well-organized minority of the cultural elite, the radical intelligentsia, moved in to fill it and organize it in its own way.

Epilogue

This essay's purpose, and hopefully its achievement, has been to illustrate the particular features and dynamics of the fundamental transformation that took place in the goals and practices of early modern European polities. I have tried to show how legislative and administrative regulations issued by the territorial sovereignties of Germany in the course of a century and a half brought about a changeover from the traditional use of political power to preserve society's "moral economy" (E. P. Thompson) in a limited world to the modern practices of rational constructivism with a high time horizon. The new policies rested on the belief that the world was infinite, its reservoir of resources boundless, and that these resources could and should be exploited to further man's spiritual, cultural, and material progress. It was felt possible to achieve this goal if man obtained knowledge of the laws of nature and exercised his will to make productive use of such knowledge to shape his destiny.

Another objective of the essay has been to show what means were selected and used to achieve these ends. More particularly, we have stressed the leadership role of state authority as embodied in the absolute sovereign assisted by a corps of professionalized officials. In the process, these officials came to view their activities as ends in themselves, not only as convenient means for their own social promotion and the transformation of their own styles of life. However, as I have also tried to show, the success of the political enterprise of the well-ordered police state depended not only on the officials but also on the Establishment's ability to enlist the participation and cooperation of already-constituted bodies. Only the members of such bodies were in a position to see to the implementation of the regulations issued to reeducate and to discipline society. Without the cooperation of such groups the .

251

efforts of the administration of the well-ordered police state would have yielded few or no results.

We have also pointed to the basic ambiguity of the entire enterprise. Guidance, supervision, and prescriptions, often taking the form of excessive regulation, were contrary to the avowed aim of developing individual initiative and energetic involvement in the process of maximizing resources. This paradox became particularly glaring in the case of Russia where the dearth of constituted bodies whose help could be enlisted led to almost total reliance on positive leadership and control by the central state apparatus. The task of organizing, disciplining, and restructuring society for productive endeavors proved beyond the forces of that apparatus. As we know, the contradiction was never fully resolved, even though some beginnings were made—especially after 1861—in restructuring elements of Russian society along the pattern of Western European autonomous corporate bodies.

The goals and practices of the well-ordered police state not only foreshadowed but endeavored to implement the notions usually associated with the Enlightenment. As far as continental European polities are concerned, the administration of the état bien policé laid the institutional foundations and identified the principles and specific goals that the philosophes subsequently proclaimed to be the moral basis for modern society. The Enlightenment gave theoretical validation to goals and practices that had been set by the seventeenth century's revolution of political culture, and it added its own contribution when it spelled out the ideology of material and cultural progress that had been implicit in the conception of the productive society envisaged by cameralism and the well-ordered police state. But instead of being only the means for greater common weal *(das gemeine Gut* or *gemeine Beste)*, progress became an end in itself for the Enlightenment: productivity as an unending process, its goal forever receding, became the ideology of the enlightened intelligentsia. These ideologues no longer evaluated the common good on the basis of spiritual ideals or religious norms, and they did not believe that in structuring society much attention need to be paid to tradition or the limitations of historical experience. If progress and the total and indiscriminate unfettering of individual productive energies were desirable ends in themselves, there was no need to respect the limitations set by specific conditions that seemed the mere unfortunate accidents of history.

Once the confusion between the means and ends had occurred and the ideology of unending progress and untrammeled individual creative energy had been unquestionably accepted (that is, by the mid–eighteenth century), the practices of the well-ordered state were themselves put in doubt and vociferously denounced, and they fell into desuetude. This brought about a revulsion from the activist and regulatory state, a rejection of the rational constructivism implicit in cameralism and the Polizeiordnungen. Indeed, by the late eighteenth century Western European society had been disciplined for production, and its individual members had largely internalized the values of ongoing productivity; would it not be more efficient, therefore, to break out of the administrative constraints? Would not ongoing progress and the benefits of material and cultural productivity be greater and individual happiness spread more widely if those who had internalized these modern values were given free rein to pursue their interests and creative drives? The demand, first intellectual and then political, was made for an end to the constraints imposed by the state: the regulations that had earlier made possible the disciplining of a productive society should be dismantled, for the energetic and enlightened individual no longer needed leading strings. "Laissez faire" became the battle cry of the ideology of progress and enlightenment that would finally realize the goals of the well-ordered police state.

Not surprisingly, the attack on the état bien policé was pursued most energetically in those societies where the internalization of the production-oriented values and the disciplining of society had gone furthest. This was particularly the case with England, which endeavored to dispense with central state administration altogether. Less overtly and less provocatively, retaining the basic Lutheran commitment to duty and social responsibility within the framework of an authoritarian sovereignty *(Obrigkeit)*, a similar path was followed in most of the Germanies. The ideal state of action became that of "benign neglect" of social and economic issues, though in the case of Prussia (with Bismarck) and to some extent under Tory governments (for example, Disraeli's in England), the government assumed again the lead in social legislation to limit those excesses of laissez-faire and selfish individualism that might threaten the polity's social harmony and peace.

The pattern of development just sketched also provides illustration of the antinomy involved in the concept of the pursuit of happiness and the progress of society, since obviously not everybody was or could be benefited by the process. The passive or negative night watchman state, while releasing individual energies, also undermined social cohesion by failing to do anything for those many members of society who could not keep pace with those who were energetic, driving, lucky, and successful. Nor did it turn out to be true that enlightenment and education, the prerequisites of successful productivity, could be taken for granted or access to them opened to all without further ado. The tension between the promises held forth by the indiscriminate release of productive energies under the benevolent abstentionism of the night watchman and the socioethical imperatives of protecting the individual and society again brought about a reversal in the political culture of the West. Beginning in the late nineteenth century, and more particularly in the twentieth, we observe a return to the directive and regulatory functions of state administration. Seen in this perspective, the modern welfare state presents us with an updated version of the basic conceptions of the well-ordered police state, while the socialist-communist regimes take to its logical conclusions enlightened despotism's ideology of unbounded material progress in a harmonious community ordered and directed by an omniscient leader and elite. Not surprisingly, Marx and Bismarck, who best embodied the values and norms of the eighteenth-century well-ordered police state, have revealed themselves, although for different reasons and with divergent social values, as respectively the most influential theoretician and practitioner of contemporary social policy.

In Russia, on the other hand, in the absence of an adequately structured society, even in the nineteenth century we note the continued role and power of an activist, constructivist state. This state, late in the nineteenth century, ushered in the dramatic economic and social transformations that for the first time created the framework for a structuring of civil society for productive purposes. But the conflict between the dirigiste state and the energetic, aggressive, and creative members of society led to tensions and clashes that were forcibly controlled by repressive autocratic measures and that prevented a constitutional settlement that would have granted civil society its fair share of participation and autonomy. The conflict was intensified by the technological transformations and pacesetting accomplishments from the West that required priming and support by the state. Eventually the way out was to be violent revolution. Yet because of the still inadequate structuring of society, the revolution swept away all the constituted bodies then in the process of formation and consolidation. The ensuing economic collapse and sociopolitical turmoil resulted in anarchy that enabled a stifling dictatorship to install itself. Ironically, the revolution brought about by the needs of energetic, progressive individuals and groups to eliminate autocratic fetters to their creative initiative resulted in a regime that proved even more directive and constrictive of their aspirations.

One might end by asking what was the place of England in the evolution of modern Europe, for England has traditionally been used as the yardstick and considered the pacesetter of the modernization of Western society and government. Some of the basic conceptions underlying the well-ordered police state had been formulated and introduced in England much earlier than on the Continent. For this very reason, England implemented these conceptions under conditions that from the start made it possible to delegate most of the functions to individuals and bodies on the local level. The Crown did not need to develop as comprehensive a bureaucratic apparatus and a corpus of regulatory legislation, so that individual members of society managed to secure the rights and liberties that enabled them to organize and further their productive energies. Thus in England individualistic laissez-faire prevailed earlier and more completely than on the Continent, where, as we have seen, its ideals and aims were taken up and implemented, more or less successfully, by the Polizeiordnungen. Under the circumstances, the transfer of the

English model to the Continent gave rise to more problems and strains than it solved and resulted in a return to state protection and dirigisme of the kind that took place in Prussia. As for France, the failure of the Old Regime to establish the well-ordered police state (aimed at by Colbert) or its successor, enlightened absolutism (envisaged by Turgot), effectively helped to bring about the Revolution in 1789. Napoleon then created his bureaucratic and rationalistic substitute, a system that performed the functions of a successful enlightened absolutism. His creation dominated French life virtually until the middle of the twentieth century (an extraordinary tribute to his genius), and though its strains and paradoxes brought about several political upheavals, they did not destroy the institutional structure of the Napoleonic settlement. By the middle of the twentieth century the turn to the welfare state occurred in France for reasons similar to those that had initiated it in Germany earlier.

In a sense, the underlying theme that our essay has tried to address comes down to one essential issue: the rate and thoroughness of a society's success in internalizing the values and norms of the modern, production-oriented, dynamic political culture whose origins, as we have argued, lay in the intellectual transformation of Europe in the late sixteenth and early seventeenth centuries. This was the dynamic factor that made the changeover from the traditional to the modern type of society and culture either a gradual or violent one. In the instances of gradual and not too violent transition the state played a major role in creating the necessary institutional and normative framework. Thus in the Germanies the compromise solution—eschewing the extremes of England and Russia—was that of the classical well-ordered police state, which gave the state primacy of initiative and guidance in cooperation with the structured bodies of society. The compromise that worked relatively well in Germany throughout the nineteenth century appeared to collapse in 1918 as a result of external factors (war). But it may be argued that its basic principles survived the First World War and left a legacy that enabled West Germany, after World War II, to renovate itself rapidly and turn into a successful and thoroughgoing welfare state, again on the basis of effective collaboration between government and society through the mediation of the latter's constituted bodies (this time trade unions and professional organizations).

My essay has called to the reader's attention the profound transformation—really a revolution—that occurred in European political attitudes and practices as a result of the intellectual innovations of the late sixteenth and early seventeenth centuries. But beyond this, I have aimed at showing the dialectical interplay between ends and means in the well-ordered police state as an instrument of social transformation and the contradiction inherent in the endeavor to foster and give full scope to the creative energies of the individual members of society by means of the state's direction and compulsion. The efforts at resolving this contradiction under varying social and cultural conditions constitute a guiding thread for an understanding of the political and social development of European polities from the seventeenth century to our day. From this perspective, modern political revolutions are the consequence of the incapacity of traditional forms of thought and behavior to integrate the values of a production-oriented society and the glorification of individual selfish interests. A just solution would have to meet the demands and expectations of the modern polity for maximized productive potential and also maintain the cultural (spiritual) values of a harmonious relationship between individual and society. The solution to this paradox remains in doubt in the foreseeable future.

Bibliography

An interpretative and synthetic essay like the present one owes much to a wide range of readings in the secondary literature on virtually all aspects of the period involved. To list even those titles that I have consulted would inflate the bibliography to unmanageable proportions. I have cited in the footnotes those books and articles that have most directly influenced my own thinking.

The bibliography below lists only the primary literature—treatises, tracts, ordinances, and codes—that has been of direct relevance to this essay and to which specific reference is made in the footnotes. The impossibly long and cumbersome baroque titles have been abridged and their highly inconsistent spellings somewhat modernized for easier handling.

The titles are listed in two sections: first, treatises and tracts; second, ordinances. The latter are arranged by territories.

Treatises and Tracts

Der Adeliche Hofemeister. N.p.: 1693.
Anastasius Sincerus [Amthor, Christoph Heinrich]. *Project der Oeconomie in Form einer Wissenschaft. . . .*, 2d ed. Frankfurt and Leipzig: 1717.
Andreae, Johann Valentin. *Christianopolis.* N.p., 1619. Modern edition edited by Richard von Dülmer. Stuttgart: 1972–. Vol. 4, Quellen und Forschungen zur württembergischen Kirchengeschichte, edited by Martin Brecht and Gerh. Schäfer.
Argenson, René-Louis Voyer d'. *Considérations sur le gouvernement ancien et présent de la France.* Yverdon: 1764.
Becher, Johann Joachim. *Politischer Discurs von den eigentlichen Ursachen des Auf- und Abnehmen der Städte, Länder und Republicken.* Frankfurt: 1668 (I used 2d ed., Frankfurt, 1673; subsequent editions in 1688, 1720, 1721).
Beck, Christoph August. *Versuch einer Staatspraxis oder Canzleyübung aus*

der Politik, dem Staats- und Völkerrechte. Vienna: 1754; 2d ed., Vienna: 1778.

Becke, F. A. von der. *Von Staatsämtern und Staatsdienern.* Heilbronn: 1797.

Berg, G. H. von. *Handbuch des Teutschen Policeyrechts.* Hanover: 1802.

B[essel], Ch. G. *Schmiede des politischen Glücks . . . darinnen viele nützliche Lehren enthalten.* Hamburg: 1669.

Béthune, Phillippe de. *Le conseiller d'Estat. . . .* Paris: 1645.

Bodey, Heinrich von, ed. [Asanius Christoph von Marenholz?]. *Fürstliche Macht Kunst oder unerschöpfliche Gold-Grube.* Halle: 1702.

Burghley, Lord [William Cecil, 1520–98]. Translated as *Heilsame Lehren so da dienen zur Richtschnur des gantzen menschlichen Lebens . . .,* by Ch. G. B[essel]. Hamburg: 1669.

C. A. K. *Allgemeine Oeconomische Maximen.* Halle: 1708.

C. B. B., M.D. [Behrens, Conrad Berthold]. *Medicus legalis oder Gesetzmässige Bestell- und Ausübung der Artzney Kunst. . . .* Helmstedt: 1696.

Court, Pieter de la. *The True Interest and Political Maxims of the Republick of Holland and West-Friesland.* London: 1702.

Cramer, Johann Ulrich von. *Academische Reden über die gemeine bürgerliche Rechts-Lehre. . . .* Ulm: 1765.

Crousaz, J. P. de. *Traité de l'éducation des enfans.* LaHaye: 1722.

Darjes, Joachim Georg. *Einleitung in des Freiherrn von Bielefeld Lehrbegriff der Staatsklugheit. . . .* Jena: 1764.

―――. *Erste Gründe der Cameralwissenschaften.* Leipzig: 1756; 2d ed., Leipzig: 1768.

Deneken, Johann. *Neu vermehrtes Dorf und Land Recht,* 5th ed. Frankfurt and Leipzig: 1739.

Dithmar, Justus Christoph. *Einleitung in die Oeconomische Polizey- und Cameral-Wissenschaften.* Frankfurt an der Oder: 1731.

Döhler, Johann Georg. *Schein und Seyn der Advocaten.* Coburg-Meinungen: 1728.

―――. *Zwey nützliche Tractate.* Leipzig: 1712.

Döpler, Jacob. *Treuer Herr/ Treuer Knecht.* Leipzig and Sondershausen: 1694.

DuBois–Hus, Sieur. *Le Prince illustre.* Paris: 1645.

Estor, Johann Georg. *Anweisung für die Beambten und adelichen Gerichts-Verwalter.* Marburg: 1762.

―――. *Nützliche Sammlung zur Erlernung der ächten und reinen juristischen Schreibart.* Marburg: 1746.

[Franciscus, Erasmus]. *Erasmi Francisci Ost- und West-Indischer wie auch Chinesischer Lust- und Staats Garten. . . .* Nürnberg: 1668.

Fredersdorf, Leopold Friedrich. *Anweisung für die ausgehende Justiz-Beamten und Unterrichter,* 3 vols. Leipzig: 1772.

Friedtlieb, Christian Werner. *Prudentia politica Christiana, Dass ist Beschreibung einer Christlichen Nützlichen und guten Policey.* . . . Goslar: 1614.

Gasser, Simon Peter. *Einleitung zu den oeconomischen Politischen und Cameral Wissenschaften.* . . . Halle: 1729.

Glaffley, Adam Friedrich. *Anleitung zu einer Welt-üblichen Teutschen Schreib Art,* 3d ed. Leipzig: 1747.

Grottnitz von Grodnow, Carl Melchior. *Teutsch gekleideter Regiments Rath.* Stettin: 1647.

Hall, Joseph. *Solomons Regir Haushaltungs- und Sitten-Kunst.* Translated by M. Andreas Beyern. Frankfurt and Leipzig: 1684.

———. *Wo gehst du hin? oder Straff Urtheil über das Räisen.* . . . Translated by Johannes Tonjola. Basel: 1665.

Hecker, O. A., ed. *Schriften Dr. Melchior von Osse.* (Schriften der sächsischen Kommission für Geschichte, no. 26.) Leipzig and Berlin: B. G. Teubner Verlag, 1922.

Heroldt, Christian. *Historischer und Politischer Tractat von Ursprung und Auffnehmen der Städte.* . . . Weissenfelss: 1683.

Heumann, Johann. *Der Geist der Geseze der Teutschen.* Nürnberg: 1761.

Hoff und Bürgerliche Reden gantz neues Styli . . . , by "A. P. v. A." Halle: 1695.

Hofmann, Johann Andre. *Unmassgeblicher Entwurf vor dem Umfange den Gegenständen einrichtungen* . . . *des polizeiwesens* . . . *im Teutschen Reiche.* . . . Marburg: 1765.

Hohberg, Wolf H. von. *Georgica curiosa* . . . , 2 vols. Nürnberg: 1701.

Hörnigk, Ludwig von. *Politica medica oder Beschreibung dessen was die Medici* . . . *zuthun.* . . . Frankfurt: 1638.

Hunold, G. S. *Der Alte und Neue Amtmann.* Leipzig and Halle: 1716.

Justi, Johann Heinrich Gottlieb von. *Anweisung zu einer guten Deutschen Schreibart.* . . . Leipzig: 1755.

———. *Gesammelte Politische und Finanzschriften.* . . . , 3 vols. Copenhagen and Leipzig: 1761–64.

———. *Grundsätze der Policeywissenschaft,* 2d ed. Göttingen: 1759.

Kopp, Carl Philipp. *Carl Philipp Kopps ausführliche Nachricht von der älteren und neuern Verfassung.* . . . Cassel: 1769.

LaMare, Nicolas de. *Traité de Police.* . . . , 2d ed., pts. 1–4 in 2 vols. Amsterdam: 1729.

Lau, Theodor Ludwig. *Aufrichtiger Vorschlag von glücklichen Vortheilhafftiger* . . . *Einrichtung der Intraden und Einkünfften.* . . . Frankfurt: 1719.

Ledderhose, Conrad Wilhelm. *Kleine Schriften,* 5 vols. Marburg: 1787–95.

Leib, Johann Georg. *Probe wie ein Regent Land und Leute verbessern.* . . . , 4 vols. Leipzig and Frankfurt: 1705–8

Lersner, Jacob. *Antwort Bericht und Beweiss Auff die Frage ob es besser sei nach gewissen beschriebenen . . . oder nach eygner Sinn Witz . . . zu regieren.* Marburg: 1542.

Limburg, Heinrich Herr zu. *Thesaurus Paternus in usum filii collectus, Darinnen eigendlich eine Unterweisung zu finden, wie sich mein . . . Sohn . . . Lebenslauff . . . geschrieben 1633, gedruckt 1670.* Appendix to Bessel, *Schmiede des politischen Glücks.*

Lipsius, Iustus. *Les six Livres des politiques. . . .* LaRochelle: 1590.

———. *Von der Bestendigkeit (De Constantia),* 2d ed. N.p., 1601; reprint ed., Stuttgart: J. B. Metzlersche Verlag, 1965, edited by Leonard Foster.

———. *Von Unterweisung zum weltlichen Regiment. . . .* Amberg: 1618.

Löhneyss, Georg Engelhard. *Bericht vom Bergwerck wie man dieselben bawen und in guten wolstande bringen soll. . . .* N.d., n.pl.

———. *Aulica Politica: Darin gehandelt wird von Erziehung. . . .* Remlingen: 1624.

———. *Hof- Staats- und Regierkunst.* Frankfurt: 1679.

May, Johann Friedrich. *Die Kunst der vernünftigen Kinderzucht.* Helmstädt: 1753.

———. *Die Weisheit der Menschen nach der Vernunft. . . .* Leipzig: 1754.

Mayer, Michael. *Hoffschul, wie man junge vom Adel aufferziehen. . . .* Augsburg: 1659.

Medicus legalis. N. p.: 1696.

Moser, Friedrich Carl. *Versuch einer Staatsgrammatik.* Frankfurt: 1749.

Moser, Johann Jacob. *Einige Vortheile für Canzley Verwandte und Gelehrte. . . .* N.p.: 1773.

———. *Einleitung zu deren Cantzley-Geschäften.* Frankfurt: 1755.

———. *Entwurf einer Staats Cantzley Academie.* Hanau: 1749.

———. *Von dem Ansehen der Rechtsgelehrten in Teutschen Staats Sachen.* Regensburg: 1773.

———. *Wiederholte Nachricht von einer Staats- und Canzley Academie.* Hanau: 1749.

Moser, Wilhelm Gottfried. *Grundrisse der Forst Oeconomie.* Frankfurt and Leipzig: 1757.

Negelein, Paul. *Vom bürgerlichen Stand welchermassen derselbige in beharrlichen Wesen erhalten. . . .,* 3d ed. Frankfurt: 1616.

Nettelbladt, Daniel. *Erste Gründe der Lehre von dem Policeyrechte der mittleren Städte in Teutschland.* Halle: 1792.

———. *Sammlung kleiner juristischen Abhandlungen. . . .* Halle: 1792.

———. *Vernünftige Gedanken von rechter Einrichtung des mündlichen Vortrages eines Lehrers der Rechte. . . .* Halle: 1744.

Der neu-aufgeführte Hoffmeister. Frankfurt: 1685.

Neu Politischer Tugendspiegel der Hofbedienten. . . . Nürnberg: 1665.

Obrecht, Georg. *Fünff unterschiedliche Secreta politica . . . guter Policey.* . . . Strassburg: 1617.

———. *Politisch Bedenken und Discurs von Verbesserung Land und Leut.* . . . N. p.: 1617.

Oldekop, Justus. *Politischer Unterricht für die Rahtsherren in Städten und communen.* . . . Goslar: 1634.

Oldendorp, Johannes. *Von Rathschlägen wie man gute Policey und Ordnung in Stedten und Landen erhalten möge.* . . . Rostock: 1597; earlier edition in Low German, Rostock, 1530.

[Ophir]. *Der wohleingerichtete Staat Des bishero von vielen gesuchten aber nicht gefundenen Königreichs Ophir.* . . . Leipzig: 1699.

Ossa, Melchior von. *Prudentia Regnativa, Das ist ein Nützliches Bedenken ein Regiment . . . zu bestellen.* . . . Wolfenbüttel: 1622.

[Philoparchus, Germanus]. *Der Kluge Beamte oder Informatorium juridicum officiale.* . . . Nürnberg: 1701.

Pisani, Octavio. *Der italienische Lycurgus / gesetze und Ordnungen durch und nach welchen die Rechte und Schleunige Gerechtigkeit verfügt wird.* Sultzbach: 1666.

Prechtl, Conrad Aloysius. *Uebungen der Gerichtsgeschäfte oder Handbuch der Beamten.* Munich: 1761; 4th ed., 1771.

Pütter, Johann Stephan. *Anleitung zur juristischen Praxi.* N.p.: 1753; 5th ed., 1789.

———. *Selbstbiographie,* vol. 1. Göttingen: 1798.

Rau, Wolf Thomas. *Gedanken von dem Nutzen und der Nothwendigkeit einer medicinischen Policey Ordnung in einem Staat.* N.p.: 1764.

Rautner, Abraham Benedict. *Anführung zur Teutschen Staats Kunst.* . . . Nürnberg: 1672.

Die rechte Reisekunst oder Anleitung wie eine Reise mit Nutzen . . . zu stellen. . . . Frankfurt: 1674.

Reinhard, Johann Jakob. *Vermischte Schriften,* 8 vols. Leipzig: 1760–69.

Reinking, Conradus. *Politikos Megalos: The Grand Politician, or the Secret Art of State Policy Discovered.* . . . London: 1691.

Reinkingk, Dietrich. *Biblische Policey.* . . . Frankfurt: 1653.

Reinkingk, Theodor. *Politisches Bedenken wie ein Fürstliches Archivum in gewisse Classes und Sedes materiarum ordentlich zu redigiren.* Zelle: 1687.

———. *Der Verjüngte Römische Reichsadler.* . . . Göttingen: 1687.

Rohr, Julius Bernhard von. *Compendieuse Hausshaltungsbibliothek.* Leipzig: 1716.

———. *Einleitung zu der allgemeinen Land- und Feld Wirthschaftskunst derer Teutschen.* Leipzig: 1720.

————. *Einleitung zur Staatsklugheit.* Leipzig: 1718.

————. *Einleitung zur Zeremonial Wissenschaft der grossen Herren.* New ed., Berlin: 1733.

————. *Vollständiges Hausshaltungs Recht.* . . . Leipzig: 1716.

Rottmanner, Simon. *Unterricht eines alten Beamten an junge Beamten,* vols. 1–3. Leipzig: 1783–87.

Schram, Johan Friedrich. *Richterlicher Gewissensspiegel.* Erfurt: 1729.

Schreber, Daniel Gottfried. *Sammlung verschiedener Schriften welche in die öconomische, Policey- und Cameral* . . . *Wissenschaften einschlagen,* 12 pts. Halle: 1755–65.

Schröder, Wilhelm von. *Disquisitio politica.* . . . Leipzig and Wolfenbüttel: 1719.

————. *Fürstliche Schatz und Rent Cammer.* . . . Leipzig: 1686.

[Schwart, Anton Wilhelm]. *Der Adeliche Hofemeister.* . . . Frankfurt: 1693.

Seckendorff, Veit Ludwig von. *Teutscher Fürstenstaat.* Frankfurt: 1656.

————. *Teutsche Reden.* . . . Leipzig: 1686.

Seuffert, J. M. *Von dem Verhältnisse des Staates und der Diener des Staats gegeneinander.* . . . Würzburg: 1793.

Sonnenfels, Joseph von. *Grundsätze der Policey Handlung und Finanz,* 5th ed., 3 vols. Vienna: 1786–87.

Spaeth (Kaspar von Stielen). *Teutsche Sekretariat Kunst.* Nürnberg: pts. 1–3, 1673; pt. 4, 1674.

————. *Der Teutsche Advocat.* Nürnberg and Jena: 1678.

Stahl, Johann Friedrich, ed. *Allgemeines oeconomisches Forst-Magazin,* pts. 1–6. Frankfurt and Leipzig: 1763–69.

Struben, David Georg, ed. *Sammlung merckwürdiger Cameral- und Visitations-Actenstücke.* . . . , 2 vols. Wezlar: 1765.

Thomasius, Christian. *Summarischer Entwurf derer Grundlehren die einem Studioso Juris zu wissen.* . . . Halle: 1699.

————. *Über die Folter.* Modern edition edited by Rolf Lieberwirth (Weimar: 1960).

Tschirnhaus, Wolff Bernhard. *Getreuer Hofmeister auf Akademien und Reisen* . . . Hanover: 1727.

Der Untadelhafte Hoffmann. . . . Lübeck: 1664.

Vattel, Emeric de. *Loisir philosophique.* Dresden: 1747.

Vetter, Johann Friedrich. *Christlicher und Wohlmeinender Vorschlag wie in einem Lande die Policey heilsamlich einzurichten* . . . *sey.* . . . N.p.: 1736.

Vollkommenere Hoffmeister. N.p.: 1707.

Weigel, Erhard. *Aretologistica: Die Tugend übende Rechenkunst.* Nürnberg: 1687.

————. *Arithmetische Beschreibung der Moralweisheit.* . . . Jena: 1674.

———. *Kurtzer Entwurff der freudigen Kunst- und Tugend-Lehre vor Trivial- und Kinder-Schulen.* Jena: 1682.

———. *Unmassgebliche Mathematische Vorschläge betreffend einige Grundstücke des gemeinen Wesens.* Jena (?): 1681.

———. *Wienerischer Tugendspiegel. . . .* Nürnberg: 1687.

Weinreich, Johann. *Wolmeinende Meinung vor Tumult und Aufruhr.* Erfurt: 1622.

Weise, Christian. *Neu Erleuterter Politischer Redner. . . .* Leipzig: 1684.

———. *Politische Fragen.* Dresden: 1708.

———. *Politischer Academicus. . . .* Amsterdam: 1685; 2d ed., 1696.

———. *Politischer Redner. . . .* Leipzig: 1679.

———. *Vertraute Gespräche wie der geliebten Jugend im Informations Wercke . . . geraten seyn.* Leipzig: 1697.

Willebrand, Jean Pierre. *Abrégé de la police, accompagné de réflexions sur l'accroissement des villes.* Hamburg: 1765.

Wolff, Christian. *Entdeckung der wahren Ursachen von der wunderbaren Vermehrung des Getreydes.* Halle: 1725.

———. *Le roi philosophe et le philosophe roi.* Berlin: 1740. English translation, *The real happiness of people under a philosopher king.* London: 1750.

———. *Vernünftige Gedanken von dem gesellschaftlichen Leben. . . .* Halle: 1721; 5th ed. (title varied), Frankfurt, 1740.

Zech, Bernhard von [Friedrich Leutholff von Franckenberg]. *Europäischer Herold. . . .* Frankfurt and Leipzig: 1688.

———. *Der Iztregirenden Welt Grosse Schaubühne. . . .* Nürnberg: 1675.

Zincke, Georg Heinrich. *Allgemeines Oeconomisches Lexicon,* 2d ed., 2 vols. Leipzig: 1744.

———. *Leipziger Sammlungen von wirtschaftlichen, Polizei–Kammer-und Finanzsachen,* 15 vols. Leipzig: 1744–56.

Zweyer Weltberümther Leute nöthige und nützliche Erinnerungen wie sich ein junger Mensch auff Universitäten rühmlich zu bezeigen habe (V. L. von Seckendorffs Instruction an seinen Vetter und D. Martinus Geier an seinen einzigen Sohn). Leipzig?: 1694.

Ordinances and Codes

Germany

Holy Roman Empire

Bergius, Johann Heinrich Ludwig. *Cameralisten Bibliothek oder vollständiges Verzeichnis derjenigen Büchern, Schriften und Abhandlungen welche von dem Oeconomie- Policey- Finanz- und Cameralwesen und verschiedenen anderen damit verbundenen Wissenschaften, auch von der dahin enschlagenden Rechtsgelehrsamkeit.* Nürnberg: 1761.

———. *Policey- und Cameralmagazin,* vols. 1–9. Frankfurt am Main: 1767–74.

———. *Sammlung auserlesenen Deutschen Landesgesetze welche das Policey- und Cameralwesen zum Gegenstande haben,* vols. 1–7. Frankfurt am Main: 1781–93 (continued by Johann Beckmann).

Kern, Arthur. *Deutsche Hofordnungen des 16. und 17. Jahrhunderts,* 2 vols. Denkmäler der deutschen Culturgeschichte, edited by Georg Steinhausen, pt. 2, Ordnungen I–II. Berlin: 1905–7.

[Koch, Ernst August]. *Neue vollständige Sammlung der Reichs-Abschiede, welche von den Zeiten Kayser Conrads des II bis jetzo auf den teutschen Reichs Tägen abgefasst worden. . . . ,* 4 vols. Frankfurt am Main: 1747.

Sovereign Territories

ALTENBURG

Sammlung von Landesordnungen des Fürstenthums Altenburg. Altenburg: 1750.

ANHALT-DESSAU

Derer Durchleuchtigsten . . . Fürsten . . . Friedrichs . . . Johannsens . . . Gebrüdern und Vettern Fürsten zu Anhalt Grafen zu Ascanien Herrn zu Zerbst und Bernburg Erneuerte und verbesserte Landes- und Process Ordnung. Cöthen: 1666.

Des Fürstenthumes Anhalt Policey und Landes Ordenung. Dessau: 1572.

Fürstlich Anhaltische gesambte Landes- und Process-Ordnung. Dessau: 1725.

Fürstlich Anhaltische gesambte Landes- und Process-Ordnung. . . . Dessau: 1777.

Sammlung Landesherrlicher Verordnungen, welche in dem Fürstentum Anhalt-Dessau ergangen, 2 vols. Dessau: 1784–1819.

BADEN

Dollmatsch, Bernhard, ed. *Sammlung sämtlicher Gesetze, Verordnungen, Verfügungen und Anordnungen, welche in . . . dem Grossherzogtum Baden über Gegenstände der Orts-Polizei seit dem Jahre 1712 bis 1832 erschienen sind,* 2 vols. Carlsruhe: 1836.

Gerstlacher, Carl Friedrich. *Sammlung aller Baden-Durlachischer . . . Anstalten und Verordnungen,* 3 vols. Frankfurt and Leipzig: 1773–74.

BAVARIA

Allerley Chur-Bayerische Landesverordnungen. N.pl., 1759–77.

Arndt, Gottfried August. *Vollständige Sammlung von Staatsschriften zum Behuf der Baierischen Geschichte. . . .*, 5 vols. Frankfurt and Leipzig: 1778–79.

Freyberg, Max Freiherr von. *Pragmatische Geschichte der bayerischen Gesetzgebung und Staatsverwaltung seit den Zeiten Maximilian I. . . .*, 4 vols. Augsburg: 1836–38.

Churfürstlich Baierische hoher und niederer Schulen Ordnung. . . . Ingolstadt: 1774.

Codex Maximilianus Bavaricus Civilis oder Neu verbessert- und ergänzt Chur-Bayrisches Land-Recht. . . ., 4 vols. Munich: 1756.

Danzer, Max, ed. *Das Bayerische Landrecht . . . vom Jahre 1756.* Munich: 1894.

Döllinger, Georg Friedrich, ed. *Sammlung aller königlichen baierischen Verordnungen in Unterrichts- und Bildungs-sachen in alphabetischer Ordnung.* Munich: 1823.

Günter, Helmut, ed. *Das bayerische Landrecht von 1616.* Schriftenreihe zur bayerischen Landesgeschichte, no. 66. Munich: C. H. Beck, 1969.

Handbuch Churpfalzbairischer Verordnungen unter der Regierung . . . Maximilian Josephs des Vierten, vol. 1. Munich: 1799.

Hübner, Ignaz. *Sammlung der wichtigsten Kurbaierischen, während der vorigen und jetzigen Regierung erlassenen Generalverordnungen.* Ingolstadt: 1783.

Kreittmayer, Wiguläus Xavier Alois von. *Anmerkungen über den Codicem Maximilianaeum Bavaricum civilem. . . .*, vols. 1–5. Munich: 1768–91 (new ed., 1844).

———. *Sammlung churbaierischen Landesverordnungen.* Munich: 1771.

———. *Sammlung der neuesten und merkwürdigsten Churbaierischen Generalien und Landesverordnungen.* Munich: 1771.

Landrecht/Policey: Gerichts Malefitz und andere Ordnungen der Fürstenthumber Ober- und Nidern Bayern. Munich: 1616.

Mayer, Manfred. *Quellen zur Behördengeschichte Bayerns.* Bamberg: 1890.

Meyr, Georg Karl, ed. *Sammlung der Kurpfalz-Baierischen allgemeinen und besonderen Landes-Verordnungen. . . .*, vols. 1–6. Munich: 1784.

Strobl, J. B. *Sammlung der Baierischen ständischen Freiheitsbriefe. . . .* Munich: 1778.

BRAUNSCHWEIG

Petersen, Walter. "Verzeichnis der Einblattdrucke und Handschriften aus dem Rechtsleben des Herzogtums Braunschweig-Lüneburg, ergänzt um den Nachweis weiterer Rechtsquellen." Vol. 1, 1475–1714; vol. 2, 1714–1807. Typescript. Herzog August Bibliothek, Wolfenbüttel.

There is room here to give only a partial list of the huge collection of printed single ordinances of the duchy of Braunschweig in the Herzog August Bibliothek in Wolfenbüttel. References to individual ordinances from Braunschweig and Wolfenbüttel are from this collection.

Cantzley Ordnung . . . Friedrichen Ulrichen Hertzogs zu Braunschweig und Lüneburg. Wolfenbüttel: 1629.

Chur-Braunschweig Lüneburgische Landes Ordnungen und Gesetze. Pt. 1, Zum Gebrauch der . . . Herrschaften Calenbergischen Theils, vols. 1–4. Göttingen: 1739–40.

Der Stadt Braunschweig Kleider Ordnung. . . . Braunschweig: 1650.

Des Durchl. . . . Fürsten Augusti Herzogen zu Braunschweig Lüneburg . . . Canzlei Ordnung. Wolfenbüttel: 1651.

Eines E. Raths dero Stadt Braunschweig Begräbnis Ordnung. Braunschweig: 1650.

Eines E. Raths dero Stadt Braunschweig Edict und Ordnung das Korn und Maltzsacken in die Mühlen betreffend. Braunschweig: 1647.

Eines E. Raths dero Stadt Braunschweig Edictum das Gevatter Brod . . . betreffend. Braunschweig: 1649.

[Sammelband]. *Landtags- Abschiede, Ordnungen, Mandate—Wolfenbüttel.* Wolfenbüttel: n.d. (reign of Herzog August, 1635–66).

[Slüter and Stisser, eds.?]. *Fürstl. Braunschweig-Lüneburgische Wolfenbüttelschen Theils Landes Ordnungen und Andere* 2 vols. Wolfenbüttel: 1729.

Unseres Augusti . . . Herzogs zu Brunswyg und Luna Burg . . . Hofgerichts Ordnung. Wolfenbüttel: 1663.

[Woltereck, Friedrich Adolf]. *Kurtzer Begriff Braunschweig-Wolfenbüttlerscher Landes Ordnungen und Gesetze . . . .* Braunschweig: 1750.

FRÄNKISCHER KREIS

Des Ernewerten Ritter Raths gantzen Franckischen Craisses verfasste Satzungen und Ordnungen . . . . n.pl.: 1590.

Des löblichen Franckischen Reichskraiss vereinte und verglichne Policey Ordnung . . . . Nürnberg: 1572.

GOTHA

Ordnung wonach sich die in diesem Fürstenthumb Gotha . . . Chirurgi und Wundärtzte oder Barbirer . . . zu achten. Gotha: 1654.

HALBERSTADT

Allgemeine Verordnung . . . auf einländische Universitäten studiren . . . legitimiren sollen. Halberstadt: 1723.
Eines Hochwürdigen Dom Capitels . . . zu Halberstadt . . . Cantzley Ordnung . . . . /gegeben April 1615/. Halberstadt: 1617.
Gesinde Ordnung Halberstadt. Halberstadt(?): 1717.
Halberstadtische Canzley Ordnung. Northausen: 1652.

HANOVER

Spangenberg, Ernst Peter Johann. *Sammlung der Verordnungen und Ausschreiben welche für sämtliche Provinzen des Hannoverschen Staates . . . ergangen sind.,* 4 vols. Hanover: 1819–25.

HESSE

Appel, C. G., and Kleinschmidt, Chr. C., eds. *Sammlung Fürstlich Hessischer LandesOrdnungen und Ausschreiben,* vols. 1–4. Cassel: 1767.
Collectiones privato studio factae, Kurhessen, in the Landes und Universitäts Bibliothek, Göttingen, contain the following volumes most useful for the purpose of this essay:

"Hessische Armen- Bettel und Gesinde Ordnungen" (1701–36).
"Hessische Cameral-Ordnungen besonders die Serviten betreffend" (1630–1740).
"Hessische Cameralordnungen das Salzwesen betreffend" (1660–1740).
"Hessische Cameralverordnungen Licenz und Akzise betreffend" (1553–1740).
"Hessische Duell Edikte" (1660–1714).
"Hessische Forst und Jagd Ordnungen" (1665–1745).
"Hessische Landes Ordnungen I" (1526–1722).
"Hessische Militärverordnungen" (1630–1755).
"Hessische Policey Ordnungen . . . Feueranstalten" (n.d., eighteenth century).
"Hessische Policey Verordnungen Marktsachen betreffend" (1631–1745).
"Hessische Polizeyordnungen über verschiedene Gegenständde" (n.d., eighteenth century).
"Hessische Verordnungen das Zuchthaus betreffend" (1720–44).
"Hessische Verordnungen der Witwencassen und Civilbedienten" (1751).

"Hessische Verordnungen die städtischen Cämmereyen betreffend"
(1695–1745).

"Hessische Verordnungen in Consistorial und Kirchen Sachen" (1627–
1745).

"Hessische Verordnungen Justizsachen und Sportelwesen betreffend"
(n.d.).

ʸHessische Verordnungen wegen Contracte, Kaufbriefe . . ." (1723–
47).

"Ordnungen wie die Rechtssachen bey denen Aemtern und Unter-
gerichten in der ersten Instanz geführet auch was dabey beobachtet
werden soll" (29.III/9.IV. 1732).

*Des Durchl . . . Ludwigs Landgrafen zu Hessen . . . wie es bei Hochzeiten . . .
gehalten soll.* Marburg: 1625.

Diehl, Wilhelm, ed. *Schulordnungen des Grossherzogtum Hessen.* (*Monumenta
Germaniae Paedagogicae no. 27.*) Berlin: 1903.

Kulenkamp, Eduard Johann. *Systematisches Repertorium aller sowohl in der
neuen Sammlung der althessischen Landes Ordnungen bis zum Ende des Ok-
tobers 1806 . . . enthalten.* 2 vols. Cassel: 1843.

Manuscript copies of ordinances, in the Landes und Universitäts Bibliothek, Göttingen:

"Hessische Gerichts Ordnungen vom Jahre 1497, 1500, 1524, 1650,
1656, 1675, 1735."

"Hessische Polizey Ordnungen—Apotheker Ordnung" (n.d.).

"Hessische Polizei Ordnungen Landstrassen und Wasserbau betreffend" (1543–1739/1743).

"Hessische Policey Ordnungen Pestanstalten betreffend" (1558–1740).

"Hessische Policey Verordnungen das Landstreicher und Raubgesindel betreffend" (1541–1720).

"Hessische Policey Verordnungen die Hude, Gärten und Plantagen
betreffend" (1647–1745).

"Hessische Policey Verordnungen Sittlichkeit, Luxus, Spielen und
Lotterie betreffend" (1526–1744).

Ordnung wie die Rechts Sachen bey denen Aemtern . . . geführet. Cassel: 1732.

Sammlung hochfürstlich Hessendarmstädtischer Landesgesetze. Giessen: 1786.

*Verordnung . . . Carlens Landgrafen zu Hessen . . . wie bei den Innungen,
Gilden . . . gehalten werden soll.* Rinteln: 1693.

HILDESHEIM

*Des Hochwürdigsten . . . Fürsten . . . Maximilian Heinrichen . . . Bischoffen zu
Hildesheimb . . . Policey Ordnung.* Hildesheim: 1665.

HOHENLOHE

Der Graffschaft Hohenlohe gemeinsames Landrecht . . . . Oehringen: 1738.

HOLSTEIN

Unsere . . . *Otten Graven zu Holstein Schawenburg* . . . *Hoffgerichts-Ordnung.* Rinteln: 1640.

LÜNEBURG

Allgemeine Verordnung des Lüneburgischen Zucht- und Werck-Hauses. (1 Aug. 1702).

MAGDEBURG

Mylius, Christian Otto. *Corpus Constitutionum Magdeburgicarum novissimarum, oder königl. und churfürstl. Brandenburgischen Ordnungen, Edicta und Mandata im Herzogthum Magdeburg* . . . *von Anno 1680 bis 1714 publicirt* . . . . , 6 pts. in 2 vols. and supplements. Magdeburg and Halle: 1719 (?).
Sämptliche Fürstliche Magdeburgische Ordnungen und vornehmsten Mandate . . . . Leipzig: 1673.

MECKLENBURG

Der Durchlauchtigen . . . *Fürsten Johans Albrechts und Ulrichs* . . . *Hertzogen zu Mecklenburg* . . . *HoffgerichtsOrdnung.* Rostock: 1570.
Der Durchlauchtigen . . . *Johannes Albrechten und Ulrichen* . . . *Hertzogen zu Mecklenburg* . . . *Policey und Landt Ordnung.* Rostock: 1562.
Reformation und HoffgerichtsOrdnung . . . *Johans Albrechten und Ulrichen* . . . *Hertzogen zu Mecklenburg.* N.p.: 1568.
Reformation und LandtGerichts Ordnung . . . *Johans Albrechten und Ulrichen* . . *Hertzogen zu Mecklenburg.* Rostock: 1558.

MINDEN

Eines Erbarn und Wolweisen Raths dero Stadt Minden Policey Ordnung. Lemgo: 1613 (?).
Policey Ordnung . . . *Herrn Christians erwählten Bischofen des Stifts Minden* . . . . Zelle: 1618.

NORTHAUSEN

Der Käiserlichen Freyen und des Heiligen Römischen Reiches Stadt Northausen Policey Ordnung . . . . Northausen: 1668.

NÜREMBERG

Erneuert und vermehrte Policey Ordnung des . . . Christian Ernsten Marggrafen . . . zu dero Landes und Fürsthentume Burggrafthums Nürnberg. Bayreuth: 1672.

OLDENBURG

Seehestedt, L. C. von, and von Ötken, F. C. *Stadt Commission Schluss, darin die zu gemeiner Stadt Oldenburg besten, in Policey Gerichts und andern Sachen ergangen . . . .* Oldenburg: 1730.

PFALZ

Churfürstl. Pfaltz Fürstenthumbs in Obern Bayern Landes Ordnung. Amberg: 1590.
Churfürstl. Pfaltz Fürstenthumbs . . . Landesordnung. Amberg: 1599.
Churfürstl. Pfaltz Fürstenthumbs . . . Landtrecht. N.p.: 1606.
Des Durchlauchtigsten . . . Fürsten . . . Johann Casimirs Pfalzgrafen bei Rhein Hertzogen in Bayern . . . christliche Policey Ordnung. N.p.: 1579.
Waldordnung der Obern Churfürstlichen Pfaltz in Bayern . . . . N.p.: 1594.

PRUSSIA

Mylius, Christian Otto. *Corporis Constitutionum Marchicarum Continuatio,* vols. 1–4. (1737–50). Berlin and Halle: 1751 (?).
————. *Corpus Constitutionum Marchicarum oder Königl. Preussische und Churfürstlich Brandenburgische in der Chur und Mark Brandenburg, auch incorporirten Landen, publicirte und ergangene Ordnungen, Edicta, Mandata, Rescripta, etc., von Zeiten Friedrichs I Churfürsten zu Branden bis ietzo unter der Regierung Friedrich Wilhelms, Königs in Preussen, etc., ad annum 1736 inclusive.* Berlin and Halle: 1737 (?).
————. *Novum Corpus Constitutionum . . . .* 4 vols. (1751–66). Berlin and Halle: 1767 (?).
————. *Repertorium Corporis Constitutionum Marchicarum [von 1298 bis 1750 inclusive] welche in Sechs Theilen und vier Continuationes.* Berlin and Halle: 1755.
One volume in Wolfenbüttel library:
Preussen, *Varia, Ordnungen.* N.p., n.d.

QUEDLINGBURG

Fürstliche Quedlingburgische . . . Constitution und Verordnung. . . . Quedlingburg: 1634.

SAXONY

Codex Augustaeus . . . Constitutiones, Decisiones, Mandata und Verordnungen enthalten . . . ., 2 vols. Leipzig: 1724.

Corpus Iuris Saxonici . . . . Dresden: 1672.

Des Durchlaucht . . . Ernsten Hertzogen zu Sachsen . . . Gemeine Fewer Ordnung. Gotha: 1651.

Des Durchlaucht . . . Ernsten Hertzogen zu Sachsen . . . Ordnungen . . . wie es auf Verlöbnissen, Hochzeiten . . . gehalten . . . . Gotha: 1646.

Des Durchlaucht . . . Ernsten Hertzogen zu Sachsen . . . Patent und Mandat die Landt Medicos, Wundartzte . . . betreffend . . . . Gotha: 9 Oct. 1657.

Des Durchlauchtigsten . . . Augustus Hertzogen zu Sachsen . . . Verordnungen und Constitutionen. Dresden: 1584.

Ordnungen Hertzog Ernsten . . . Albrechten . . . Moritzen . . . Augusten Ordnungen . . . Sachsen Chur und Fürsten zu Sachsen . . . in Sachen Policey, Visitation Hoffgerichte . . . . Dresden: 1583.

TYROL

New Reformirte LandesOrdnung der Fürstlichen Grafschaft Tirol. 1573.

WÜRTEMBURG

Dess Herzogthumbs Würtemberg allerhand Ordnungen . . . . Anjetzo theils wegen Ermangelung der Exemplarientheils abgangener unterschiedlicher Ordnungen wiederumb zusammen in dieses grosse Format gebracht. Stuttgart: 1670.

ZELLE

Zellisches Stadtrecht, aufs neue übersehen . . . ., 2d ed. Zelle: 1739.

France

Isambert, Decrusy, Taillandier, eds. *Recueil général des anciennes lois françaises depuis l'an 420 jusqu'à la révolution de 1789*, 29 vols. Paris: 1821–33.

Ordonnance du Roy sur le faict de la Police générale de son Royaume . . . . Paris: 1578.

Peuchet, Jacques, ed. *Collection des lois, ordonnances et règlements de police depuis le XIIIe siècle.* 2d series, *Police moderne de 1667 à 1789.* Paris: 1818.

Lorraine

Ordonnance pour l'administration de la justice du mois de novembre 1707 (Code Léopold). Nancy: 1708; new ed., 1777.

Russia

Doklady i prigovory sostoiavshiesia v pravitel'stvuiushchem Senate v tsarstvovanie Petra Velikogo, vols. 1–4. Edited by N. V. Kalachov. St. Petersburg: 1880–91.
Manuscripts in the Tsentral'nyi Gosudarstvennyi Arkhiv Drevnikh Aktov (TsGADA), (Central State Archive of Ancient Charters) Moscow:

Razriad (section) XVI, "Pravitel'stvuiushchii Senat"
Fond (collection) 248, "Zhurnaly i protokoly Pravitel'stvuiushchego Senata"

Pamiatniki russkogo prava, vols. 6–8. Moscow: 1957–61.
Polnoe sobranie zakonov rossiiskoi imperii, 1st series. St. Petersburg: 1830–39.
Sbornik imperatorskogo russkogo istoricheskogo obshchestva, 148 vols. St. Petersburg: 1867–1916.
Voskresenskii, N. A. *Zakonodatel'nye akty Petra I,* vol. 1. Moscow and Leningrad: 1945.

Index

Absolutism, enlightened, 31, 71, 223, 256
Academy of Sciences (Russia), 236
Administration, 15, 38, 50; dynamic, 4, 22, 41–42, 147, 171; ordinances re, 146–66
—Russia, 187, 188, 221, 222, 228; administrative function of colleges, 201–02, 203, 225–26, 228; bureaucratized, 190–91, 217; under Catherine II, 222, 223–24; centralized, 221, 246, 252; fiscal, 197–98; of foreign settlements, 231–32; Petrine, 201–03; provincial, local, 227–29, 240–44 (*see also* Estates: in Russia); urban, 243. *See also* Westernization: of Russia
Administrators, 20–23, 33–34, 44, 56, 150; as distinct class, 166; functional separation of, 43, 159–61; at local level, 165–66; ordinances re, 160–61; prestige, status of, 161–62; professionalization of, 21–22, 92, 128, 129, 156, 159, 164; recruitment and training of, 48, 158–59, 164, 165, 166; refashioning society, 22–23, 38, 40, 41; Russian, 209–10, 211
Agriculture, 12–13, 65, 84, 212, 224; ordinances re, 92–93, 111–16, 169; populationist policy and, 70, 71–72; Russian, 230–32, 234
Alexis, tsar of Russia, 182, 184
Anabaptists, 67, 68, 168
Anne, empress of Russia, 220
Apprenticeship(s), 103–05, 164
Architecture, 124–25

Ardant, G., 118
Ariès, P., 78n74
Aristotle, 35
Arnauld, Antoine, and Pierre Nicole: *Logique de Port Royal*, 36
Attitudes, 28–29, 33, 151; disciplining of, 87–88, 92; toward future, 40–41; toward human life, 136, 145–46; routinization of, 34–36, 38–39, 41; transformation of, 56, 84, 145, 257. *See also* Social transformation
Austria, 31, 167, 222
Authority, 3, 5, 7, 20, 43, 56, 86; conspicuous consumption essential aspect of, 82, 86, 87; delegation of, 156, 215–16; implementation of legislative, 154–57; leadership role of, 28–29, 127, 251; legislative, 152–54; moral, 53; of sovereign, 112, 148–49, 152–53, 154, 156, 161, 207; transcendent, 179
—Russia: centralized, 201, 204, 217; loose structure of, 185–86; moral, 189, 190; personal aspect of state, 207, 208, 221–22, 241–42

Banking and credit, 119
Bavaria, 9, 48n8, 59, 142
Beccaria, Cesare Bonesana, Marchese di, 136
Beggars, begging, 88–91, 135, 144, 168
Behavior, patterns of: elimination of traditional, 85–86; legislated change of, 53–54, 206. *See also* Social transformation

275

Napoleon I, 134, 256
Naturalism, 24–25, 26
Natural Law, 27–28, 38, 39, 40, 88, 152, 192, 207
Nature, laws of, 26–27, 40, 41, 88, 152, 164, 175, 247, 251
Neoscholasticism, 35–36
Neo-Stoicism, 27–29, 37, 38, 88, 164
Netherlands, 34
Nicole, Pierre, and Antoine Arnauld: *Logique de Port Royal*, 36
Nikon, Patriarch, 183
Nobility, the, 80, 157, 229. *See also* Elites
—Russia, 184–85, 218, 232, 249; as estate, 239–42; in service system, 209–11, 212, 215, 222; Westernization of, 213–14
Norms: ethical, 169; legal, 52; legislative, 50; social, 38–39, 41–42; traditional, 74

Oestreich, Gerhard, 87
Old Belief, Old Believers (Russia), 183, 187, 188–90, 193, 215
Ordinances (German territories), 4, 5, 6–10, 41–42, 43–56, 85, 92, 163; areas of concern of, 54–56, 167, 168–70, 175; compilations of, 47–48, 55 (*see also* Codification); didactic, 84, 103, 122–23, 126, 127, 128, 168–69, 170; differed from Petrine legislation, 205–06; re education, 139–40, 142; evolution in tenor of, 61–62, 65, 69, 81–82, 84–85, 89, 116, 123, 133, 135, 137–38, 159–60, 167–79; form and style of, 45–46, 48–55; justification of, 148–50, 168, 176–77, 222; and modernization, 166, 167–79; negative, passive, 99, 112, 113, 167–68, 169, 171, 177; paradoxes/ambiguities in, 79, 99, 108–09, 119; positivist, constructivist, 169–70, 176; publication of, 46–47, 51–52, 163–64; re religion and church, 56–69; repetitive, 50–54, 55, 76, 106

Orphans and abandoned children, 69, 73, 145; in Russia, 238, 242
Orthodoxy, 65–66

Paraguay, 30–32
Paternalism (state), 85, 113, 153–54, 157, 176; in Russia, 231–32, 244, 247–48; in trade, 95, 97–99 (*see also* Protectionism)
Peace of Augsburg, 65
Peasants, 12, 13, 80, 85; education of, 139, 140, 142; paternalism toward, 85, 97–98, 112–13, 115, 244
—Russia, 185–86, 188, 198, 199, 215, 218, 219, 232; estatelike structure for, 243–45; reaction of, to Petrine reforms, 217; relation with state, 230; social mobility of, 219; unrest among, 222, 229. *See also* Serfdom
Peddlers, 96–97, 143
Peter I (the Great), tsar of Russia, 4, 65n46, 71n60, 145, 181, 189, 224, 233, 246; death of, 218, 220; failed to grasp nature of police state, 215–16; personality of, 195–96, 199–200, 205; reign of, 182. *See also* Petrine reforms
Peter II, tsar of Russia, 202
Peter III, tsar of Russia, 221–22
Petrine reforms, 186, 187, 193, 194–95, 196–202, 221–22; improved by Catherine II, 225–27, 237; results of, 216–21
Pharmacy, 132
Philanthropy, 145
Philosophes, 32, 222, 252
Philosophy, 25–28, 32, 36
Physiocracy, 93
Pietism, Pietists, 33, 67
Piety: routinization of, 34–35
Planning, 20, 100, 173
Poland, 187, 194
Political culture, 18–19, 152–54; modern, 256–57; revolution in, 252, 254, 257; in Russia, 182–84, 192–93, 208
Political institutions, 1–2, 5–7, 28; con-